blue
rider
press

FORGETTING
TO BE AFRAID

FORGETTING
TO BE AFRAID

WENDY DAVIS

BLUE RIDER PRESS
a member of Penguin Group (USA)
New York

blue
rider
press

Published by the Penguin Group
Penguin Group (USA) LLC
375 Hudson Street
New York, New York 10014

USA · Canada · UK · Ireland · Australia
New Zealand · India · South Africa · China

penguin.com
A Penguin Random House Company

The author gratefully acknowledges permission to reprint the following: William
Stafford, "A Ritual to Read to Each Other" from *The Way It Is: New and Selected
Poems*. Copyright © 1960, 1998 by William Stafford and the Estate of William
Stafford. Reprinted with the permission of The Permissions Company, Inc., on
behalf of Graywolf Press, Minneapolis, Minnesota, www.graywolfpress.org.

Library of Congress Cataloging-in-Publication Data

Davis, Wendy, 1963–
Forgetting to be afraid : a memoir / Wendy Davis.
p.   cm.
Includes index.
ISBN 978-0-399-17057-7 (alk. paper)
1. Davis, Wendy, 1963–   2. Legislators—Texas—Biography.   3. Women
legislators—Texas—Biography.   4. Texas. Legislature. Senate—Biography.
5. Texas—Politics and government—1951–   6. Political candidates—Texas—
Biography.   7. Women political candidates—Texas—Biography.
8. Governors—Texas—Election.   I. Title.
F391.4.D48A3   2014   2014025482
328.764'092—dc23
[B]

Printed in the United States of America
1   3   5   7   9   10   8   6   4   2

BOOK DESIGN BY AMANDA DEWEY

For my daughters, Amber and Dru
and Tate,
who taught me a love deeper than I believed was possible.

For my mom,
who taught me the blessing of service above self.

And for my dad,
who taught me to be awake . . . while still dreaming.

Become so wrapped up in something
that you forget to be afraid.

—LADY BIRD JOHNSON

FORGETTING
TO BE AFRAID

INTRODUCTION

I was given a thorn in my flesh, a messenger of Satan, to torment me. Three times I pleaded with the Lord to take it away from me. But he said to me, "My grace is sufficient for you, for my power is made perfect in weakness." Therefore I will boast all the more gladly about my weaknesses, so that Christ's power may rest on me. That is why, for Christ's sake, I delight in weaknesses, in insults, in hardships, in persecutions, in difficulties. For when I am weak, then I am strong.

—2 CORINTHIANS 12:7–10

WHEN I WAS a YOUNG GIRL, we moved quite a bit, crisscrossing the country twice before we settled in Texas for good when I was ten. Mostly we moved to follow my father—where his job took him, it took us, too—but wherever we lived, we tried to spend as much time as we could with my grandparents. We never had a lot, but what we had was what mattered most: family.

My mother's parents still lived in the panhandle of Texas in the small town of Muleshoe. My grandfather, Nealy Stovall, made his living for most of his life as a tenant farmer, and when he was in his mid-sixties, he suffered a massive stroke. From that moment forward, he lived the rest of his life in a nursing home. He was partially paralyzed, and as a result he had a very difficult time forming words.

When my mom and my siblings and I would pile into my mom's old Volkswagen hatchback to visit him in Muleshoe, we would pick him up at the nursing home and take him to be with us in his real home for the weekend, the home he had shared with my grandmother. On several of those occasions, my grandfather would beckon me into the kitchen and I would sit with him at their old Formica table—the kind with the silver band that goes all the way around. He would bring out a piece of paper, point very determinedly at it, and I knew my task—he wanted to "dictate" a letter to me so he could communicate with a friend.

As you can imagine, him sitting there in his wheelchair and me with my skinny legs stuck to the plastic chairs in their kitchen on a hot summer day—it was a lot of hard work. Those hours with a pencil and paper, decoding and deciphering the words he was trying to say, were slow and difficult and challenging, not just for him but for me as well. Nothing could have been more important than the task he'd entrusted me with. So much was riding on my getting it right; so much depended on both of us working hard to do what needed to be done. Watching him struggle made me even more determined. If my grandfather had the fortitude to try to speak despite the broken pathways in his brain . . . well, then I could certainly do my part.

Invariably on those occasions, he would start crying, which meant that I would start crying, too. It's a very hard lesson for a ten-year-old to witness the despair on her grandfather's face. One of my favorite photos of the two of us was taken on one of those bittersweet weekends. He's in his wheelchair with his right arm in the gray sling he always wore after his stroke, and I'm leaning in to him on the edge of his chair with my little arm around his big shoulder. I'm smiling, and he is, too, if only just with his eyes.

Of all the memories that have stuck with me, and formed me, and made me who I am, the ones from spending time with my grandfather are among my most cherished, because the experience drove home such a powerful point to me: the importance of having a voice, how painful it is to lose it, and how important it is to speak up for those who can't speak for themselves, and to be true to what they would say if they could.

I couldn't possibly have known then that years later I would be leading a historic nearly thirteen-hour filibuster in the Texas state senate to defeat an anti-abortion bill, giving voice to thousands and thousands of women pleading to preserve their access to lifesaving health care and reproductive rights. As much as was written about that day—the sneakers I wore, the battle over the rules of order, the dramatic closing of the capitol building in Austin that night because it was filled to capacity with people in opposition to SB 5—and as much as I will add to that account later in this book, the true power of that day transcended anything I could have expected.

June 25, 2013, was an awakening. It was an awakening that went beyond reproductive rights. It was an awakening for a group of citizens, all over the state of Texas, and all across the country, who understood that night that when people *do* stand up and when they *do* cry out, they *can* be heard and they *can* make a difference. And even though that bill passed just a few days later when a second special session was called, people were empowered by what they had been able to accomplish that day. They saw that we cannot continue to cede our values simply because we may not win every time we speak out.

It was also an awakening for me.

As I was finishing my third hour on the floor, I began to read another letter aloud—one of thousands and thousands of letters that had poured into my office via e-mail from women all across Texas who wanted to share their deeply personal testimony in the hopes of stopping the bill. This particular letter, from a woman named Carole, described how she learned twenty weeks into her pregnancy that the precious little girl she was carrying was dying in her womb of a rare and fatal prenatal condition, and it shared the unfathomable decision she and her husband then faced: wait and deliver their daughter as a stillborn, or take measures to terminate the pregnancy in order to spare themselves the agony of waiting for nature to run its inevitable, but unendurable, course.

It was a heartbreaking letter, so raw and honest and painfully sad that I could barely get through the reading of it. Each paragraph and detail of Carole's tragic story and her eloquent plea to consider the emotional well-being of parents facing such devastating choices and losses as well as the humanity of the unborn baby, undid me, and I had to stop several times to wipe my eyes and to regain my composure. And each time I did, I felt something deep inside me loosen. Giving voice to the human stories behind the bill we were fighting had emboldened and empowered me to push on through all those hours on the senate floor; it had made me realize fully how the passage or failure of that bill would affect the lives of women and their families all across our great state.

But reading Carole's letter touched me profoundly and connected me to the moment, and to the issue, in a way I see now I hadn't expected and that I had, whether consciously or unconsciously, tried to ignore. It made me understand why I was there and how all the paths in my life had led me to be in that place, at that exact moment in time, to fight that particular fight. Giving voice to the truths of so many women made me see that I needed to give voice to my own truths, the truths that had made me who I am and had brought me to stand there that day, and not yield until my job was done.

I had a story to tell, too.

A story I had never told before.

And it was finally time to tell it.

ONE

All God's angels come to us disguised.

—JAMES RUSSELL LOWELL

M Y DEEPEST ROOTS grew in Texas, but my story starts in Rhode Island, where my father was raised, where my parents met and married, and where my brothers and I were born, one after the other, after the other.

It's where my parents fell in love. It's also where my father broke my mother's heart for the first time.

There are Texas ranches the size of the state of Rhode Island, where my dad, Gerald "Jerry" Russell, grew up. He was born in 1936, an only child, and lived just outside Providence in West Warwick, a once-thriving center of the water-powered textile industry. Stone and red-brick mills, some with castle-like clock towers, twisted up and around the hills surrounding the Pawtuxet River, mills with faded-glory histories and names like Royal, Riverpoint, and Valley Queen. It's where Fruit of the Loom started, where some of the world's best velvet and lace and corduroy were made, and where generations of

Irish Catholics and immigrants from Canada and Europe worked the looms side by side in sweatshops.

My father's ancestors were among those immigrants who came to work in the textile mills. My dad's grandfather, Pepé, had emigrated to West Warwick from Quebec. He spoke only French but was determined to raise his family in the ways of their new country, speaking only English. Like many French-Canadian immigrants, Pepé worked in the textile mills. Eventually he opened a barbershop, and after my father graduated from high school and spent a short time in the United States Air Force, he became a barber, too. My dad's father eventually joined the barbershop, but not before devoting much of his adult life to working in the textile mills as well. As my mother tells it, my grandpa lacked the skill at haircutting that his father and son possessed. Perhaps it skipped a generation. Nonetheless, news articles from the West Warwick paper saved by my grandmother stand as evidence of the "Three Generations of Barbers" that were my dad, my grandpa, and Pepé.

Whatever my grandfather lacked in barbering skills, he more than made up for in warmth and physical affection, which was lucky for all of us, especially my dad, since his mother, Doris Friar Russell, was very much the opposite. She seemed to temper every gregarious gesture of Grandpa's through her own more tepid, quiet manner and tone. Both her parents were English, and while she was loving and thoughtful in her own way, she was much more reserved. She was careful in her manner, and though she carried herself on the most beautiful legs I have ever seen, her style of dress reflected that reserve. Given her measured nature, I always marveled at how outgoing and confident my dad was. He was warm and physically affectionate, particularly with his own children. He was, in all ways, his father's son.

Biology doesn't always trump environment, though. Our deep

childhood hunger becomes our destiny. Often, we spend the rest of our lives answering to the combination of who we were "born" to be mixed with the environment that played a role in shaping that fate. My father grew up with a sense of confidence generated from both of these influences. He was an only child of two parents who loved him dearly. He was their center, their pride, even if my grandmother wasn't as generous in her ability to demonstrate that. He was well liked by his peers and seemed, though not classically handsome—he had an oversize nose and an unruly mane—to attract all manner of people into his fold. His laugh, his energy, the way he owned a conversation without seeming overbearing, were, I'm sure, all traits that eventually attracted my mother to him.

These traits also kept her deeply drawn to him, even when he hurt her. Even when he deeply hurt her. His was a bravado that allowed him the ability to disengage from that, from what he left in his wake. And along the way, he would leave several women in his wake. But there was something magical about him, too. Something incalculably endearing, for he always managed a reconnection, even if only through friendship, with the women he loved. Perhaps it was because his true passion was always something beyond and outside what his amorous connections could fulfill. Was it ambition? In a sense. More accurately it was a hunger to live the one thing that overrode his passion for all else—performing on a stage.

In 1922 my mother's mother, Lela Agnes Crandell, met my grandfather, Nealy Stovall, in Scipio, Oklahoma. He was born and raised in Wills Point, Texas, but had moved to Scipio not long before meeting my grandma. She was thirteen and he was eighteen, and because her parents wouldn't give her permission to get married, they eloped on stolen horses to Fort Smith, Arkansas. When they returned to Scipio in a covered wagon three years later, they brought with them their firstborn, my Uncle Will, to whom my grandmother had given birth when she was only fifteen.

To illustrate the immaturity that my grandmother brought to the early task of parenting, my mother loves to tell the story of her parents' return trip to Oklahoma. Traveling by horse-drawn wagon, her young parents camped outside at night along the way. One night a group of Gypsies set up camp near them. My grandmother was absolutely terrified of Gypsies, mostly because she'd heard rumors that they were in the habit of stealing children. Only a teenager herself, my grandmother worried that she would be stolen, consequently deciding to place my infant Uncle Will outside the buggy in his sleeping basket. If they were going to steal a child, they could steal him instead. Telling this story on herself to my mother years later, my grandmother couldn't help but see the black humor in how ill equipped she was to be a mother at such a young age. But her penchant for hard work, the responsibility she showed in clothing and feeding the brood of children that she was eventually to bear—these were the characteristics that came to truly define her as a mother.

My grandmother was half Native American, descended from the Cree tribe. For a long time, until one of my cousins began an ancestral search just a few years ago, we didn't know even that because that piece of her heritage was something she refused to acknowledge or discuss. When asked about her dark complexion, she would offer only that her father was "Black Dutch" and no more. Such was a reflection of the time in which she lived, because discrimination against Native Americans, especially in Oklahoma and the panhandle of Texas, made it more favorable to be viewed as Black Dutch than Native American. Later my grandmother would privately admit that her mother was Native American, but she would offer no more information than that. My grandmother was private, part of a generation that preferred leaving the past in the past—she preferred to talk about almost anything besides herself.

My granddad—"Pop," as his children called him—was the child of an Irish mother and a Dutch father. Their family history isn't one that my mother recalls with any clarity, only that her pop was one of six children, five boys and one girl, and that his father worked in a saw-mill in Oklahoma. His coloring was clearly influenced by his mother's heritage—red hair and fair, ruddy skin. And his temper matched the stereotype—easy to flash, quick to forgive. He and my grandmother were prone to arguing in a way that was rather dramatic. My mother recalls heated screaming debates in which it wasn't uncommon for my grandmother to chase him out of the house with her cast-iron skillet in hand, but they loved each other and were devoted to the familial responsibilities that bound them.

My mom, born Virginia "Ginger" Stovall, grew up literally hun-gering for more. Raised by parents whose livelihoods were lashed to the opportunities made available to them by farm owners who needed help on their land, theirs was the transitory life of tenant farmers. Following work, they lived for a time in Oklahoma, in South-ern California, and in the panhandle of Texas. One of fourteen chil-dren, only two of whom were girls, my mom didn't really have a place she called "home" until, when she was twelve, her family relocated to Muleshoe, Texas, and stayed planted there. Eventually, after a stint at raising pigs, my granddad went to work at King Brothers' grain eleva-tor facility as a grain elevator operator, and when he did, his family finally had a more stable home, a place where they could put down their own roots rather than planting on behalf of others. Having lost their last child, a son, shortly after he was born, my grandparents lived the struggle of providing for the needs of their remaining thirteen children.

Muleshoe was a quintessential West Texas town, a ranching and farming community founded in 1913 when the Pecos and North Texas Railway laid track for the Farwell-to-Lubbock line. Named for the nearby Muleshoe Ranch, which was founded in 1877 by Civil War veteran Henry Black, it is now home to the National Mule Memorial and the biggest mule shoe in the world.

Mules are known for the best traits crossbred into them—the endurance and surefootedness of the donkey, the courage and strength of the horse—and it's said that people who rely on working animals prefer mules to horses because they have thicker skin and need less food and water. Perhaps, like the tenant farmers in West Texas, they were just trained to need less. My mother's family made do with almost nothing because almost nothing was all there was, but I'll never believe that they truly got used to it. Hunger grew in her like dark shadows, because of what they all lacked in sustenance but also likely because of what she herself lacked in the way of physical attention or affirmation.

My mom was born smack in the middle of the birth order. "Lucky number seven," she says with a sarcastic but somewhat wistful tone. The only girl for a while (her sister was the third-from-last to be born), hers was a life filled with intense daily responsibility. Expected to pitch in on the farming, but mostly to help with the laundry, the cleaning, the cooking, and the canning of vegetables that sustained them through lean times, my mother didn't know anything other than hard work. And unlike my doted-upon father, my mother had an upbringing that was devoid of any opportunity to be self-interested or to feel she was in any way the focus of her parents' day-to-day lives. Even her education had to yield to the demands that such a large family placed on her. She left high school toward the beginning of her tenth-grade year when her mother became ill and she was needed to care for her younger siblings. When she was only sixteen, she married for the first time, more than anything as a means of escape. With her new husband, who was seventeen, she moved to Arizona, but not for long. Within three years she was back under her parents' roof, living once again with them in Muleshoe.

My mom's early years were spent as part of a family who farmed other people's land while living on it. Every day was a struggle for survival, and they just barely scraped by. They had nothing. Literally nothing. They were the family where the kids slept head to foot in bed because there were so many of them. My mom said they had only two bedrooms in the house where she spent much of her time growing up, with one mattress in one room, one mattress in the other room, and a third mattress in the kitchen, where her parents slept. The children must have looked like an odd assortment, stacked end to end—some of them bearing the dark skin, hair, and eyes of my grandmother, others as fair, freckled, and redheaded as my granddad. At Christmas, if they were very lucky—and often they weren't—they might each get a piece of fruit, like an orange, grown somewhere warm and picked by other hands. Though a modest gift by modern standards, to them it was an exotic and coveted treat. Citrus doesn't grow in West Texas, and almost none of their food was store-bought.

They were poor their whole lives. They grew almost all their own food, canned every vegetable they coaxed out of the earth, and, when they had them, killed one cow and one pig each fall to get them through winter, even after my granddad found more stable work at the feedlot. Despite their best efforts, my mother recalls a time in Muleshoe when my granddad was still looking for work and they were living on "water gravy" and "water biscuits." "It was like eating glue," she says, remembering how it was to live for weeks on end in a state of unabated hunger with only water and flour to sustain them.

It was such a difficult life. I think about that whenever I think about my mom—how what she went through and how she was raised hardened her in ways that would make it challenging for her to know how to be demonstratively loving and warm with her own children. Her childhood had left her deprived and wanting for so many things. Like the parched panhandle soil she'd grown up on, there were parts of her that water never reached.

W hen my mom was in her very early twenties, after her brief three-year marriage and divorce, it was the same Uncle Will, the one my grandmother had set outside the covered wagon on the night of the Gypsies, whom my mom followed east to Rhode Island. The navy had taken him there, and my mom went to live with him and his wife and children for a while with the intention of trying to find herself.

Whether she did or not, I don't know, but what she did find for sure was my dad. A friend of hers had dated him first, and when she realized she wasn't particularly interested in him, she'd introduced him to my mom. My mother, just nineteen years old, had beautiful high cheekbones and was far better read than her ninth-grade education would imply, though she lacked confidence regarding her intellect, always self-conscious about not graduating from high school. My dad was handsome, charismatic, and confident—from his high-school yearbook, which I found among his things after he died last year, it was clear he was already a standout: popular, voted onto the student council, and named "Best Orator" by his senior-class colleagues. He was also in all the stage productions and already involved in community theater outside school. Again, acting was his deepest passion. And ultimately he would follow that passion wherever it led, straight to the end of his days.

By the time he'd met my mother, he'd been honorably discharged by the air force because he had asthma. He had also already married once and divorced, but unlike my mom's early marriage, his had produced a child, his first daughter—my half sister, Kathy Russell, whom I would be lucky to get to know later in life. In spite of their radically different upbringings, or perhaps because of them, my parents fell in love, and in the span of only one year they married in West Warwick and had my brother Chris when my mother was only twenty-two; my brother Joey, and then I, followed in quick succession.

I wish I could say that their union was happy from the start, that my father only had eyes for my mother, and that he would never break her heart, or ours.

But that's not how the story goes. All marriages have their ups and downs, their twists and turns, their times of bounty and drought.

Theirs had more than most, I think. And with our wagons hitched to theirs, so did our childhoods.

When my mother became pregnant with me, I was not an expected child and my parents didn't greet the news with great happiness. Their marriage was already on rocky ground, and when I was born Wendy Jean Russell on May 16, 1963, I was not a child who came into the world and started life in a happy, stable situation. As my mom recalls it, she weighed only ninety-eight pounds when she gave birth to me. Her doctor would tell her to drink beer and milk shakes: anything with a high calorie content, to try to get her to put weight on. But she was too depressed to eat. Her energies were focused on her failing marriage, a marriage that she desperately wanted to succeed. Her emotions were focused on my father, whom she loved with all she had. During her pregnancy with me, and after I was born, she had no capacity to nurture me. Instead she was dealing with the devastation of having lost the man she loved and with the responsibility of having to care for three children under the age of four with little if anything at all left in her emotional reserves. Not very long after I was born, when I was only a few months old, my parents separated and then divorced. It would be their first time to do this, but not the last.

My dad had met someone else and fallen in love. And we were left in his wake.

I don't know the particulars of that situation, but getting involved in community theater wherever we lived and then falling in love with his leading lady would become an unfortunate pattern of his. Years later a marriage counselor would tell my mother that my father had a hard time creating an appropriate separation between himself and the characters he played and that that was why he got so caught up in the parallel universe of whatever new world he entered as part of his stage persona. But at that time, in West Warwick, after only a few brief years of marriage to a man she loved and adored, all she knew and all that mattered was that he was gone.

It makes me so sad to think of my mom then—to imagine how awful and depressed she must have felt. Here she was, the daughter of tenant farmers, who had picked cotton until her fingers bled when she was only a child, who was now far removed from her real home in the Texas panhandle, alone in Rhode Island, in the small house where my dad had abandoned her with only her brother and sister-in-law to lean on and three small children to take care of all by herself.

Joey, who is just one year older than I am and to whom I've always been incredibly close (I'm the only one who still calls him Joey and the only one he allows to do so), has a remarkable ability to recall memories from when he was just two and three years old. I remember none of those years, but Joey does. He remembers the vineyard behind our house. He remembers he would crawl around the vineyard and pick the grapes and eat them and that when he did, the old man whose vineyard it was would come out on his upstairs back deck and holler, "Get out of my grapes!" He also remembers that I got a toy lamb with wheels for feet that was too tall for me to ride and that on one of his visits to see us, my dad took a handsaw and cut the tail off the lamb so it was low enough for me to climb on and roll around on.

But even Joey doesn't remember understanding the depth of my mother's despair. Even when she acted on it in a way that likely would have ended all our lives, he didn't understand why it was that she put the three of us kids in the trunk of her car—Chris, four; Joey, two; and me, not quite one—in the garage, with the intention of getting in the car with us and starting the engine. As she told me many years later, without my dad she didn't want to live anymore. But she didn't want to do something to herself and leave us behind, not knowing what would happen to us.

Joey remembers that the car was one of those old round fifties models, a Pontiac or Chevrolet Bel Air, with a great big trunk. He remembers her laying us down in there as if it were a little bed, and he remembers actually being excited about it, not scared, as if it were some kind of game. But sometime after she'd gotten us all into the car, the doorbell rang. It was a neighbor, a gentleman who was not in the habit of visiting but who'd come to the door that day, he told her, because he wanted to check on her. They sat in the living room and talked for over an hour; then they prayed together. When he left, she'd gotten past that terrible dark spot she'd been in, so she took us out of the open car trunk and brought us back into the house.

I've long believed in angels on earth, in a higher power, in moments when someone or something comes into your life out of the blue and saves you from the dangerous path you're on. Like that one. Whether the neighbor saw something strange or just sensed that something wasn't right and felt the need to reach out and check on her, we'll never know, but I absolutely believe that an angel saved my mom that day. And us.

I was a young adult when my mother first told me that story; she talked about it again when my father was dying last summer and we were all gathered at the hospital during his final days. It was an up-setting and disturbing story for me to hear, of course, especially as the mother of two daughters, but as I've processed it, I've moved from my initial feeling of horrified disbelief—*How could she have thought about doing that to us?*—to one of compassionate astonishment—*How incredibly depressed and desperate must she have been to want to do what she almost did.*

As I look back at that time in her life, my heart breaks for my mom. She loved my dad so much, and he had started a relationship with someone else while she was pregnant. That meant her time car-rying me and delivering me and caring for me as an infant must have been so sad and painful and traumatic for her. Was she also suffering from postpartum depression and severe hormonal changes—neither of which was regularly treated at that time? Likely. Dealing with what her body was going through biologically, together with what she was going through emotionally because of my dad, had put her in a state of absolute despair—enough to want to end both her own life and her children's.

I think that the state of her mental health contributed to her in-ability to truly bond with me during that time in my life. Though she is the most loving and giving of mothers now, back then I don't think she had the capacity. I don't have memories of her being physically affectionate. Because her parents were not the demonstratively nur-turing sort, combined with the fallout from the pain that losing my dad caused her, my mother was never one to show much in the way of physical affection to either me or my brothers. That all changed when her grandchildren were born. Today you would never know she had a hard time connecting with her ability to show love. I understand all that now. But for a small child, it created a void.

We spend our lives trying to fill the empty places in our souls that love never got to, where there wasn't enough water to reach our roots; it's those deficits that often have the biggest impacts on us and that shape us the most. Whatever the void created in those early formative years, I think it's part of who I became as an adult. I think it contributed to my drive, to my toughness, and to where my public-service energies ultimately have led.

TWO

Things fall apart; the centre cannot hold.

—WILLIAM BUTLER YEATS,
"The Second Coming"

SHORTLY AFTER MY PARENTS separated and sometime during their divorce, while my grandparents were still living in Muleshoe, my mother left Rhode Island with us and moved back there. It was the mid-sixties by then, and Muleshoe had grown since my mom had finished ninth grade—well on its way, by that point, to being a town with two hospitals, two banks, a library, a newspaper, a radio station, and a wide and thriving Main Street, where big-finned American cars angle-parked nose-in on both sides. I doubt that her decision to move back there had anything to do with such chamber-of-commerce selling points, but I imagine it had everything to do with desperately wanting to escape the painful memories of her life with my dad and wanting to be near her family.

How hard that must have been for her. She was twenty-six when she had three children under the age of four to take care of all by herself, and a badly broken heart. Going home to such a small town couldn't have been easy under such circumstances—the shame of divorce was still visited upon women then. Whispers must have rustled through porch and parlor conversations like wind through the fields my mother once worked. It must have been depressing and humiliating for her to move back in such a sad state of defeat.

I'm not sure if her plan went any further than moving home to Muleshoe—I know from my own experiences that some plans are like that, because that's all you can see from where you are in that tough moment—but unlike her putting us in the trunk of her car on that darkest of days for her, this move was a step forward toward a new life. Whether she knew what she'd do after that or not—and I suspect she had absolutely no idea what she was going to do next—there had to have been a very small part of herself that trusted she'd figure it out.

I was so young when my parents first separated and divorced that I don't even remember a time in my early years when they weren't together, when my father wasn't around. I had to be told that later on. Occasional blank spots in memory are blessings, I suppose, but just because I don't recall those days of his absence, that doesn't mean they didn't happen or that my mom, and especially Chris, didn't feel them intensely. Three years is a long time for a young family to be without a husband and father.

But while memory might be fallible, pictures don't lie. Old family photos tell stories we sometimes only vaguely recall or don't remember at all. When I look at the picture I found of myself from that time, I see clearly what I was too young to know then. I'm about two, and I'm standing outside my grandparents' house in Muleshoe, wearing one of those terry-cloth diapers babies wear when they're potty training. I'm crying, and I look scruffy and unkempt and lost in a way that would come to feel familiar as we moved around the country and lived in houses that never quite felt like home. I may not have been conscious of it, but on some level I knew that things had fallen apart and that without my dad our center did not hold.

For a while we lived in that home with my grandparents. Eventually, with the fifty dollars a week that my father was sending to my mom, we moved into a small house of our own on a corner dirt lot. It was a sad-looking little two-bedroom house. We were living there when my older brother, Chris, started first grade. And it was a letter my mom wrote to my dad about Chris's first day in school that ultimately led to their reuniting.

That letter came about two years after my mom had moved back to Muleshoe. And it wouldn't take long before it prompted my parents' reunion. But there was a complication. My father had married the woman for whom he'd left my mother in Rhode Island—his third wife—he'd even had a son with her, a child he would never know beyond infancy and who would never know him either, or us— but in time he'd had a change of heart. He missed my mom—he missed us all terribly—but more than anyone, I think he missed my brother Chris.

My mom's letter was not a plea for his return. Instead it was short and informational. She told him that Chris had started school and gave him a few updates about Joey and me. He answered her instantly. And thus began his journey back to us.

He followed that first letter with more, each imploring my mother to allow him another chance. He must have told her that he loved her, that things would be different this time, that he'd changed. Despite his written pleas and phone calls, which were undoubtedly persuasive, she refused to let him come back unless he was divorced.

That's when he found out about Juárez, Mexico, and made a plan to meet my mother, and us, in Arizona, where he would collect us and take us to El Paso with him.

Juárez was the home of the "quickie" divorce, the place that could "untie marital knots with speed and ease." In Mexico they were called *divorcios al vapor*—divorces granted quickly as marriages were evaporating—and in the 1960s, travel agencies north of the border offered packaged trips to Juárez, nightclub tours and gossipy tales of the vaporous celebrity divorces: Johnny Carson, Marilyn Monroe, Elizabeth Taylor, Richard Burton, Norman Mailer, Lauren Bacall, to name just a few. Until the law was changed in 1970, an unhappy spouse could cross the border from El Paso into Juárez in the morning, sign the court clerk's ledger at the Municipal Palace, and pay one dollar for a slip of paper that gave the petitioner instant residency, instead of having to wait six weeks for residency before a divorce in Nevada or Idaho. In two hours, one's divorce papers were ready, along with the freedom to remarry later that same day in the same courtroom, all while the other person involved in the divorce wasn't even there.

My father drove from West Warwick to El Paso and then on to Juárez in the old Volkswagen Beetle he owned then. And my mother loaded us into that same sedan she'd had since we lived in Rhode Island and drove us to Arizona to live for a while with her brother Raymond. There we would wait the few months it took for my dad to establish himself in El Paso. He took a job at Der Wienerschnitzel and lived at the YMCA for three months, working to save up enough money to rent a house for us. Once he accomplished that, he took all the seats out of his VW Bug except for the driver's seat, then drove to Arizona, where he loaded our belongings into it and towed it behind his newly reunited family in the sedan. I was almost four. And I finally had a father.

Like most of West Texas, El Paso is flat and dry and hot, with the rugged terrain of a small nearby mountain range—the Franklin Mountains. Many of the streets then were dusty, lined with small box houses with cement yards and dirt driveways and chain-link fences, but unlike other parts of Texas, it's home to two of the biggest military complexes of the United States Army: Biggs Army Airfield and Fort Bliss. We moved into one of those small box houses, onto a street called Vulcan Drive, in an area where a lot of military families lived, and started over. My dad continued his job at Der Wienerschnitzel, back then a popular and growing chain of fast-food hot-dog restaurants—I distinctly recall him leaving for work in his little paper hat, and I recall even more distinctly the Tijuana Brass album that he brought home as a free gift from the restaurant and that we played over and over and over again. The tunes are forever emblazoned in my mind, and hearing Herb Alpert's trumpet is an instant path back to that time in our lives, the first memories I have of us as a real family.

It didn't take too long before my dad began to pursue something more for himself than his hourly-wage job. He began to seek a more "grown-up" job, one that would better support our family, and when he was around thirty, he got one with National Cash Register. It was a job he wasn't qualified to get, much less even apply for. The company had tried to turn him away, telling him that they didn't hire anyone without at least two years of college—he had only a high-school diploma—but true to form for my confident, optimistic father, he didn't take no for an answer. Instead he convinced them to let him take the test they gave to prospective hires, and he landed the highest score anyone had ever gotten on the test. Needless to say, he got the job.

That story sums up exactly what my father was all about. He was brilliant, truly brilliant, and he never, ever gave up. Once he was determined and fixated on accomplishing something, nothing could get in the way of it. That was true of his pursuit of acting roles. It was true of convincing my mother to reunite. It was true in the job arena. And it was true with his amours.

When he started that job, his motivation was to make a good living and a nice life for himself and his family. Later his motivation would change and he would have other, less practical goals, goals that had nothing to do with financial stability—his or ours. His focus would become all about following his heart, his true passion, and he would sacrifice everything to pursue the thing he loved most in the world—the theater. Following his dream would change his life, and ours, in ways we never could have imagined.

But in those early days in El Paso, the hum of daily life continued. My brothers and I spent most of every day playing outside together in the hot, dusty yard; my father went to work and came home; my mother had her good days and her bad ones. Soon my sister, Jennifer, was born. What had fallen apart had been put back together; the center was holding. We were, for better or worse, a family again.

One of my mother's favorite shows to watch on television when we lived in El Paso was that strange, campy soap opera *Dark Shadows*. Sometimes she would let us watch it with her in the afternoon. I was absolutely terrified of Barnabas Collins, the "romantic" lead in the form of a bat who transformed into a vampire, and watching the show gave me nightmares. "I'm not going to let you watch it anymore!" my mother would say, annoyed, whenever I'd had a bad dream. And every day I'd beg to watch it again: "Please, please, please!" I'd plead. "I promise I won't get scared!"

But I always did get scared. Bats flew through our yard most nights at dusk in El Paso, and when they did, I was certain that one of them was Barnabas Collins and that he was coming to bite me.

What haunted me even more than Barnabas Collins were the dark shadows of my parents' marriage, the volatility of their relationship, which manifested itself most prominently in my mother's reactivity to my father's behavior. The years in El Paso marked another difficult time in my mother's life, and thus in her children's.

Whenever they would fight, it was my mother who would become hysterical—screaming and crying and throwing things—while my father would remain calm. He never argued with my mother, never raised his voice at her—or at us—which was probably maddening to her and made things worse. It must have felt to her that he was being dismissive of her feelings. In one of my most vivid early memories, I'm standing at our small bathroom sink, giving my one and only doll a bath, her blond hair straw-like as I worked a bar of soap through it. My mother is screaming. She is crying. And before I know it, as I cautiously peek into the kitchen to see what's going on, she's out the back door with our dinner plates in her hand, throwing them one after the other at the concrete wall. I still remember seeing her there, shards of our Pyrex plates all around her, crying, her anger faded and her sorrow taking its place. And my father—still in the kitchen—calmly looking out the back door to examine the damage he had indirectly wrought.

On another occasion, when my dad had returned from rehearsing a play in which he'd been cast, I recall a similar outburst on my mom's part—this time she met him at the front door with his suitcase packed, throwing it out onto the front lawn, where it broke open, his clothing spilling out everywhere. I did not understand it then. But I came to as I grew older. Typically these episodes arose as a result of some jealousy on my mom's part. I can't say with any certainty whether they were motivated more by fear or reality, but I do know that my mother suffered from a deep insecurity because of my father's history.

If he gave her cause, and he likely did, to believe that he was ro-mancing someone on the side, I can hardly blame my mother for her rage and anger, but living with her tirades was traumatic.

As her fiery parents did to keep their brood in line, sometimes my mother's fire would direct itself at us. Like many parents of the era, she did not believe in sparing her children the rod. My brothers and I have vivid memories of being on the hurting end of a belt or a switch when we would spark her anger.

"That's just where she came from," Joey's always said. "Her daddy made part of his living training mules—tying them to what they called the 'snubbing post' and teaching 'em who was boss. That's how they horse-trained back in the old days. And that's just the way things were. It was a hard life."

Eventually, though, my mom rejected that perspective. I distinctly recall an afternoon, having been told to go get a belt of my dad's from their shared closet, the three of us—Chris, Joey, and I—lined up for an expected spanking. But instead, my mother waved us away and began to cry. She never laid a hand on us again.

Sadly, I do not have memories of my mother nurturing us in any physical way during that time. Though I know she loved us. She made sure we always had books to read, and she encouraged our love of them. She was a stay-at-home mom, who provided for our basic needs without fail—three meals a day, a clean house and clothes.

I believe that even though my parents managed to survive what-ever it was they were going through at that time, my mother's unhap-piness continued to impede her ability to love us demonstratively. She just didn't know how. And because she felt so intimidated by her lack of formal learning, she'd never really ventured into the world to try to create a life for herself outside of us, which was pretty typical back in the sixties—a lot of women were stay-at-home mothers, though they weren't called that then, and there was no shame in it at all. Only, she wasn't the kind of stay-at-home mom who participated in our schooling or got involved in volunteering or any other kind of parent-and-child-oriented activities. She lived a very isolated life; the only time she would ever come into contact with other adults was when she would go watch my father rehearse at the theater.

We spent quite a bit of time doing that—watching a show being blocked and seeing the way a production unfolds over time. I don't remember a time when my dad wasn't performing, and it seemed perfectly normal to me that that's what he did. I thought that's what everyone's dad did. I idolized him and thought he was a total superstar because he always had the leading role. We never failed to go to the production itself when it was presented in front of a live audience, and he'd invariably get lots of acclaim and applause. I was so proud of him.

I know that my mom was proud of him, too. She and my dad had made a simple coffee table out of unfinished wood, affixed legs to it, painted it avocado green, and had a piece of glass made to fit the top of it exactly, and it was under that glass that my mother put newspaper clippings from all the different shows he was in. That table followed us to at least four of the cities we would later live in as my dad's job transferred us from place to place. And in each one the collection under the glass grew. All those memories collected as a daily reminder for us of my dad's talents and our pride in him. Ultimately, when my parents divorced for the second and final time, my father would take the coffee table with him and we would be left with neither him nor our collection of shared memories from his plays, captured in newsprint under the glass.

THREE

You have to do your own growing no matter
how tall your grandfather was.

—ABRAHAM LINCOLN

CHILDREN WHO MOVE FREQUENTLY adapt in different ways. Either they try to overcome the social awkwardness of always being the new kid and never knowing anyone in the room by being very outgoing, or they retreat into themselves and become painfully shy. I was the latter of the two, and "painfully shy" does not even begin to describe me. They say practice makes perfect, but I don't think that saying applies to moving. It never got easier for me.

Each time we moved was traumatic, each first day at a new school terrifying. Up until my first day of school in El Paso, I hadn't had much contact with other children, or other people, outside my family. For some reason my mom hadn't sent me to kindergarten in El Paso, and, looking back, I realize that my siblings and I had never really been socialized because she herself had not ventured out into the world very much. Except for playing with my two older brothers—especially Joey, who was just one year older than me—I hadn't interacted much with other people. None of us did. Which meant that even the most basic and fundamental social skills most children have at that age were a complete mystery to me. I had no idea how to play and make friends with other kids, and, more important, I had no idea what it felt like to be comfortable in my own skin around others.

My first day of school ever was my first day of first grade just down the street, and while I have no actual memory of that day, I do know we would have walked there, Joey and Chris and I—we would always walk to school, no matter how young we were or what the weather was. But I do remember being entirely reliant on Joey. We'd always been constant companions, and now that I had to go to school and be around other people—people I didn't know—I needed him even more. I'm not sure how I would have survived without him.

However acute and painful the adjustment was to my first new school—and it was acute and painful—it didn't last long. Before I'd even finished first grade, National Cash Register transferred my father to Oklahoma City. There we lived in a modest house, but in a nicer, more suburban-style neighborhood than where we'd lived in El Paso. I finished first and started second grade there. My first-grade teacher was Mrs. Gary, and I thought she was the most beautiful, wonderful woman I'd ever seen. She was nurturing and kind, and she had a thick head of long red hair that she wore down, and she loved to read to us. My favorite of the books we read together was *Charlotte's Web*, and we named our school guinea pig Wilbur at my suggestion; she praised me for thinking of that. Mrs. Gary was also very impressed with my reading skills and often would have me read to the class when she needed to step out for some reason or other. She made me feel special, loved, and smart. It's funny how you remember small things like that, little kindnesses that adults show at a time you need them most. I was so hungry for that kind of encouragement, and I soaked up every ounce of it.

While we lived in Oklahoma City, my paternal grandparents came to visit, and though I didn't know it, it would be the last time I would ever see my paternal grandfather. He was such a kind and warm man, and I loved him so much when I was a little girl. I have vivid memories of the special way that he treated my brothers and my sister and me. Because my dad was an only child and we were all my grandfather had in that regard, he just adored us. We were the light of his life.

My grandfather always loved showering us with little treats, and I remember on one occasion during that last visit going to the 7-Eleven with him. He instructed us to just go in and get whatever it was that we wanted. Of course, we were the kind of children who had never been told anything like that before, and we didn't really know how to respond, so we each selected a few pieces of candy. I selected one of those magnetic toys where you move the iron filings around with a little pen and put a beard and hair on a face. When we got home my mother scolded him for spoiling us, but with enough of a smile on her face so that we knew she wasn't really upset.

Oklahoma City is also where I recall my mother doing something really thoughtful for me. Birthdays were never a big occasion in our home. My mother didn't believe in making a fuss over someone's birthday, and I have no doubt that's because when she was a child there wasn't the possibility or the privilege or the luxury of providing any kind of birthday recognition for her many brothers and her sister. So in our family the same was true. Usually my mother would make us a Betty Crocker cake mix, plus a can of frosting, and we could pick out the one we wanted at the grocery store with her. But on this occasion, when I was in second grade, my mother had taken me earlier in the day to buy a new pair of sneakers, and when my dad came home from work and we were at the dinner table, my mother said, "Show your father what you got for your birthday today."

I showed him my sneakers, but I was secretly disappointed because I had really been wanting a pair of roller skates. And then my mother put a bag on the table. "Here," she said. "This is for you, too." Inside was a pair of roller skates, the kind you just slip your shoe into and tighten up with a key—not exactly the ones I wanted, but I was happy nonetheless and spent the rest of that evening and many days afterward trying to learn how to skate. It was one of my few memories of my mom showing some warmth and an attempt to do something special for me when I was that young, and it's always been a cherished memory.

Within a year, though, my father's job transferred him again, and we left Oklahoma City for California—Chula Vista, a suburb just outside San Diego. As they had been in Oklahoma, things were calmer at home there than they'd been in El Paso, but my experience at our new school knocked me off the sense of balance, confidence, and calm I'd been settling into in Oklahoma City. Joey and I went to an experimental, open-concept kind of school—there were a lot of new education concepts at that time—and this school had four classrooms that opened up onto a central and circular kind of "pod." I was finishing my second-grade year, but we weren't really classified in that way. We worked at our own pace without any formal or traditional structure to our learning day. Instead a mix of elementary-school-aged children worked by floating from room to room to room around the pod, depending on the subject area and our skills and ability in that area.

Structure gives children a sense of certainty, the knowledge of what to expect and count on throughout the day, and a feeling of order and continuity and security. The unstructured architecture and teaching style there completely distressed me. I remember going to the individualized reading box and making my way through all the colors of the graded reading material—the purple group and the red group and the blue group and so on—and if I spent too much time with the reading box, someone would gently try to steer me toward science or math. But no matter how self-motivated I was, I never got used to the lack of direction and guidance and the absence of an imposed schedule—things that are so important and so comforting at that age, especially to the kind of child I was. For me, the lack of structure was deeply disturbing and had a profoundly unsettling effect on me. As bizarre as it may sound, I was anxious and scared the whole time I was there, too timid to even ask to use the bathroom, since regular times to go line up weren't set aside the way they normally are for children that age. As someone who craved stability and predictability, I felt utterly lost at the lack of walls and limits and a regular daily schedule.

The silver lining in the open-classroom concept was that I could be with Joey when I needed him. Which was all the time. Seeing him gave me such an enormous sense of relief and comfort. He was my touchstone. Many days we worked alongside each other because our learning skills were at similar levels. We ate lunch by age group, and afterward I'd stand outside the lunchroom and wait anxiously for him for "free time." Almost always, he'd appear and rescue me from my misery and we'd go to the playground together, but on the occasions when he didn't show up, I wouldn't go out for free time by myself. I'd just wait until it was over and go back to the classroom.

But I have happy memories of our time in Chula Vista as well. During the time that we lived there and always, my father absolutely loved to surprise us, and I remember one of his best surprises came on an Easter Sunday in San Diego. We observed Lent, and even as small children we were expected to give up something—I recall that I usually gave up eating anything sweet. We always had an Easter Sunday outfit and went to church, and an Easter basket would inevitably await us when we came home—nothing too fancy, just the cellophane-wrapped kind you'd buy at the store. But on this particular Easter, when we came home from church, my dad was really excited.

"You need to look in the backyard," he said. "I think the Easter Bunny might have come."

We all ran out into the backyard, and there was a badminton net, and badminton racquets for each of us, and of course we immediately started playing with my dad. Because the weather was always perfect in the San Diego/Chula Vista area, I have many memories of us playing badminton out there—it was usually the three of us older kids (as Jennifer always seemed just too young to do the things the rest of us were doing) with my dad—he would come out to play with us on the weekends and on some evenings when he'd get home from work. And every now and then, even my mom would give it a try. He'd created an opportunity for us to bond as a family in a way that we hadn't before.

One of our happiest surprises from my dad while in San Diego came in the form of a dog, Mr. French.

One morning when my father left for work, he told us that he was going to have a surprise for us when he came home. We had no idea what it would be and anxiously awaited his return. When he came home, he walked in the door with Mr. French, who would become the most beloved dog our family would ever have.

Mr. French was actually the second dog we'd had. When we lived in El Paso, we had a little dachshund whom my mother named Lady Bird, for Lady Bird Johnson, but, for whatever reason, Lady Bird didn't make the trip from El Paso to Oklahoma City. I'm not sure who my dad had claimed him from, but Mr. French, a medium-size poodle, needed a new home. He was suffering from some pretty bad ear infections and wearing the Cone of Shame when he arrived that first day, and we were beyond delighted when he came to live with us. He quickly became very special to us—he was incredibly smart and fun and so cute, and, because we never groomed him like a regular poodle, he was always shaggy in a most endearing way. We loved him tremendously. And for a shy girl like me, he was especially important. To this day, I believe it was my love for Mr. French that fostered my enduring love for and need to always have a dog companion in my life, filled in for the past eleven years by my much-adored Labrador, Moots.

S adly, though, while we were in Chula Vista, my paternal grandfather died, less than a year after that last visit in Oklahoma, during which I think he must have known he was ill. He had lung cancer, and to this day I believe it was likely a by-product of his many years of working in the textile factories and inhaling toxic materials. Of course, they didn't have the same health standards in place that they do today, and though I recall him every now and then puffing on a pipe, he wasn't a real smoker the way my dad was. He was very young when he died—only in his late fifties—though in my memory, from the perspective of a six- or seven-year-old child, I believed he was elderly.

What I remember was coming to the breakfast table on a weekend morning and my parents sitting the four of us down and telling us that he had died. Up until that moment, we had not even been made aware that he was ill, so we were all just devastated by the news. To comfort us, my dad made sure to tell us that when our grandpa died, he had all of our photos with him in the wallet that he kept in his shirt pocket, keeping us close to his heart right up until the end. The

next day, my father left to go to the funeral and to help my grandmother settle my grandfather's very modest estate, and then he returned, and that was that. As was the tradition back then, children
didn't attend funerals and weren't invited to play a role in those rituals the way they are today, so we didn't have the kind of closure that
a funeral would have brought us. It was our first loss of a loved one,
and we all took it very hard.

Sometime before or right after I'd started third grade, NCR, as
National Cash Register was now called, transferred my father to
New York. We moved to a town called Pearl River, a bedroom community in Rockland County, twenty miles north of midtown Manhat-
tan, where he worked, and just shy of the New Jersey border. It is the
second-largest hamlet in New York State, green hills giving it the
lushness of Ireland and attracting a population that's now more than
half Irish-American exiles from New York City.

Its current topography is a far cry from the swamps and woods the
Dutch found in the 1600s, when they settled there and called it Muddy
Creek. So is the name, which was changed either because a town
resident supposedly found small pearls in the mussels of a brook or
because the powers-that-be in the late 1800s knew that "Pearl River"
would roll off the tongues of train conductors and prospective residents infinitely better once the railroad came and ran through it.

I'd like to think it was because pearls were found in the brook,
since living there was the pearl of my childhood. It was the place that
would feel most like home to me until we moved back to Texas and the
place where I would have some of my happiest childhood memories:
where Joey and I played in the rural wonderland around our house
every day; where my mother, aided by the help of my paternal grand-

mother, who came to live with us after my grandfather died, tried to create a sense of structure and routine of traditional family life. But, like everywhere else we'd lived and every other part of my life so far, those years we spent in Pearl River also held some instability, so some of my saddest memories of my childhood come from there, too. Maybe it was because I was becoming old enough to understand the tension in my parents' marriage. Maybe it was that it was the actual beginning of the second unwinding of their marital bond. In either event, I was aware in New York that my parents' relationship was beginning to unravel.

The house we rented belonged to Basia Hammerstein, the daughter-in-law of Oscar Hammerstein, of Rodgers and Hammerstein fame, which I think now is such a strange and wonderful coincidence, given the fact that musical theater was one of my father's great passions. At the time it felt as though we were living in the home of a celebrity, and I remember bragging to the few friends I had at school about it. There was a separate garage across the driveway with an apartment above it that Basia maintained, and from time to time she would come to stay there. There was a piano in the apartment and another piano in the house itself, and on the rare occasions that we weren't outside, Joey and I would fiddle around with the music books and try to teach ourselves to play.

The house itself was set in a rural area, up on a hill surrounded by several acres of heavy woods that seemed endless. For Joey and me, who were complete nature lovers, it was heaven. There was a beautiful little brook that ran down toward the bottom of the driveway, and every day we would follow it for hours and hours, fishing and playing and having some kind of adventure, Joey with a red rag hanging out of his pocket and both of us getting filthy in the process. We were always together and always outside, and, like any respectable adventuresome duo, we gave each other nicknames—Buddy Girl and Buddy Boy. There was always some stray cat we were taking in or stray dog we were trying to bring home. There was even a horse we discovered one day while walking far enough down the brook—we'd go through our yard with giant Hefty bags and pick leaves off the trees and go back down to feed him. Sometimes we would catch fish in the little brook below our house. I have a picture of us on the back patio cleaning one, and I was as comfortable doing that as I was doing anything—that's the kind of tomboy I was.

Mr. French also loved the adventures that he'd make for himself day to day, wandering around the woods that surrounded our home. We never had to worry about having a fence where Mr. French was concerned, because he loved his family and returned home to us every night even if he'd gone off for a long escapade of his own during the day. But he did return several times after having been sprayed by a skunk, and my father would use the old-fashioned remedy of filling the bathtub with cans and cans of tomato juice and dousing him with it to get rid of the smell. Mr. French also came home one day with a BB in his hindquarters, which I'm sure meant that he had been up to creating some nuisance in someone's yard.

Because my paternal grandmother lived with us, my mother was able to take a job outside our home for the first time in my childhood, at a ShopRite grocery store not far from where we lived, and as a result I spent a lot of time with my grandmother after school. The house wasn't huge, but it was laid out well, with an attic space on the partial second floor where she was able to have her own living area: a bed and dresser, a small sofa, and a little round wooden table with four chairs. Almost every day after school I'd go up there and play gin rummy with her for hours. It didn't take long before I got really good at the game and started beating her with fair frequency, so every now and then I would let her win. If she caught me, though, which she sometimes did, she would get mad at me and make me leave her room.

When it snowed, we'd have to shovel the driveway, which was incredibly arduous because the driveway was so long. We'd come home after school and get started, doing just two paths for the tires, my grandmother beside us, working as hard as we were. Luckily, sledding the unshoveled strip in between the tire tracks was always our reward. And when we would finally come in, she would make hot chocolate for us and help my mom with the house. Even though she was reserved and contained, in her own way she was very nurturing and spent quality time with all her grandchildren, especially me.

Pearl River is also where I first recall us attending church regularly; no doubt my grandmother's presence helped to drive that. She and my grandfather had raised my father in the Catholic Church, but he and my mother chose to raise us in the Episcopal Church—"Catholic-Lites," as we referred to ourselves. Regular attendance usually consisted of twice-weekly Mass, every Wednesday evening and Sunday morning, with my grandmother always accompanying us. I went through my confirmation process there, as did my brother Joey. On the few occasions that we expressed a desire not to go, my dad would be so disappointed in us. Apparently even Episcopalians still went heavy on the guilt.

By then, as I was growing a bit older and probably because I spent much more time playing with my brothers than I did with my younger sister, I was still quite a tomboy, so for me it was a fate worse than death to have to wear a dress. Maybe that's why I remember so vividly the long, pale blue dress I wore for my First Communion in the Episcopal Church, which my mother had bought me for the occasion, and how she'd actually gone to the trouble to fix my hair in sponge rollers. Looking at those pictures now, I think how uncharacteristic it was for me to appear so well dressed with my hair so kempt; back then I didn't have a lot of everyday casual attire, nor did I care that much about it. I had jeans and a couple of shirts, which I would repeatedly wear to school, and I wasn't at all concerned with what my hair looked like. But because it was so long and so curly, it was frequently very disheveled, since my idea of doing my hair was to just brush over the top of it, leaving the back pretty gnarly, and sometimes I'd get teased at school because of it. My mom didn't pay much attention to that, and though my grandmother tried, she didn't have much success in focusing my attention on my appearance.

I attended third and fourth grades in Pearl River, and in third grade I had a wonderful teacher named Ms. Thomes. Like Mrs. Gary, she was young, kind, and very nurturing. She was into some alternative teaching methods and would introduce them to us as part of our class: making mellow music with bamboo sticks and bouncing red rubber balls. She was very modern in the way she dressed and in the way she related to us, talking to us and treating us almost as if we were grown-ups. It was from her that I learned about the homeless. "Hobos" was the term she used, not intending to disparage or be unkind. She explained to us that she once invited a hobo into her home for a meal and a bath and that thereafter there was a fairly constant stream of transient homeless people who would come to her door. She believed that they had marked her house in some way so that others would know, a secret code that they shared.

I didn't have a nurturing teacher in fourth grade, nor did I have many friends, but I didn't care, because I always had Joey, at least during recess and lunchtime hours. Just as in San Diego, in Pearl River he was my buddy during the school year and during the summers, when we would spend the majority of our time together.

———

The years in Pearl River also gave me some of my fondest memories of my dad really enjoying being with us. We were his first playmates, his first siblings—as an only child, he'd never really had the experience of family peers.

My dad wasn't usually home too early in the evening—I'm sure the commute was long, and once again he'd gotten involved in community theater. One production he did in probably every city we lived in was *The Music Man*. My brother Chris often played Winthrop Paroo to my father's Professor Harold Hill, and when I was eight, I had a small part in the Oklahoma City production—a tiny, frail, timid girl wearing a band uniform, with my little fist swallowed in the bell of a French horn. During the last performance there, the theater where we'd performed honored my father with an award, and I remember crying when he got it, telling him how proud I was of him as he carried me out to the car. But being in New York City was an opportunity for my father to really try to do something more professional in the acting arena. And he did snag some bit parts—he had an agent, and he was getting some voice-over work. He even did a water-bed commercial and had a tiny role in some movie we saw at a drive-in theater after we left New York and moved back to Texas.

The older and smarter we got, the more fun he had teaching us how to play chess and other strategic games. But it was while he was listening to comedy tapes on his reel-to-reel tape player with my brothers and me that we truly had the most fun—*The Best of the Flip Wilson Show, Stan Freberg Presents the United States of America*, to name just a couple. They were absolutely hysterical, and we would sit and listen to them and laugh and laugh, and then my brothers and I would get them out again and listen to them while he was at work. I'm not a funny person but I'm a wonderful audience, and I'm sure my sense of humor and irony formed from listening to these recordings. My dad also loved riddles and enjoyed presenting them to us. On his commute home from the city each evening, he listened to a radio show that would pose a riddle to its listeners. My dad enjoyed asking us these same riddles at the dinner table and would wait for us to figure them out on our own. Sometimes it took us all week.

I still remember one of them to this day:

A traveler is lost on a journey, and he meets two gentlemen at a fork in the road, one of whom always tells the truth, and one of whom always tells a lie. But the traveler knows only that about them: he doesn't know which one is the liar, nor does he know which one always tells the truth. And he is able to ask only one of them one question to determine the correct path to take. So the riddle is this: What is the *one* question the traveler can ask one of the gentlemen in order to determine the correct path to take?

The answer to the riddle was that the traveler could ask either of the gentlemen this question:

"Which path would *the other one* tell me to take?"

If the traveler asked the man who always told the truth, the man who told the truth would know that the liar would tell the traveler the wrong path to take. If the traveler asked the liar what the truthful man would say, the liar would lie about what he thought the truthful man would say. So in either case, the traveler should take *the opposite road* of whatever he was told to take.

It was one of the riddles we could never figure out—my dad finally had to tell us the answer.

While I loved having my grandmother live with us, I do remember some tension between her and my mom around little things. It must have been difficult for both of them to find themselves sharing the role of "woman of the house." So after about a year, whether it was because of those tensions or because she missed her home community, my grandmother moved back to Rhode Island, where her friends and relationships were, and lived in a small apartment. Sadly, a couple of years later, after we had moved to Fort Worth, she was diagnosed with late-stage colon cancer. The summer after she had a colostomy as part of her treatment, when I was around eleven or twelve, I went to stay with her for a couple of weeks. My mom knew that of all her grandkids, I was the closest to her, and my mom wanted me to be some company for her. But my grandmother was embarrassed for me to see her struggles with her colostomy bag, and so, every morning, she'd spend an hour or two secluded in the bathroom to deal with it before getting dressed. She was sad and didn't talk very much. I think she missed my grandfather desperately and, with her newfound health problems, simply lost the will to live. She passed away shortly after my visit, far too young, just like my grandfather.

Back in New York, on the surface, things seemed tranquil, but to me there was a palpable sense that the situation was once again becoming unstable between my parents. I was beginning to grasp, I think, from the innocent perspective of the child that I was, the fact that my father had friendships—relationships—outside their marriage.

C hildhood memories, like all memories, are unreliable, distorted by desires and dreams of the past and a need to see things as we wish they'd been, not necessarily how they really were. For a long time, our Pearl River house existed in my mind as enormous and expansive, but years later, when I returned to it with my second husband, Jeff, during a trip to visit friends in Connecticut, it was much less grandiose than I'd remembered it and described to him on the way there. There was no huge home, no vast acreage, no movie-set estate grounds—just a modest stone house badly in need of paint. Much of the expanse of trees had been replaced by houses where the adjacent land had been sold off and built on over the years. Other than the house, all that remained of the first place that had ever truly felt like home to me was the brook and the heavily treed area alongside it, which looked exactly the same.

Some things are indeed as we remember them.

When I walked down the hill to its banks, the brook's peaceful babble sounded just the way it had all those years ago with Joey always at my side. And for a brief moment, the serenity and simplicity of that time, born of hours of rock hopping and watching squirrels, feeding horses and rescuing rabbits, all flooded back, and I reached into the water for a rock, a souvenir of the past, a pearl of memory to bring with me. Nostalgia and sentimentality might have distorted size and proportion, but the essential truth of my memories was still intact:

Home is where you always leave a little bit of your heart behind.

Our lives are full of paths we choose to take and paths we don't and people, fellow travelers, we meet along the way. Though I didn't know it then as a child in Pearl River, a fork in the road would soon appear. But unlike my father's riddle, here there would be no truth tellers or liars to help solve the question of which path to take. When the time came, depending on choices that only he would make, my father would decide on his road, and thus on ours as well.

FOUR

All you need is love.

—JOHN LENNON AND PAUL McCARTNEY

BOTH OF MY PARENTS handed down little superstitions that they followed. My mom's were fairly typical. If you spilled salt, you had to grab a pinch and throw it over your shoulder to ward off bad luck. Found pennies were only good luck and only to be picked up if they were "heads up."

My dad had only one superstition, but he adhered to it resolutely. If one of us kids was walking alongside him and we were separated by an object, whether a light pole or a person walking between us, my dad always muttered, "Bread and butter." To him that momentary and physical break threatened a more permanent break between himself and us. But the words "bread and butter," in his mind, were enough to reconnect us.

When I was an infant and my parents divorced for the first time, it was the pain of not being with his children that ultimately drove their reconnection. I wonder, while we lived with my grandparents in

Muleshoe and my dad was far away in Rhode Island, with all that physically separated us, whether he whispered those words to himself. And again, when my parents separated and divorced for a second time. Did my dad repeat his "bread and butter" mantra?

Whatever the cause, and despite the periods of physical separation and absence that were the by-products of my parents' divorces, I always felt a closeness to my dad. I knew that he would never let anything break the seal between us, no matter the time or distance. Like butter on bread, our bond was seamless.

To know me is to know I absolutely adored my dad, and to have grown up with him was to understand what it meant to be cherished and loved unconditionally. He had the most amazing eyes—big, warm brown eyes—and if there's one thing I wish everyone could have growing up, it would be a dad with eyes like his. He could literally hug you with them. Feeling so adored by him and connected to him is, I'm sure, one of the reasons I was able to pull through so many trying times and to thrive in spite of them.

My father was fun. My mom had come up hard in a farming family of fourteen children, so for her, understandably, life was about pragmatism, about taking care of the tasks at hand: feeding, bathing, cooking, laundering. But for my dad, who grew up without siblings, raising his children meant an opportunity to be a kid again himself, this time with playmates.

He created rituals with us, making sure we always sat down as a family to watch the cartoon specials that came out during holiday seasons—the stop-motion animation *Rudolph the Red-Nosed Reindeer, How the Grinch Stole Christmas*, the *Peanuts* specials during Christmas and Halloween, and most important to me, *Winnie the Pooh*, from which my father, and then my mother, drew my nickname. From that point forward, when they were speaking to me fondly, I was Pooh.

Christmas was a big deal to my dad. A really big deal. He loved Christmas as much as—if not more than—we kids did. Each family celebrates Christmas in its own way. In ours, we always went to midnight Mass, and then Santa would come on Christmas morning. The presents that the family got for you were wrapped, and the presents that Santa brought just suddenly appeared under the tree that morning, unwrapped. Those few years when there were stacks of presents, my dad was always as excited as we were when Santa would finally arrive, leaving a little pile of treasures for each of us. Dad's deep brown eyes would sparkle with mischievous pleasure, watching us discover some unique surprise that we weren't expecting amid our bounty. One of my favorite Christmas memories was our first Christmas in Fort Worth, when my dad snuck out of church while we were at midnight Mass without our knowing and was waiting to take pictures of our excited faces when we got home and saw what had "arrived" under the tree. Without fail, every Christmas morning he would join us on the floor beside our artificial silver Christmas tree, or in later years the live trees he would insist we have, and immediately start playing with us and our toys, whether it was air rifles for my brothers, a little typewriter for me, or games for everyone to share.

In the summertime there was always a trip in the big green-and-white Pontiac, and later, in our maroon Ford LTD, heading for an adventure that he had designed and painstakingly planned—complete with games in the car that he would play with us to keep us entertained along the way. He was really wonderful about occupying our time and attention when the drive would get long and we would grow antsy and irritable: challenges to spell names out of license plates, seeing who could spot ten Volkswagen Beetles first, and more. He was just so patient and so much fun, which I find amazing—being crammed in a hot car for miles and miles and miles with four young kids would try a saint's patience. But the one thing he wouldn't stand for during those car trips was stopping. He was bound and deter- mined that we would never stop along the way—no matter how long the trip—even if that meant, literally, peeing in a jar, as my mom re- minded us all recently. My siblings and I can tell you that this was good bladder-control training that's come in pretty handy at times.

Our summer trips were almost always to theme parks— Disneyland and SeaWorld and, of course, Six Flags after we moved to Texas. But we also went to the Alamo, New York City, and Carlsbad Caverns, among others. At each, particularly at the adventure parks, the first thing that always happened was that my dad would ask for a map of the park, sit down on a bench, and—as we all begged and clamored to get started—plan the entire day for us. He was a planner. If we were going to spend all that money to be there, then by golly we were going to see every damn show there was to see and we were going to ride every damn ride there was to ride. Before long he would have the whole day sketched out, and off we'd finally go, experiencing every single adventure the park had to offer.

I love the photos of us in those places, faded now and in boxes that I keep promising myself I'll organize into proper albums. I love those vacation photos, because I know it's him standing on the other side of that lens, capturing scenes of us having fun, not only on film but in his eyes and in his heart, too. On rare moments when he wasn't squinting into the camera, I would catch my dad looking at us that way. Soaking us in. Literally soaking us in. With so much love. So much love.

I have such wonderful memories from when I was a young girl of my dad sitting at the dinner table with us, doing homework. If we got stuck on something, he would take our book—whether it was algebra, science, or anything else—read the material (essentially learning it for himself), and then guide us through our sticking point. He was a whiz at math—even the "new math" that he'd never been taught in school. And he was a master with words. He loved doing the *New York Times* crossword puzzle and, when he got older, completed it every day—to a timer.

No matter where we lived—El Paso, Oklahoma City, San Diego, Pearl River, and finally Fort Worth—there were the games, from badminton to croquet, gin rummy to cribbage, chess to Risk and Monopoly and Speculation and Yahtzee. His favorite kinds were strategic games, and he loved watching us puzzle things through as we developed our own strategic sensibilities. We earned our wins; nothing was given. Through those games my father taught us all, in the safest, most loving of environments, about winning and losing. How to find and embrace a competitiveness that would contribute to our strength as the people we were to become. And, perhaps most important, to know that we were going to be loved, win or lose, though we all much preferred winning.

In the midst of all of that, there was always the backdrop of my dad the actor, the performer, the artist. My grandmother, and also my mother, put together numerous scrapbooks over the years of news clippings that stand as enduring testament to the many, many hours he performed in theaters throughout the country. Again, in each city where we lived, his first mission was always to seek out the community theater and get involved, almost invariably in the leading role.

My siblings and I grew up in that world—that world of theater. That world of watching our father, from our earliest of memories, bigger than life onstage. Chris and Joey both carry with them that kind of talent, each having had his own impressive stage experiences alongside my dad. My sister and I to a lesser degree, but we, too, were no doubt infected with his enthusiasm. Jennifer shared his love for baseball, raising her two boys as fine baseball players and competing with my dad for who was the bigger Texas Rangers fan. As for me, my dad and I shared a passion for people, for justice. And later, for politics.

Both our parents instilled in us a deep work ethic; both valued education and the good grades we always brought home; both raised us to believe there wasn't anything we couldn't accomplish if that's what our hearts were so inclined to do. And while my dad was far from perfect, he is truly the person who always made me believe in myself.

It's fitting to me, then, that the last role my dad ever played on-stage, in the spring before he died last year, was that of the title character in *Clarence Darrow: A One-Man Play*. That was the third time he'd done it in his career, and it was one of his most beloved roles. In the play, Darrow says, "If I became anything at all, I owe it to my father's patience and his books." I hope, as my father repeated that line in rehearsals and in those performances, he understood that those are the words I'd said before, and that even though he has now passed, I still say to myself and to others:

If I became anything at all, I owe it to my father.

There's a term for the imaginary lines drawn from the farthest seats in the back of the theater to the stage: "sight lines." Where the action takes place on the stage depends on them, so that everyone can see everything that's happening onstage from every angle and from every seat in the house.

I think that people looking at our family then, from the outside— from right up close or from far away—if they'd watched us racing through the theme parks we visited those summers, or if they'd peeked through our windows at dusk while my mother was putting dinner on the table and afterward, when we were reading in the living room, or listening to comedy albums, or getting help with our homework—I think they would have seen what we saw then: a happy family. And for that brief time, from the furthest reaches of my heart and mind, that's what I saw, too. The journey to that point had been rocky for all of us, but finally, at the ages of ten and eleven, my view was clear and unobstructed from every angle. For the first time in my life, I had a hopeful anticipation of what might happen next.

Our last move would take us back to Texas, to Fort Worth, where my dad was transferred right after I finished fourth grade. I was turning ten. As always, we packed up the big green-and-white sedan and drove there, all four of us kids in the back with Mr. French and my dad refusing to stop unless it was absolutely necessary until we got to our destination.

It was the summer of 1973. The year had started with the first American POWs being released from Vietnam after the peace accord, Lyndon Johnson passing away on his Stonewall Ranch in Texas, and *Roe v. Wade* overturning state bans on abortion. By the time we drove west, and south, from Pearl River to Fort Worth—a sixteen-hundred-mile journey that would have taken us at least twenty-four hours of solid driving time, stopping and overnighting somewhere only once along the way—inflation was in full swing, the Watergate Hearings were already being televised from the United States Senate, and *Paper Moon* and *American Graffiti* were the big movies. I didn't know much of what was going on in the country during that time when America was growing and changing in ways big and small; all I knew was that we were moving again and starting over, which to me meant only one thing: having to go to another new school.

Once we got to Fort Worth, we lived at the Holiday Inn for about a month while my dad found our house and got everything settled. That meant we were in a swimming pool every single day, which we all thought was the greatest thing ever. The house we moved into was on Scranton Drive in Richland Hills, a blue-collar suburb just northeast of Fort Worth; the families whose parents worked at Bell Helicopter tended to live in the slightly newer, more upscale part of the adjacent community of Hurst. My parents paid around twenty-one thousand dollars for that house. It's the last house we lived in as a family and the one my mom still lives in to this day.

We joined St. Stephen's, an Episcopal church nearby with a wonderful priest, Father Parker, who would hug everyone warmly as we filed out of church. I just loved him. One night he came to our home and went out to dinner with my parents, which I thought was so unusual—*A priest was coming over to go have dinner with my parents!*— but it turns out the night he took them to dinner was the night that he remarried them. It was quite a shock when my mom told us about it much later, since we'd all assumed our parents had gotten remarried in El Paso, right after my dad's quickie Mexican divorce. I don't think my younger sister even knew she'd technically been born out of wedlock.

So, as my parents were settling into being a married couple again, I would be settling into the place that would become my forever home—Texas. For all my usual dread and anxiety about starting another new school, fifth grade at Glenview Elementary was a real turning point for me; it's where I came out of my shell. It's the first time I remember an actual first day of school (I was nervous and excited, instead of nervous and terrified), and it's the last time I would have to endure that first day as the "new kid." I cannot tell you a single name or a single distinct memory of friends other than Joey that I had before we moved to Texas, but everything started to change in Fort Worth, and I finally began making my own friends. It was a warmer place to be from the get-go—people in Texas are just friendlier, they really are—so kids were friendlier to each other, too. The street we lived on had several families with kids who were our age, so we would play together outside at night, riding bikes around the block or having games of hide-and-seek, and it gave us the classic experience of growing up in small-town, blue-collar America. It didn't take long before I finally become more comfortable in my own skin.

Glenview was the first school where I ever remember feeling really happy. It was only a few blocks from our house on Scranton Drive—Joey and I walked there, of course, and my brother Chris walked to the junior high school that was on the same street but in the opposite direction, less than half a block away. My fifth-grade teacher, Mr. Vance, had long, dark sideburns and longish dark hair. He used to tease me in front of the other kids about being so thin, in a way that hurt my feelings, but I thought he was pretty cool, even though he gave me terrible marks in conduct. I was smart and would finish my work quickly and then cut up and keep others from doing theirs. I became a bit of a class clown. Although my grades were excellent, those poor conduct marks used to make my mother crazy. Respect was terribly important to her, and she felt that my acting out in class was disrespectful.

Fifth grade was also important because for the first time I felt a real connection to a school and got involved in it. When we moved to Fort Worth, people knew my dad was in theater, and because they assumed that singing and acting abilities ran in the family, I would be selected to sing solos in the school plays. But just like my grandfather's hair-cutting skills, skills having to do with acting and carrying a tune skipped a generation with me. I recall playing a dunce in one of the plays, and undeserved solos in two of the school musicals: Dorothy's "Over the Rainbow" in *The Wizard of Oz* and "O Holy Night" in the Christmas play. My dad told me later in life that my "O Holy Night" solo was simultaneously the most terrible and beautiful sound he had ever heard. But he was still proud. Even when I was awful—and I assure you, *I was awful*—he was always proud, though he didn't ever try to falsely convince me that I had talent.

If not for phys ed, everything would have been almost perfect. I was the painful cliché, the one always picked last for sports teams— kickball, softball, basketball—every single time. Waiting for the inevitable moment when my name would finally be called, with the picker giving a grimace and an exaggerated eye roll at being forced to have me, made me feel like a complete and utter loser. The dread and embarrassment are feelings I'll never forget, and that's what kept me from attempting to participate in organized sports at school, though I did love playing four square at recess. It was only after my second husband, Jeff, encouraged me to play golf that I discovered I had an aptitude for sports after all—and I later also came to love running and biking especially.

B ooks were a whole different matter. I read constantly. Whether we used it as an escape or a form of entertainment, we were all avid readers, especially my parents. Though her formal education was limited, my mom was a voracious reader, particularly of biographies and mysteries—anything she could get her hands on. She started each of us out with collections that were uniquely ours. Mine was the Nancy Drew series, Chris read the Hardy Boys mysteries, and Joey tore through the Bobbsey Twins. We all read the Encyclopedia Brown series and every one of the Boxcar Children books. At school I gravitated toward the Caldecott and Newbery Medal winners—*A Wrinkle in Time* is still one of my favorite books.

Before my parents divorced, we'd sit in the "formal" living room of our home in Richland Hills, reading. The living room, unlike the den, had no television, and my parents would spend many evenings with my dad's reel-to-reel playing some popular music of the day—Henry Mancini, Nat King Cole, Petula Clark—in the background. Joining my parents during their quiet reading time with our own books was a joy. I still love putting music on in the background, sitting in my own formal living room, and reading.

During that period in Fort Worth, my mother made an attempt to pay more attention to my clothes than she had before. I was painfully skinny at a time when it wasn't cool to be skinny—even though the stick-thin Twiggy look was popular among adults, girls my age wanted to look like Marcia from *The Brady Bunch* or Laurie from *The Partridge Family*—and I desperately wanted a pair of hip-hugger jeans with the big flare legs that were the style then. I wanted them so badly that my mother finally relented and let me get a pair, but unfortunately, with my skinny, boyish body, I didn't have the curves for them. To go with the jeans, my mom sewed a little gathered top for me with shoestring ties at the shoulders, made out of fabric with *Peanuts* characters on it, and then, as a surprise, she cut out some of the characters, like Snoopy and Lucy and Peppermint Patty, and appliquéd them to my new hip-hugger pants. It was such an incredibly sweet thing for her to do, but I was a preadolescent and therefore completely and utterly mortified that she'd done that to my cool new jeans. But they were all I was going to get, and I wore them often.

For a while, our life was very comfortable, and very normal. My dad was making a good living as a regional manager for NCR—he'd bought a nice used car, a big Cadillac sedan, which he was really proud of—and he always dressed well for work. When he was in a play, things weren't quite so routine and predictable, but still, there was a welcome stability to our life. He'd come home from work at five-thirty or six; my mom would have dinner on the table at the same time every night; Chris and Joey and Jennifer and I would do our homework, and read, or watch sitcoms on television, before bed. In the mornings my mom would get up with my dad and make bacon and eggs and toast and sit at the kitchen table with him while he ate before leaving for work. She'd already have gone back to bed by the time we got up, so we'd pack our own lunches—bologna sandwiches with a package of Hostess cakes, usually—and walk to school. I can see now how hard my mom was trying to create her version of a happy home life for us. She'd sewed that top for me and decorated my jeans, and our family life was more structured and predictable than it had ever been before. She was really making an effort to be a good home-maker and a good mother. More than anything, probably, she was trying really hard to be a good wife.

I wish I could say that her efforts paid off, that my father wouldn't break her heart—and ours—a second time when he left again a year and a half later for someone else. But that's not how the story goes.

I don't think I'll ever fully understand his compulsion to look for love elsewhere when he was so beloved at home, by my mom and all of us—his family—and when I know he loved us all so much, too. What he was trying to find each time he left my mom and each time he left the women he'd left my mom for, why the urge to escape and release himself from the confines of marriage and home life was so strong inside him—I'm not even sure he understood. For someone like my father, who wasn't tethered by conventional wisdom or by the limitations of familial expectations, I suppose there was something about being bound by paper after my parents remarried, instead of being bound by choice, that made him feel the need to escape.

FIVE

I will show you fear in a handful of dust.

—T. S. ELIOT,
"The Waste Land"

EVEN IF FATHER PARKER, the priest who remarried my parents, had known the Spanish term for the divorce my dad got in Juárez before he came back to us—*divorcio al vapor*—I doubt he would have known that what he was performing for them that evening in Richland Hills could have been called a *matrimonio al vapor*—a relationship that evaporates after marriage. Which is, in my mother's version of things and from her perspective, exactly what happened: marriage was what made my father feel trapped, and feeling trapped was what always motivated him to escape. Ironically, getting remarried would mark the beginning of another end.

That end came in the fall, about a year and a half after we moved to Fort Worth. One morning, as we were leaving to go to school, my mom told us to come straight home that afternoon.

"I have something to tell you," she said.

I was excited—I thought it was going to be something good—but of course it wasn't. Later that day, when we'd come home straight from school just the way she'd asked us to, she sat us all down in the living room and told us the news:

"Your father left last night."

All children are devastated by divorce, and that proved no exception in our house, but my brother Chris and I were particularly crushed. We were the ones who fell apart right there and right then. And we were the ones who struggled most to find our way through the loss. I think Chris and I felt most attached to the importance of our dad in our lives. He was so important to us—almost every happy memory, every loving memory, came from our dad, and the reality that our family as we'd known it was suddenly over seemed unfathomable. What would it be like without him? He was so focused on us when he was at home with us in the evenings. He was so engaged in our lives, even if it was just to ask us to share a particular television show with him. Playing those strategic games all the time and seeing that gleam of pride in his eyes when we got good enough to beat him. Getting his help with our homework, the way he could teach us anything, even if he didn't know it, just by sitting down and reading through a few chapters in the textbook—the way he'd taught Chris his algebra. The evening bike rides around the neighborhood that he and I had started taking together, just the two of us. It was impossible to comprehend his absence when his presence in our lives was so strong. What would happen to those moments? How could they just stop?

Either from shock or disbelief, or both, the first thing I did after my mother told us that my dad had left was to jump up and look for his things. His reel-to-reel tape deck was gone from the living room. I ran to their bedroom and opened the closet. All his clothes were gone. I ran to their bathroom. His shaving stuff was gone. I went to where all his record albums were—all the record albums were gone. Everything was gone.

There was no presage. There was no warning. Given that my father refused to engage my mother in a fight, we didn't even have the histrionics of arguing to foretell what was to come. He had moved out. And he wasn't coming back.

At some point that evening, we were made aware that my dad was seeing someone else—I don't recall if he told us or if our mom did, but when he came over later and took us aside one by one to try to talk to us about it, I didn't want to have anything to do with him. If you had asked me that evening what I was feeling, I would have told you that I was angry. At least that was how I reacted to his attempts to soothe me. All I wanted was to shut him out. But, truth be told, I was mostly scared. When he tried to speak to me, I ran away from him and out into the backyard, where he followed me. It's a moment I remember still so vividly: me with my face in my hands, crying hysterically, my father with that ever-calm voice of his trying to reassure me that everything was going to be fine.

But it isn't fine! I wanted to scream at him. *And it's not going to be fine!*

But I didn't say anything. The person I treasured and worshipped most in the world was abandoning me. That's how I felt. I was terrified at what I would do and what *we* would do without the balance that he brought, and I didn't yet have words to put to my fear.

We didn't sit down to a meal together that night, my mom and us kids, maybe because we were already on our way to defining the new version of who we would be as a family. We drifted to separate places in the house—my mom to her room for the rest of the evening, the four of us to our shared rooms: Jennifer and me in one, Chris and Joey in the other. Our modest house, the three bedrooms all huddled

close together off one hallway, was filled with the sounds of our muf-
fled sobbing. Unlike the last time my dad had left and they'd gotten
divorced, when I didn't know or remember a thing, I was now old
enough to keenly understand what was going on. My dad was gone.

I'd suffer more this time.

We all would.

It was Chris, I think, who suffered the most. Like me, Chris had
always been a fairly sensitive child. And our dad was such a source of
calm and support for him. Joey was always the most secure of our
trio. Practically born with a permanent smile, Joey had and still does
have an ease about him that is rare. He loved our father deeply. But
perhaps he depended on him a bit less. Jennifer was only five or six
at the time. She didn't truly comprehend what was happening. But
Chris suffered the loss of our father's everyday presence in our life in
an acute and simultaneously chronic way. So much so that even my
parents soon came to see that he needed some counseling to help him
through it. He was fourteen. Without ever really discussing it, we—
Joey particularly—understood that Chris needed our extra love and
care. Talking about it years later, Joey would say that he felt that he
needed to step forward and be the man of the house. The schism that
opened up between my father and Chris from that point on created a
deep wound for Chris that was hard to heal. And for the second time,
following my parents' second divorce, I think my father suffered most
from the loss of Chris. His firstborn son, with whom he shared a
birthday. His love for Chris was always particularly keen.

Despite what had happened, my mom *never* spoke an ill word
about my father. Not then and not ever. And she wouldn't allow
us to either. It simply wasn't tolerated. Even at our most hurt, even at

our most angry, she gently guided us to be free of our anger at him. She wouldn't let us go to that place of being mad at him or saying bad things about him. From that first night, whenever I said that I couldn't believe he'd done this to us and that I hated him, she would stop me.

"Your dad is a good person," she'd say. "He loves you—he's still your dad, that hasn't changed. This is between him and me."

I marvel at that now, and I marveled at it even then. Once again he'd left her. And once again, at least it seemed to us, for a paramour, someone he'd been in a play with, someone he'd fallen in love with and moved in with—he'd gotten a house, near Texas Christian University, and moved in with her—but still my mother would not say a negative word, though there were times when she certainly could have. She could have made us feel so bitter about him, but she didn't, and I have a profound admiration and respect for her and consider it one of the greatest gifts she gave us as a mother: that in neither of their divorces did she ever, even for a split second, do anything or say anything to adversely color our perception of our dad. She gave us permission to love him, despite all his faults and flaws, and to find our own way of discovering how to forgive him.

I had no way of knowing what an important life lesson she was teaching me—that the behavior she was modeling would be something I'd seek to emulate in my own life, with my own children, after my divorce years later.

I now know that the unwinding of relationships in general, and of my parents' in particular, is much more complex than can be summed up by a single cause. And as I grew older, I came to see that my parents' relationship had likely held together much longer than it otherwise would have, because they worked to make it last for their children. Their mismatched personalities, no doubt an attraction at first, finally weighed more heavily than even the love of their children could sustain. My father, the optimistic, gregarious, ambitious, driven force of nature that he was, simply wasn't the right fit for my self-effacing, less secure mother. But the bewilderment and loss I felt back then wasn't shaped by the more objective lens I can view it through today. And there were times when it hit me hard enough that even in public places I couldn't hide its impact. Even after I'd started junior high, it would weigh on me to a degree that demanded an outlet, like a pressure valve in need of release. I distinctly recall crying in the school hallway, feeling lost and alone. But my dad worked hard to melt through my anger, my hurt, and my fear, and eventually I began to soften.

Ironically, his way back to me and Chris (the hardest to break through with) came through a play, in the very theater where he had met his new girlfriend. He cast the two of us in *The Miracle Worker*, a play he was directing at the Scott Theatre; Chris was cast to play Helen Keller's older brother, and I was one of the blind students at the school Helen attended for a time. My scene was very short, but I had to be there for each and every rehearsal, and I remember feeling reluctant and hesitant to be in his world, afraid that I'd be sucked back in. Which I was, of course, by the end of the first evening's rehearsal. The irony of the play's title and of my role in it notwithstanding, I wasn't blind to his faults or to his ability to work miracles in softening my heart. I just wanted to get past them.

It took about a year for me to make my peace and to get to a comfortable place with him again. I didn't want to stay with him for quite some time—I refused to do so while he was living with the woman he was currently in a relationship with, the woman I felt he'd left my mother for. But after a while they went their separate ways, and I started spending a weekend night every now and then with him, sometimes alone and sometimes with Jennifer.

My dad was patient. He worked hard to make his way back to us. And he waited for each of us to be ready to make our way back to him.

Chris, though, would probably tell you that he was an adult before he really did get all the way there again. The break he experienced with my dad at that point was one that didn't seem to entirely mend until my dad was in his last days. And even then I could see Chris struggling to make his peace. It was poignant watching him near the end of our father's life, finally giving in to how much he loved my dad and allowing himself to be present for that and to feel that so he could give him that love before my dad left us, before he took his final breath.

M any years later I read that, right around the time we'd moved to Fort Worth from Pearl River, one of the longest total solar eclipses ever recorded occurred. Like most things in life, eclipses are relative: what you see depends on where you are when they happen. Seen from the earth, the moon passes in front of the sun, and for a few short minutes—in this case, seven minutes—the moon blocks out the sun and the world goes dark.

Eclipses can happen only when all the planets are on the same side of the sky—in syzygy, from the Greek meaning "yoked together." Technically, syzygy is when three celestial bodies in a gravitational system are in a straight line. Loosely defined, which it often is, it describes times when all the planets are on the same side of the sun, even if they aren't in a straight line.

That's what it was like when my parents divorced: for me and Chris and my mom, the world went dark when my dad left.

We all experienced the divorce differently, from different vantage points and by different degrees, but our lives, individually and together, were forever changed. And though the planets in my family would never be in a straight line ever again, we always remained on the same side of the sun. We were yoked together, as families are, bound by love, and loss, and the grace that comes from finding the healing of our deepest wounds.

SIX

All children, except one, grow up.

—J. M. BARRIE,
The Adventures of Peter Pan

L ESS THAN A YEAR after my dad and mom divorced, NCR told my father that he was going to have to choose between them and the theater. Travel was an important part of his job as a regional manager of their sales force, and when he was in a play, which he almost always was, he couldn't travel. When they first sat him down, he agreed to stick with his job and not do theater. But soon after making that promise, he stole away to nearby Irving and did a community-theater production without telling them. He became so worried they were going to find out about it that he finally faced his lifelong question: Was he was going to continue living his dream in the shadows or was he going to follow his heart, his passion, and his optimism and do something brave and bold?

He chose his passion. He went bold.

But as a consequence, just like that, literally overnight, we were thrown into poverty. Up until then my dad had really tried to do the right thing by us financially. He made a generous agreement with my mom to continue to help take care of us and keep our lives going—more modestly, of course, because now he had his own home expenses to deal with, too. But he regularly paid child support and helped my mom with the house payment and groceries. Once he made the decision to leave his job for the theater, though, life as we all knew it ended abruptly. We'd never lived with excess, but we'd always had enough for clothes and school supplies and the electric bill and our yearly trip. Now we didn't.

The first thing he did was open a little sandwich shop in downtown Fort Worth—the Stage Door Deli—with probably the only savings he had. He named all the sandwiches on the menu after characters in plays. The best-known sandwich was the Irving R. Feldman, named for an offstage character who owns a delicatessen in *A Thousand Clowns*, a play in which my dad had performed the lead role of Murray. In 1978, when he found out that the space next door to the sandwich shop was available, he knocked the wall down and put on his first play there, Edward Albee's *The Zoo Story*. The sandwich shop didn't last long, but the theater became the focus of his life's work. The success of his first productions allowed him to open Stage West, a tiny sixty-five-seat theater, in 1979. He built it into one of the best-respected professional Equity theaters in Texas and it's now in its thirty-fifth season.

From that moment on, he didn't look back. He would never have the benefit of financial resources again, but he would live a life of incredible happiness and fulfillment. And it's not like he was living with and we were living without—he was living without, too. Of course, this was back before the days of punitive measures to force the payment of child support, but even if my mother had had that legal option available to her, she never would have done that to him. He was truly the love of her life, and the idea of taking his dream and his passion away from him and forcing him back into another salaried position—in order to pay child support—is something she never would have asked of him. I'm absolutely sure of it. Theirs truly was a unique situation, since in most divorces, women would justifiably pursue their ex-husbands for financial support.

But her support and understanding of his financial stresses did nothing to relieve the fact that things became very hard for my mom and for us. With just a ninth-grade education and only a year's experience working as a cashier at the ShopRite in Pearl River, my mom had no real skills to get a job, but she had to figure out a way to find work. And she did. First she went to secretarial school and began working as a secretary for a local manufacturing company. Not long after that, a new Braum's Ice Cream and Dairy Store—a family-owned regional chain based in Oklahoma that had grown out of their earlier business, Peter Pan Ice Cream—was opening up not very far from where we lived. She applied for the job of assistant manager and got it, which meant a pay increase from being a secretary. Eventually she became the manager of the store.

My mom worked really long hours, and even after the store would close at 11:00 p.m. she'd often have to stay to do inventory, counting the many gallon buckets of all the different varieties of ice cream in the freezer and recording how much milk and butter and everything else they'd sold. Braum's was a dairy, an ice-cream parlor, and a neighborhood grocery, all in one, which meant they sold everything from fruits and vegetables to frozen pizzas to loaves of bread— all packaged with their private label. They had stores only within a three-hundred-mile radius of the family farm in Oklahoma—in Texas,

Kansas, Arkansas, and Missouri—close enough for their truckers to make deliveries every day for freshness but still be back with their families at night, which is why taking frequent inventory was necessary. A lot of times, we kids would go there and help her do the inventory—we'd get into the freezer with her and help her count everything up as best we could so she could come home just a little earlier.

She provided for us as best she could, but as hard as she worked and as little as we asked for—we knew enough by then not to ask her for what we knew she didn't have—we continued to struggle. While we didn't starve, there were times when our meals had to stretch enough to leave us with less than we otherwise would have eaten. Everything we'd always taken for granted continued to disappear. There was no more shopping for school supplies and buying four or five outfits every September to start the year. Now if we wanted to buy lunch at school, or clothes for school, or go on a field trip, we had to figure out how we were going to make money to get those things for ourselves. Having enough money to pay for rent, food, and utilities just got harder and harder and made the seemingly small things that went wrong, like getting a flat tire fixed, feel catastrophic. My mom even had to take our dog, Rosie, to the pound after my dad left, because we couldn't afford another mouth to feed and didn't have the time to take care of her. She left instructions with them to call us if no one adopted her, but Rosie was a beautiful Irish setter, so we never got that call.

The most significant change for all of us was that we went from having a stay-at-home mom to having one who was rarely home anymore. Working at Braum's meant working many nights and lots of weekends, so even though she'd never been the traditional baking-cookies kind of mom, it used to be that every night at six o'clock, while my dad was still around, there was always dinner on the table when he came home from work. Now, all of a sudden, that baseline of normalcy and stability was gone.

More than that, we went from always having a parent around to not having parents at home anymore. From when my sister was seven, I was twelve, and my brothers were thirteen and fifteen, my mom was almost entirely our financial provider, which meant we had to do without her much of the time, leaving us all to pretty much raise ourselves. At least Chris and Joey and I had a base, a foundation that my dad had given us and that had created a stability we could draw upon, but my little sister didn't. Jennifer was almost six years old when my dad left and around seven when my mom went to work, and she was saddled, in many respects, with the responsibility of raising herself. Those years were especially hard on her as a result.

That my mother would end up supporting herself and her four children, alone, by working for a company that had originally been named after the Boy Who Would Never Grow Up—just like my dad—especially after naming me for the girl in *Peter Pan*—is one of the sad ironies of that period. I'm not sure if she knew the origins of the store's name, but even if she didn't, and even though she never, ever complained, she must have thought about my dad's choices and wished he'd made different ones. And she must have been disappointed, even if just secretly, that he hadn't ever stopped being Peter Pan. For my father the world might have been made of faith and trust and pixie dust, but for my mom and us kids it was made of very different things. We didn't have the luxury of not growing up in the world we lived in.

In fact, we grew up too fast.

We all started working to try to help out, and I was fourteen when I got my first job—selling newspaper subscriptions for the *Star-Telegram*. We got a dollar for every one we sold. A woman would pick Joey and me up in a van, and the two of us, plus three or four other kids who'd be working, too, would get dropped off in a neighborhood, usually in Arlington, to fan out and go door-to-door. Sometimes guys would invite me into their apartments, and, not knowing any better, I'd actually go in. My mother would have been horrified to know this at the time. Fortunately, I was never truly endangered, but it probably wasn't the wisest way for a young girl to try to earn money. When we had a good night, the woman would take us to a go-cart place on the way home as a fun reward.

When I was fifteen, I got a job at Orange Julius at the North East Mall, because they'd hire you even if you weren't sixteen yet—and when I actually was sixteen, I went to work at Braum's, the same store my mom managed. Teenagers don't often work after-school jobs with their parents, so they don't often see, as I did, the tough choices and difficult sacrifices parents make to provide for their children. Our daily survival depended on my mom working long hours, which meant she wasn't home much and we weren't able to be together as a family. But she did what she had to do and because she did we got through it. To this day I'm amazed at the example of selflessness she set for us—an example that inspired me years later when I, too, was a single parent.

We didn't spend a lot of time with my dad during those years, because he was busy doing his thing—and we were busy doing ours. The relationship he was in after my parent's separation didn't last. And we all paid a huge price for his decision to follow his dream. But, over time, we came to see the silver lining in watching my father answer his passion's calling. And, through that, we learned an invaluable lesson: that there are things in life bigger than us and that there are some dreams worth following, even if those dreams come at a great cost. I have no doubt that my father lived with the shadowy regret that comes from having caused pain in the lives of those he loved. He was incapable of acting with chagrin where we were concerned. My mother, on the other hand, seemed to answer only to a voice that called her to put sacrifice above self. Both experienced pain as part of the essence of who they were as people. Watching my parents, through their triumphs and their struggles during that time and beyond, I learned what it must have meant to them to become present to the reality that they were imperfect. As parents, they gave us their best while also answering to the deepest calling of who they were as individuals. And, just as I've learned and grown from my own triumphs and mistakes, from my own humanity, I learned and grew through theirs. I've suffered some of the very same costs in pursuing a calling that has often felt bigger than me, something beyond self, something that couldn't be quieted. As I'm sure was the case for my dad, following those pursuits has not been free of collateral damage—damage that has left me with an aching regret for having caused pain to the people I love most in the world.

All parents question their parenting and the decisions they've made. Looking back now at the parent I was, I think about the challenges I faced, the choices I made, and all the things I wish I could have done differently. The experience of having children forces you to reflect on your own behavior, just as it gives you the perspective and the grace of understanding and forgiveness of your parents' flaws and weaknesses. We are all human—as parents, most vulnerably so.

Amid the complexities of who my parents were, how different they were, and somewhere in the emotional push and pull of their successes and failings with each other and as parents to my siblings and me, I have grown as an adult to have immeasurable love and appreciation for them both. Had we been raised by only one of them, I think it would be harder to say that. But theirs was, truly, a yin and yang of parenting.

The way they raised us was a reflection of how they were each raised. My dad, the idolized only child, had parents with a more sophisticated understanding of how to bring him up healthy and whole. My mom, though very loved by her parents, grew up with so many other siblings and so many demands on her from such a young age; her parents knew how to provide for basic physical needs, but not much more.

My dad grew up in a world that gave him permission to pursue his passions, my mother in a world that taught her there was no place for that kind of frivolity. Fortunately for us, we got a foothold in both.

There is no defending my father's amorous pursuits. And yet we and all his loves ultimately forgave them, for without his passion, his zest for life, the magic that was my dad wouldn't have existed at all.

And he was magic. Everyone—and I do mean everyone—who had an opportunity to come close to him grew to love him with abandon. I was no exception. In fact, I was the rule, a blazing neon sign of unconditional love. I forgave him every fault and loved him almost blindly. The reason was simple: He loved me, and he was the only adult for most of my childhood life who knew how to demonstrably show it. I have so many memories of his warm hugs. Of dancing with him to the music on his reel-to-reel, my bare feet on top of his wingtip shoes. Of the Old Spice smell of him. Of being told by him that I was smart. Of being reassured, during a terribly awkward teenage stage when I was painfully thin, that all the French models were thin and that I was beautiful like them. I have memories of his hearty laugh, and of what it felt like to be taken in and so visibly loved by those deep brown eyes of his. Even when we were distanced through the space and time that followed the divorce, I knew that he loved me. And I knew he was never going to let me go.

And he didn't.

Most girls seek out their mothers for advice. Until I became a mother myself, I always sought out my dad. My mom just couldn't quite seem to connect with us, though she so clearly loved us. She sacrificed everything to provide for us. While she struggled to overcome the barren emotional upbringing she'd endured, her wrenching heartache over the fact that my father was never able to sustain an unfailing love for her left her with a depression so deep that there were times it could be unimaginable.

After my parents had been divorced for a few years, I have a vivid memory of my father coming to the Braum's Ice Cream and Dairy Store where she worked. I don't remember why he came, but I do remember that it was when I was working there, too, and that my mom and I had gone out behind the store to say hello to him. His car still running, he had stepped out to greet me. "We missed you!" my mother said jubilantly as I was engulfed in his hug. Instinctively, she reached out to him, and when she did I saw my dad's subtle but obvious recoil. I could see what he was doing. It was a boundary he didn't want to invite her to cross. And she could see it, too. That brief moment said so much about them. It said that my mother was still in love with him and that he recognized allowing even the smallest physical connection would be painful for her. He knew how vulnerable she was to him and he knew to draw a boundary that wouldn't create a place for her to fall into again. And it made my heart ache for her.

No, my mother was not the nurturing sort with us. But she gave us so very much nonetheless. She was our safety net. She was never going to let us fall. And she sacrificed herself completely for us following her second divorce from my father. At the time, I thought she was old. I couldn't imagine that she still had the desire to be loved, to be held, to be intimate with a man. But of course she had those desires. She was only thirty-seven when they separated for the second and final time, and though she went out occasionally with a girlfriend or two, country-western dancing at the Stagecoach Ballroom, and though I'm sure she had some brief flirtations, she resolved not to bring a man into our home until we were grown and gone. Her concern about exposing us to someone who might turn out to be more harm than good for us was ultimately much more important to her than satisfying her own human needs for companionship, for love.

Never was there enough in any way of financial resources for much beyond food on our table and a roof over our heads after my parents' divorce. But she did make sure that we had those, which usually meant that she herself did without. During that time, I can't recall her treating herself with a new dress or a new hairstyle. But she took care of her children. And when we became parents ourselves, she took care of her grandchildren as well.

In the last couple of years that I lived in my mother's house, before I turned seventeen and moved out, Jennifer and I were there much of the time alone. At sixteen, Joey had moved to Nashville to live and work with my Uncle Jesse, who had moved there after he graduated from Christ for the Nations. Chris, at eighteen, three years older than me, had moved out as soon as he had a paying job and could afford to do so. He married young. Joey married even younger, as did I. Joey and I had our first babies within one month of each other. I was nineteen and he was twenty when his son Daniel and my daughter Amber were born.

And from the day each of them was born, my mother transformed into someone whom none of us recognized. All the love that she'd so obviously had for us but had been unable to show came spilling out of her like water trapped behind a logjam for decades. If you were around my mom today, particularly on occasions when she is surrounded by her children and her grandchildren (and now a great-grandchild), you would see a woman who seems completely happy. She married twice since she and my dad divorced, for twenty years to a dear man named Ira whom her grandchildren called Poppy. She lives a simple life punctuated by the pains and joys that she feels at her children's and grandchildren's occasional sorrows and at our happinesses. She has reconnected to a deep faith in God and prays for each of us continuously. Never for herself. Selfless, as always. But at peace and happy in a way that she probably has not been since she was a young girl on the farm.

SEVEN

Some day you will be old enough to start
reading fairy tales again.

—C. S. LEWIS

THOSE YEARS AFTER my father moved out of our home and before I would do the same were filled with challenges. And though
they were difficult, looking back on them, I realize that these challenges formed an important part of who I was to become. In the first
few years, until I was almost fifteen, I spent a great part of my time
assuming my mother's role since she was working so much, just
as Joey felt he had to become the man of the house after my dad
moved out.

I took over the duties and responsibilities of keeping house, doing
the cleaning and laundry, skills I gained in the two summers I spent
with my maternal grandmother after my parents' separation and
eventual divorce. These were the summers between my sixth and
eighth grades, the summers when I hadn't quite yet let go of being a
child.

Like the one-on-one time I was able to spend with my paternal grandmother playing gin rummy when we lived in New York, my summers with my maternal grandmother, "Grandma," were rare treats for me, especially given the dozens of first cousins from her twelve living children with whom I typically had to share her. The chance to spend an extended period with her, all alone, was perhaps the most beneficial fallout of my parents' divorce.

Grandma Stovall was a quiet, steady, calming force—and she *was* a force—at a time when I needed a steadying hand. Her days were filled with the calm that routine and certainty bring. The morning always began with the smell of a hot breakfast, usually bacon and eggs, and the crackling of the grease in which she would fry them. She always cooked in a heavy cast-iron skillet, and, ever the miser, she kept an old Crisco can on her stovetop in which she would collect the grease to use over and over again until it would become too pungent. (Even then, only half of it at a time would be tossed and replaced with fresh shortening.)

After breakfast, beds were made, the kitchen was cleaned, and the real work of the day would begin. Regardless of where my grandma lived, she always kept a large garden. It was the only thing she knew. Growing, canning, storing, and benefiting from the hard work of spring and summer harvests were in her blood. The hot summers of the Texas panhandle and, later, when she moved to McAlester, Oklahoma, to be near her sister, required that the work be done each morning before the heat of the day became unbearable. Grandma Stovall's gardens were meticulous. Corn grew in straight, neatly lined-up rows, with potatoes, turnips, carrots, and onions growing alongside in the shadows cast by their tall stalks. Tomatoes were neatly staked. Green beans occupied an enormous portion of the garden, as did black-eyed peas, steady staples for canning. And never, ever was a weed allowed to take root and thrive. A portion of the backyard was always reserved for her chicken pen, and one of my favorite jobs during those summers was collecting eggs from beneath the warm feathers of the mama chickens. Tending to all this right beside her, the quiet way in which she went about her work—these were the most still of times I had experienced in my entire childhood. The schisms between my parents, the constant moving from one place to another when I was very young, and even just the tensions of sibling rivalries—all of this was quieted for me in the escape of those times spent with my grandmother. Each day with her was rhythmic, predictable, safe.

Afternoons were reserved for the caretaking of the house, and my grandma was meticulous in her attention to detail in keeping it clean. Meticulous is actually an understatement. She was a germophobe, and her obsessiveness required that the floors be swept and the kitchen and bathroom floors mopped several times each week. Coiled rugs were taken outside and beaten with a wide paddle stake that she kept just for that purpose. Nary a speck of dust would ever be seen on a flat surface, and one of my favorite jobs was removing the lamps and starched green-and-white doilies from atop her sofa tables and nightstands to spray them with Pledge and wipe them down with an old diaper.

As the sun would fade over a typical day, we would retire to her back porch, owning the reward that came from looking out over a neatly mowed lawn, listening to the hum of the cicadas, and taking in the scent of summer. Sweet iced tea, brewed fresh from whole tea leaves in the little yellow enamel-covered metal pan that was reserved specifically for that purpose, and a fresh, round homegrown tomato eaten apple-style with a salt shaker in hand were a typical treat as we sat in her wooden rockers side by side. Thinking back on that now, I can smell it all. I can hear the quiet, punctuated only by our rockers *creak-creak*ing ever so slowly on the wooden porch floor.

When it was time for canning, our days would end with us snap-ping beans or slicing cucumbers for pickling. Hour after hour of snapping beans, until blisters appeared on my tender, city-girl hands. I knew not to complain, though. My grandma had no tolerance for weakness in any form. The snapping would be followed the next day by her stovetop pressure cooker *hiss-hiss*ing as it readied the beans. And it would not stop until mason jar upon mason jar had been filled with the contents that would take her through the fall and winter.

There are times when I long for those days. Days when I could step back and see, literally see, the results of a hard day's work. A tangible outcome that is not so easy to find in my adult work world. The only thing that has come close to matching that has been my public-service work, particularly in the arena of economic development, where I could literally stand back after helping to make a project possible and survey the outcome—the jobs, the human energy and activity, the improvements to quality of life—much like sitting on that porch with my grandmother, looking out over the results of having tended her garden. Rarely was this routine interrupted. When it was, it was usually to walk to town to pay a utility bill or to the grocer. My grandmother did not drive, never had. But she was assiduous about the routine of paying bills on time and using a walking trip to maximum benefit. Never do I remember her putting a stamp on a bill and mailing it off. Instead our legs could carry us to accomplish this task. And whether it was to the "light company," as she called it, or to the telephone company, we delivered her bills by hand, stopping at the Piggly Wiggly on our way home to buy what little she ever purchased in the way of groceries.

At night we would sit together at her Formica kitchen table, that same one I sat at while taking dictation from my granddad, and play Parcheesi or Chinese checkers. Sometimes, but not often, we would turn on her black-and-white television, adjust its rabbit-ears antenna, and tune in to the news, but never for long. Having spent most of her life farming, Grandma believed in rising with the sun and retiring with it when it went down.

The first summer that I stayed with her, my Uncle Jack lived there, too. He was freshly divorced and worked in town. During that summer, and while he occupied the second bedroom, I slept on a cot in my grandma's room. Or rather *tried* to sleep, as she could literally snore the paint off a wall. Sometimes I would give up and move to the sofa in the front room, where her snoring could still be heard but where the *tick-tock* of her cuckoo clock would work to drown it out, all the while lending its own interruption to my sleep. *Tick-tock. Tick-tock. Tick-tock.* Steady. Eventually sleep would come. And when it did, I would sleep the sweetest of sleeps. Safe. Everything in order.

Leaving her home those two summers was as hard as just about any hard day I'd ever had to endure up to that point. Though my grandma was not a physically affectionate person as a rule—there was the one kiss when I would greet her after a long absence and the one hug as I departed to head for home—I still remember what it felt like to be drawn and held to her bosom. Pushing my face deep into the floral housecoat-style cotton dress that was her typical attire, taking in the smell of her rose-milk skin, feeling the roughness of her hand as it touched my tearstained face to draw me near before I would board the Greyhound bus for the journey home—these are some of my most poignant childhood memories.

The need for the civility, the calm of the order I learned working alongside my grandma was instilled in me during these summers and stayed with me when I would return home. And that is where the care-taking of my mom took root and formed into something that became all-consuming for a time. It became important to me to re-create, in my mother's home, the safety of order that I'd discovered with my grandma, for my mom *and* for me. I found that I had come to need it.

And it made me feel good to be doing it for my mom, who was working so hard for us.

While my mom was working late at Braum's, I would clean the whole house, and then I'd write her a little note and put it on her pillow for her to read when she got home around midnight:

> *Dear Mom,*
>   *I cleaned and vacuumed the living room and*
> *vacuumed the den. I cleaned the bathroom and swept the*
> *kitchen and dining room. I cleaned the house tonight so*
> *that you wouldn't have to do anything but pick it up*
> *tomorrow.*

Sometimes the note was an apology:

> *I'm sorry I was too tired to clean the house today, so*
> *tomorrow I'm gonna do a good job.*

Or a promise:

> *Tomorrow I am gonna clean this house so spotless that you*
> *ain't gonna believe it! And that's a promise!*

Or a reminder:

> *Just a note to say I love you. Sleep well!*
> *Remember your pills tomorrow!*

And every once in a while, my note had nothing to do with cleaning and everything to do with the emotional pain that was underneath it all:

Dear Mom,

    Right now I'm sitting crying so hard that it's pathetic.
I realized tonight how much I love and miss Daddy. I
want him back so bad that it really hurts. I love you more
than anyone in this world. Thanks for being a mother to
me. Thanks for working so hard just for our family. Just
thanks for being my mom.

I love you,
Wendy

I see now that my caretaking in our home didn't help just my mother: it helped me, too. I was trying to find a way to feel good about myself, and I felt good about myself when I did things for her, when I was useful, when I was able to make her life just a little bit easier. Cleaning was an outward response to my parents' divorce and the pain I was struggling with. It was my way of controlling one small aspect of my life, when everything else felt completely out of my control. It became my way of bringing order to chaos, and I would carry that behavior well into my adulthood.

I wish I could say that this need to please my mother had held, that it was a pattern I followed until I finished growing up and left home. But after a couple years of that, my teenage desire for social interactions and my normal adolescent desire to separate myself from her took hold. And the rebellion that grew out of it, that grew out of the years of on-again, off-again stability, was something I was at a loss to contain.

I was around twenty when my grandmother passed away, and my mother asked me if I wanted to have any of her belongings. My mind went back to those summers I'd spent with her, to all the little things in her home that were forever part of my memories of those precious moments: I thought about the stiff, starched, green-and-white doilies underneath her knickknacks; the large velvet wall hanging of a hunting scene with brown-and-white spotted dogs; the coiled rugs; the collection of salt and pepper shakers, including the ones shaped like an old man and woman; the miniature donkeys bearing the inscription MULESHOE, TEXAS.

Despite the sentimental value I attached to each of those items and so many more, what I wanted most was the little yellow enamel pan that she used daily to brew iced tea in.

The pan was not an heirloom, of course. It held no value for anyone other than me. But it represented the smell, the color, and the feel of my childhood and the summers I spent with her, all the work we did, everything we accomplished every single day. To this day, I use it to brew tea or to warm soup when I'm not feeling well. That pan reminded me of a time when I understood what it felt like to know my purpose in life, to know exactly why I was here, and to fulfill that purpose matter-of-factly, without drama, without complaint, on a daily basis. Those days were never easy, but the meaning I learned to find in them through her example was simple: Life was about the value of an honest day's labor and the good sleep that followed it.

Hard work was the silent prayer she taught me.

It's a prayer I learned by heart.

EIGHT

His was a great sin who first
invented consciousness.

—F. SCOTT FITZGERALD

WITH MY FATHER GONE and my mom working nights and weekends, we didn't have parents at home anymore. We became latchkey kids, coming and going on our own, fending for ourselves and looking after one another. My sister, Jennifer, who was so young when they got divorced and so much younger than the rest of us, was very much on her own in many ways. She didn't have the benefit of all those years of sibling solidarity and tradition that Joey and Chris and I shared, and I'm sure that made her experience even more difficult and painful than ours.

There was a fearfulness in not having an adult around, in not being parented anymore, in having such a sudden role reversal. Practically overnight we'd gone from being taken care of *by* our mother to taking care *of* her. While I assumed the role of caretaker, doing all the housework sometimes with Jennifer's help, Joey and Chris as the de facto men of the house assumed the role of her protectors. The normal structure of our family had collapsed so quickly and dramatically that all we could do was try to fill the roles vacated by our working parents and keep things going.

N ature abhors a vacuum, and so, I think, do children. When an important person leaves, you try to fill the emptiness with other people, to glue the broken pieces together. In part, I attempted to fill that emptiness through a series of relationships that exposed me to and set me on a path of religious observance that was distinctly different from the Episcopalian upbringing my parents had fostered.

My mother's youngest living brother, Jesse, moved to Dallas to go to Christ for the Nations Institute, a non-denominational Christian Bible college with evangelical roots, in the hope of entering a church leadership role. Services there were the kind where people speak in tongues, have hands laid on them to be healed, and sometimes even collapse onstage. It was all very dramatic, full of the devout belief in the ever-present power of God and a strict adherence to all the historic and original writings and teachings of the Bible, and I became heavily influenced by it.

Since New York, we'd always been faithful churchgoers, going to Mass on Wednesdays and often twice on Sundays, and we'd been very involved in Sunday school. But the Episcopal religion is very ritualistic, without any of the drama I would come to observe through the Christ for the Nations church, and its services were completely predictable. I'd always liked and felt comfortable with the predictable aspect of our religious upbringing, especially when I was young. It was consistent and therefore felt safe.

Jesse was my favorite uncle, and from time to time my mom would take us to services at Christ for the Nations' church on Sundays, and afterward we'd have lunch with him and the woman he was dating, Carole, who became his wife while he was going to school. They were both so sweet and warm and loving, and he became very much like a father figure to me, Jennifer, Chris, and Joey.

Whenever Uncle Jesse would come to our house for a meal, he'd always bring something to contribute to it, sometimes boxes of dented canned foods that he'd bought at a discount from the grocery where he worked part-time. He also loved to tease me, and I remember particularly one Thanksgiving, as I was happily eating my dinner, he looked at me across the table and asked me if I was enjoying my meal. When I said yes, he started laughing and then revealed to me and the whole table that he had given me the turkey butt to eat. Mortified, I jumped up from the table and ran off crying to the living room, with him following and apologizing profusely. "If I didn't love you so much, I wouldn't tease you so much," he'd often tell me. His brand of showing love toughened my hide.

Because he was such an influential person in our lives, the church became really influential in our lives, too. I took in those beliefs and the perspective they offered, even if they didn't always make sense to me. I would try so hard when I was in services to have the Holy Spirit speak through me, and I would wonder why it wasn't happening. Carole, my new aunt, would be standing next to me, speaking in tongues, and I would struggle to let the Holy Spirit flow. But it didn't happen that way for me.

At about the same time, Joey and I had, on one of our neighborhood bike rides, discovered a little art guild, housed in what had once been a private residence on a block of homes that had been cleared to make way for a park. Ever curious, we parked our bikes outside and went in to see what was going on. Before long we had convinced our mom to let us take some art lessons there after school. While it became pretty apparent that I was not a budding artist, I enjoyed getting the adult attention we received there. After a few months, the art guild folded and the house assumed a new purpose, this time run by a woman we would come to love dearly, named Jackie. She was about my mom's age, and she had an inspirational manner that drew people to her. We became part of a cluster of young people who would informally gather there and receive her guidance, particularly her religious guidance. Jackie was and still is a person of deep faith, and her faith radiated from her with a love and warmth we were hungry for. She and my Uncle Jesse shared the same perspective on biblical teachings, and she, too, spoke in tongues during worship services.

Jackie had an amazing influence on my life and on Joey's. She was one of the first outsiders to see that we needed an adult who would give us the kind of nurturing and attention we weren't getting elsewhere at that critical time. Later on, as Jennifer got older, Jackie became an incredibly important part of her life, too. Even after Joey and Chris and I had all moved on and gone away, Jackie still made sure to spend time with Jennifer, giving her some attention every week, because she saw how desperately she needed it. Jackie is still close to all of us, but especially to Joey, who continues to visit with her when he returns to Texas from his home in Tennessee. My mom was very grateful for Jackie's presence in all of our lives—especially in Jennifer's—and she and Jackie became close, too.

I'd also made a good friend in middle school who shared those same deeply held religious beliefs. She was a flute player in our band; I started playing the clarinet. Her father was a high-school band director, and her family was devout. One Sunday while attending church with Donna and her family, I found Jesus Christ as my Lord and Savior. That experience opened me up in ways I could not have expected. My newfound faith would soon be severely tested, and in the years since has grown and matured.

In some of the notes I wrote for my mom, I told her that I'd found

Jesus Christ as my Lord and Savior, and I tried to convince her to go down that path with me, too. But it wasn't until some years later that her faith became a central part of who she is and continues to be. To this day she attends a Baptist church in her neighborhood—where believers receive eternal life through the acceptance of Jesus Christ as their Savior—that more appropriately reflects her religious perspective than the Episcopal church did, and her faith is an incredibly important part of her life.

But for me, the walls around which that type of religious observance had been built began to crumble. I became doubtful about some of the things I was seeing at Christ for the Nations' services. And a particular incident at one such service planted those seeds of doubt and disillusionment in my mind. My maternal grandparents were with us as part of a brief visit to Fort Worth. During this particular service, my granddad sat beside me in his wheelchair on the aisle while the pastor was calling people up to the stage one by one to be healed. As I sat there, I prayed as hard as I could that my grandfather would be chosen. No matter how hard I prayed and no matter how hard I cried, my grandfather was passed by as church deacons left the stage and walked among the audience, deciding whom to select. Looking over at him, slouched in his wheelchair, his arm in its sling, I saw tears streaming down his face. I will never forget the disappointment and disillusionment that settled over me that day. Why had God chosen to heal those other people? Why had my grandfather been overlooked? My adult self can reflect on that question today with less of a sense of hurt and distrust than my young self felt all those years ago. But on that day, and for long afterward, my faith suffered a deep blow.

It was the first time I really began to question what I was being taught, and my sense that I was not being told the whole truth of God precipitated a slow but sure fading of that kind of religious observance from my life. And while I never really returned to that particular brand of faith that I'd found as a teenager, I credit it with being a refuge for me at a time when I needed it most. Today I belong to a Baptist church, but I mostly worship in a variety of denominational churches in the African-American community in the senate district that I represent, where the message is focused on the power of God in our lives for good instead of on damnation, and where the sermons are ones of aspiration and forgiveness. I tend to cry when I sing in those churches, during those services. The songs open a door I try to otherwise keep closed and force me to be in touch with my vulnerabilities and my understanding of how small I am in the construct of God's power. My faith now is built upon a mixture of all I learned as a child and all I've experienced as an adult. I do believe. And I do believe that God has a hand in our lives, though not always in the way we would have asked for it. Even in my darkest moments, even when I could not see it, that connection to God that I found as a teenager has never left me. I've found that it's impossible for me to look back over my life and not see his hand in all that brought me to where I am today, to see his grace in difficulties that became my greatest blessings.

A fter I put that phase behind me as a teenager, my life started to move in a whole new direction. School was still easy—I didn't have to study very much to make good grades—but something in me had shifted. Part of it was a normal teenage desire for independence and freedom; another part was a sense of rebelliousness and frustration that was born out of the financial stress we were always under and dealing with collateral damage from my parents' divorce. At some point my need for my mother's approval and happiness fell away, and I stopped cleaning the house obsessively and leaving her notes to tell her how much I'd done to help her.

And that's when my rebellious phase really started. From the fifth grade up until ninth grade, my best friend was Tracy, who lived what I thought was the most perfect life in the world. Tracy and her twin brother were both attractive, happy, popular kids who were really good students. They lived in Hurst, where most of the houses were newer and bigger and had modern layouts. Her parents were married, and her family, which included two younger siblings, had none of the soap-opera dynamics and drama that mine had had. Her mom didn't work outside the home and was always well dressed, and her father, like most of the people who lived in that area, worked at Bell Helicopter.

I often spent the night at Tracy's house, which I loved to do, and on many Fridays her mom would pick us up at school, looking amazing, with perfect hair and makeup, and always acting so warm and welcoming to me. We'd get in the back of their station wagon, the leather smell of which I'll remember forever, and we'd sit in the rear facing the back of the car until we got to their house. Often, when we'd get to Tracy's room, there would be a new outfit laid out on her bed that her mom had bought for her, which was such a foreign experience to me based on my own life. There was something so grounded and stable about their house and their family, and I loved being part of it. I really looked up to Tracy—because she was such a good student, she helped inspire in me a healthy sense of competition in school. Where my edges were rough, hers were smooth, and we had a wonderfully solid and stable friendship for several years.

In the last year of junior high school, though, when I was fourteen and so much was happening at home, I made a new best friend, Lori, and that's when I stopped being that girl who was so perfect and well behaved. Lori also came from a great family—her father worked at Bell Helicopter, too, and they lived in the same neighborhood as Tracy—but despite her stable home life and family, Lori was a rebel, a bit of a wild child, and that fascinated me. I was mesmerized by her; she was beautiful, and, like Tracy—and me—she had wild, curly hair. Up until then I'd always tried desperately to tame mine, getting up at five-thirty in the morning to try to straighten it each day before school. I desperately wanted Marcia Brady hair. But with Lori, for the first time, I let my hair go natural, owning more of who I really was.

Lori would remain my best friend all through high school, and during that time she and I went down a path of cutting class, smoking cigarettes, and sneaking out of the house at night. It's while we were hanging out and wandering around when we shouldn't have been that I began my very first relationship with a boy, Steve, a nineteen-year-old. I was only fourteen and in middle school, and Steve had already graduated from high school. He had a Grand Prix, and one of his friends had an even newer Grand Prix, and Lori and I were totally impressed. They were older, they had cars, and they could take us to parties.

You may find it hard to believe that my mother let me go out with someone so much older—five years older—but a lot of the time I made sure she didn't know what I was really up to. She had a deep sense of concern about what she saw happening with me and the way Lori and I behaved, but because she worked so many nights and didn't know what to do, her way of dealing with my newfound rebelliousness was to try as hard as she could to contain me so I wouldn't get into trouble. Of course, the more she tried to control me, the more I rebelled. I'd lash out at her and lie to her about where I was or who I was with, just wanting to break free.

Toward the end of my junior year in high school, I started dating Frank Underwood, who would become the father of my eldest daughter, Amber. Frank was two years older than me and had already graduated. He came from a much more traditional family than I did, and one with more earning power. They lived in the newly developing area of Northeast Tarrant County; his father was part owner of a manufacturing company, and his mom was a stay-at-home mom who had gone back to school to get a master's degree. She was a thoughtful, smart, articulate person and one of those adults who could look you in the eye when you were only seventeen years old and talk to you with respect and treat you as though she was sincerely interested in what you had to say.

Frank was outgoing and funny and extremely good-looking—he had chocolate-brown eyes and a great smile like the one that Amber has now, plus a dimple like my brother Joey's. He was the perfect kind of bad boy—a boy from a good family who also had a rebellious side, which I found very attractive. I don't remember how we connected—in school he was popular with the football players and the cheerleaders, which certainly wasn't my group—but I do remember our first date: we went to one of those driving ranges where you hit golf balls.

I had never in my life known anyone who played golf, and I thought to sit and watch someone who actually knew how to hit a golf ball was the most sophisticated thing in the world. That's how he'd been raised—he even had his own golf clubs. I couldn't believe it. I mean, who had their own *golf clubs*? I was captivated by him. He was very smart, but he was one of those kids who didn't excel in school; his report cards were not a reflection of his intellect. He didn't handle authority figures well at all, which perhaps explains why he went through several different jobs while we were together.

Lacking confidence in the academic side of his intelligence, Frank decided not to pursue college as his two older sisters had, even though his family would have provided for him if he'd wanted it. Instead he enjoyed working, particularly on or with anything that had a motor.

When we were first dating, he had a job driving a forklift at a nearby plant, and he'd already begun to look for an apartment for himself. When he told me he was moving out of his parents' house, he asked me if I wanted to move in with him. We would share the rent, and all would be good.

It was the summer between my junior and senior years of high school. And I said yes.

Like so many impulsive decisions young people make, mine to move in with Frank at the end of my junior year of high school was all about escape and rebellion. I'd become immune to my mother's understandable attempts to control me. I'd reached my breaking point. I didn't want all the responsibility of our home life anymore. I didn't want to be the caretaker anymore. And I didn't want my mom telling me what to do. I just wanted to be with my friends and have fun.

Understandably, my mother was very upset when I told her I was leaving, but after I moved out, I think it was a relief for her. She didn't have to worry every minute about where I was and what I was doing: she could put it out of her mind somewhat.

"I placed you in God's hands now," she'd told me, completely resigned. "I trust that God will take care of you."

It's not so much that she felt she'd failed me, but that she couldn't control me anymore. I was such a driven, determined person that even though she never doubted that I would always work hard, I'm sure she was also afraid of the danger I would put myself in now that I was living on my own. Mothers worry about their girls because they know the things that they've been vulnerable to—they worry about them in a way that's different from the way their dads do. And, while my dad acted nonchalant when I told him the news, I remember that the first time he came to the apartment after Frank and I moved in together, he clearly felt awkward and uncomfortable. He might have been fine with it in the abstract, but when he had to be in the actual physical space where his unmarried seventeen-year-old daughter was living with a boy, he had exactly the kind of reaction most dads would have under the same circumstances. But for the most part, my dad, ever the optimist, always had trust that I was a smart, mature kid who was going to find a way to take care of myself.

The truth about me would lie somewhere in the middle.

NINE

Where there is no struggle, there is no strength.

—OPRAH WINFREY

F RANK AND I MOVED into a tiny apartment in Hurst in May of 1980, the cheapest one we could find. A grim, dingy place that's since been torn down, it had a bedroom with a sliding glass door that opened directly onto the frontage road of Highway 183, a little galley kitchen, and ugly green shag carpeting. Frank had gone to pick out the apartment while I was at work one day and asked me whether I wanted brown or green carpeting—the apartments came with one or the other—and I'd said brown. On move-in day, though, when we got to the apartment with our meager belongings, I saw we had green carpeting and was surprised to learn the reason behind the apparent mistake: Frank was color-blind.

I brought with me my clothes and my bed from home. Frank brought with him his clothes, a used sofa set that his parents gave him, and an assortment of some dishes, pots, and pans. Even though I was there because of the difficulty I'd left behind, I was excited: I was the only senior at school with my own place. It very quickly turned into party central—not surprising when two teenagers are on their own and away from their parents. Friends were always dropping in, and there wasn't much time to sleep or be by myself, but I remember that first feeling of self-sufficiency, a strange combination of pride and bitterness. At seventeen I already had no illusions about the world. I knew there was no easy way through life, that it was a struggle, and that we all had to find our own joy and make our own success, even if success meant just managing to pay the rent.

It didn't take long for me to realize that all I'd done by moving across town was to trade one set of problems for another.

Life had been hard for me before, but now in my senior year, while I was going to school and working two jobs, it had gotten even harder. I'd started waiting tables at my dad's theater the previous year, after his sandwich shop became a preshow dinner service. It was tough, low-paying work—we worked for tips only, and there were some nights when I would make less than twenty dollars—but it came with the added benefit of getting to spend a lot of time with my dad again, seeing him become so many different people through the characters he played onstage, and watching him persevere and refuse to give up even when things were financially tough for the theater.

It also gave me the opportunity to connect with him in a way that I hadn't been able to since my parents had separated and divorced; I have some very fond memories of that, including the fact that for a while I started calling him Jerry. I looked up to him and admired him for what he was doing with the theater, and now that I was working for him, I started calling him by his first name the way everyone else there did. For me, calling him by his first name meant a recognition that we now had a relationship that had moved beyond one of just father-daughter. During this time I saw him in a whole new light: I now understood that he was living his passion, and I had a newfound respect for his willingness to do without everything in the way of financial success in order to achieve that dream. Calling him Jerry was a recognition of that respect and a demonstration that I didn't just see him in the role of my father. I saw him as the extraordinary human being that he was, working so hard, and with such dedication, and against so many odds, to bring this theater to life when it looked as if it wasn't possible that it could continue to survive.

My siblings never really appreciated or understood my calling him by his first name, particularly my brother Chris, and it wasn't long before I once again settled into calling him Dad. I don't remember why, but perhaps it was that once again he became who I needed him to be to me—a parent—more than a singular human being to admire and marvel at from a distance.

I'd also started working as a receptionist for two pediatricians—it was part of my high school's vocational-education program, because my dream was to become a doctor. This meant going to school during half days in the morning, then answering phones at the doctors' office in the afternoon, then waiting tables at my dad's theater at night. While I stayed at the doctors' office on and off for a few years, Frank went through several jobs during the brief time we lived together—sometimes due to layoffs, sometimes due to a disagreement he had with a superior—either way, it added to the rockiness of our partnership from the get-go. Frank brought a unique cleverness to everything he took on, meaning that he had a hard time conforming to the way others thought he ought to do things. He was very particular in how he approached tasks and projects, and sometimes that didn't match up with how his boss wanted things done. Almost always there would be some kind of confrontation, and he'd lose his job—he'd either quit or be fired—and then get started on finding another one.

Despite his employment issues, Frank always wanted to work. He was very smart and very hardworking, and it was his hope—which was certainly exhibited in his efforts—to provide partnered financial support for me. He typically drove heavy equipment, like forklifts in a warehouse setting or backhoes in a road-building capacity, which was very much in keeping with who he was and what he loved. He *loved* automobiles. Frank was the kind of person who could take something apart, figure out how it worked, and reassemble it, never needing to read a manual. I recall his mother telling me that he had been doing that since he was a little boy: taking his toys apart, figuring out how they worked, and reassembling them. Looking back, I wish he'd had the opportunity to find the right career to match his interests and his talents. But, at least for the time that we were together, that didn't happen.

In May of 1981, a year after I'd moved in with Frank, I graduated from Richland High School. I was a member of the National Honor Society, but I don't remember ever studying. I made it a point to go to school most days, hardly ever skipping class. That sense of obligation to follow through was driven deep into me by my parents and grandparents. And though they weren't physically around to make sure I adhered to my duties, they were there in my conscience nonetheless. As had previously been the case, I did well academically even after I was living on my own. I was blessed with a very good short-term memory, for which I credit my dad, so I was one of those students who could just show up and take a test and do well, remembering whatever work we'd done in class well enough to regurgitate it on an exam. English was my main interest, born from the love of reading that my mother had passed along. But math was always one of my strengths, too, especially calculus and elementary analysis and trigonometry; by the time I was in eleventh grade, I'd exhausted every math class my high school offered. I credit my father's constant problem-solving quizzes for shaping my analytic thinking. But though I was blessed with natural aptitudes and developed talents, I was lost when it came to understanding how to navigate my way into college when I graduated high school. I applied to only one—the University of Texas at Arlington (UTA)—because it was one my dad and I agreed we could best afford. Part of the U.T. system, it had a sprawling urban campus and most of its students then were commuters. It was close enough for me to continue working part-time at the doctors' office, but because I was running back and forth from work to classes, I wasn't able to connect with the school community and feel socially rooted there.

After I started taking classes, Frank and I moved to a slightly nicer apartment and worked hard at starting a stable life together. I was still committed to my dream of becoming a pediatrician, as was my dad—he'd wanted it so much for me, in fact, that he'd scrimped and saved enough money to help me pay my first semester's tuition. But soon after that, in November of my first semester, I got pregnant with Amber, and I did not return for a second one.

It was a difficult decision and one that I never really forgave myself for, but there was no way around it: I wasn't able to work full-time at the doctors' office when I was in school, and Frank and I needed my full-time paycheck. I still remember what I earned working there—$960 a month, before taxes. My half-time amount—when I worked in the morning and had afternoon classes or worked in the afternoon and had classes in the morning—was significantly less. Even though I was still waiting tables, the instability of Frank's work situation and the cost of going to school made it impossible for me to afford to continue. Especially now that we had a baby on the way. And honestly, the whole thing felt pretty overwhelming to me. It was difficult for me, as a first-generation college student, finding my footing in that first entrée into college.

O f course, I hadn't planned on becoming a teenage mother.

But one day that fall, while shopping with my mom in JCPenney, I suddenly got dizzy and had to hold on to a shelf in the store to gather myself. My mother immediately knew what I had not yet recognized for myself.

"Oh, my gosh," she said, looking at me. "You're not pregnant, are you?"

As it turned out, I was. I was eighteen. Still a child myself, and now presented with a level of responsibility I could not fully appreciate until I first held Amber in my arms and understood, as only a mother can, how very real, how very overwhelming, that responsibility would be.

I know that my mom worried about my financial capacities and that Frank and I were in a relationship that likely couldn't sustain the responsibilities of both marriage and parenthood, but at the same time, from the moment that I confirmed that I was pregnant, she was completely supportive and demonstrated that she was going to be there for me. The nurses at work did as well, comforting me with their advice and their warm support. I had a very real sense that, surrounded by people who I knew were going to help me do this hard thing, somehow it was all going to be okay.

D espite our financial circumstances and the fact that I was only eighteen, my emotions turned quickly from overwhelming fear to excitement. I was going to have a baby. And I determined to be grateful for the opportunity to become a mother. It took Frank a little longer to adjust to the idea, but once he did, he decided we should buy a mobile home so we wouldn't keep throwing money away on rent. It was only after we picked one out and signed on the bottom line that we realized, too late, that we had to find a place to put it. Two kids, we hadn't thought about the difficulty of finding a mobile-home park that we could afford. No one had mentioned this fact to us while we were in the process of buying it, probably because they assumed we were smart enough to know that for ourselves . . .

There were no mobile-home parks in the area of Richland Hills and Hurst, where I had grown up and where Frank and I were currently living—and certainly none nearby that we could afford. In order to find an affordable one, we had to move quite a distance away—about a twenty- to twenty-five-minute drive from my mother's house, off Loop 820, in southeast Fort Worth, where there were two mobile-home parks. One was the "nice" one that had a pond with ducks and parklike grassy areas and where people had potted plants on their decks and a little bit of a yard. And then there was Lakeview, with poorly done asphalt roads and older, smaller mobile homes that were much lower in quality. Lakeview was farther out of town than we would have liked, but it was all we could afford; we made arrangements to rent a spot there starting in late January. I still laugh when I recall the name of that trailer park. Lakeview? Ha. The only view from those trailers was of each other, families struggling to make ends meet. Good people who, like Frank and me, were doing the best they could.

On January 24, 1982, Frank and I got married at my father's theater, while my mom sobbed audibly in the front row through the entire ceremony—and not because she was happy. My best friend, Lori, who was my maid of honor, had driven me there that afternoon, and on the way I remember telling her that I feared I wasn't doing the right thing.

"Then don't do it!" she kept saying.

But I didn't know how not to do it.

I didn't know how to have a baby and not be married—in the world I'd grown up in, women didn't choose to do it that way, have babies on their own. But if my present self could have advised my eighteen-year-old self, she would have told me this:

Don't do it.

Just move back in with your mom and have your baby.

Don't go down this road.

However, of course my present self *couldn't* save my eighteen-year-old self from going down that road. And as I look back on my journey, I know that going down that road was an important part of shaping who I became. As we mature, most of us look back on things that we would have done differently, but if we're lucky enough to be proud and happy with the person we've become, it's hard to second-guess our decisions, no matter how ill-advised and unwise they appeared at the time. Yes, I would have told my younger self to do so many things differently, but I cherish the fact that it was those very decisions and challenges that made me the person—and the mother and the public servant—I eventually became.

B ut that night, on the way to my wedding, even without the benefit of hindsight, I knew I was making a mistake. I knew that Frank and I weren't long-term-marriage material. Though I loved him, I could already see clearly the hurdles that we would confront as a couple. I knew that we were different. I had dreams for myself, and I was driven to make them happen, and I could tell that he wasn't going to go along on that journey with me. It wasn't the journey he wanted to be on.

When we first met, I was in high school and just as excited about having parties every night as he was, but now I was already growing past that. It was a phase for me, but Frank wasn't ready to outgrow it. His frequent partying became a real source of conflict for us, and not just because he was spending money on something like that when we had a baby on the way and were always struggling to pay the bills.

I knew that I wasn't on the path I wanted to be on, but I didn't have the fortitude to call a time-out in order to reconsider. So there, on the same stage where my father had played so many different roles and where he, too, had gotten married—to Suzi McLaughlin, who became my stepmom—we took our vows and drove to our new mobile home in Lakeview as Mr. and Mrs. Frank Underwood.

L akeview Mobile Home Park had a rule that you must have a skirt around your mobile home, but we couldn't afford a ready-made one. Instead ours was a skirt cobbled together from metal sheeting that Frank had bought at the hardware store and that covered only about the front quarter of the trailer. Thankfully, the management of the park didn't press the issue because we couldn't afford to address it. And so we began our marriage and tried our best to make a home to bring our baby into. We both worked during the day, and I worked many nights as well. And we settled into our pattern as a married couple. Frank's real passion was working on cars, especially his beloved yellow-and-black Trans Am, so there was always an old car up on blocks beside our trailer, with its hood up and its motor parts strewn around on the ground. We would eat a dinner of either spaghetti, fried chicken, frozen pizza, or pork chops (the four things in my "cooking" repertoire). Frank would work on his car. On the evenings I was home, I would work obsessively on keeping our trailer clean. And we awaited the birth of our child.

Living in Lakeview was a foreign experience for me. Though we were only a twenty-minute drive from our previous home and from our parents, it felt as though we had moved into an entirely different life. I didn't recognize myself in it and found a hopelessness settling in on me. At least when we'd lived in the apartment, I still felt part of the community I'd grown up in, but now we were out in a trailer park that was far removed from anywhere.

That was certainly a difficult time. I'd left my community. I was in a marriage I didn't think was going to work out. And we had a mortgage and all the other responsibilities that came along with "home ownership" even if that home was one on wheels. It required a whole new level of maturity for me that came at a time when I was already dealing with a lot: being pregnant and feeling the disappointment of college not working out after I'd completed just one semester.

As always, there was the stressful distraction of having to earn a living. Chasing a job with a better opportunity for advancement, I left the pediatricians' office and started at Dresser Industries, with the help of a former co-worker who had also gone to work there. Though the commute was long, the pay was slightly better, there was an opportunity to work my way up the ladder, and, most important, there were health-insurance benefits. Without them I wouldn't have been able to afford maternity care. Frank and I were overwhelmed at the prospect of paying for any of that.

Dresser Industries was a good company, one that supplied parts for drilling rigs, from the smallest of gaskets to some of the most complex machinery parts. I worked in the requisition department, and it was my job to take an order, bring it out to the floor, have it filled, and get it sent off to the customer.

But getting to my new job presented another set of challenges. I commuted to Dallas and had a car-pool arrangement with my former co-worker, who'd encouraged me to apply for the job, and her husband. They lived in Arlington, east of where I lived and in between where I lived and Dallas. To be at work by seven or seven-thirty, I'd get up at four-thirty in the morning, leave my place at five-thirty, then pick up my friends and head on into work. We took turns driving from Arlington to Dallas and, at one point during that commuting period, when every precious penny counted for me, my car began experiencing serious engine problems, and Frank was unable to fix it properly. Unable to afford a solution, I continued to drive it for a few months after that. This terrified my friends when it was my day to be the driver, because I couldn't get it to accelerate above fifty miles per hour, making things pretty precarious when I tried to enter a freeway ramp.

Frank and I then decided to do something that in hindsight was extremely irresponsible. We bought a new car, the dealer's model that had been test-driven quite a bit, so the price was lower, but it was still far more than our budget allowed us to afford. I cannot believe the dealership was willing to sell it to us. It's likely that Frank's parents had to co-sign for us, though I don't recall that with any real clarity. It was a gold Pontiac Grand Prix with cloth interior, and it was only a matter of days before Frank burned a hole in the front seat with a cigarette. It was the first new thing I'd ever owned, and I was really proud to have it, but a car payment on top of our other obligations added an unbelievable burden to our already stressful financial situation.

And then, out of the clear blue sky, I was facing the prospect of losing my job. I was about six months pregnant, and Dresser began downsizing in response to a decline in the oil and gas industry. Because I was so newly employed, I was caught in the first wave of layoffs. But one of my co-workers, a young woman with two children and a husband who had a steady job, gave me her position and took the layoff so I could keep my job and, more important at that juncture, my health benefits. She wanted to take the opportunity to be home with her very young children, and she also wanted to help me—

it was an incredible act of kindness that moved me to tears. She was an angel in every sense of the word, and I will never forget the sacrifice she made to help me. Sadly, though, even her sacrifice didn't save me from the next round of layoffs. Within another month, her job—which had become my job—got cut. My immediate supervisor understood very clearly what this layoff would mean to me and my pregnancy. In what was the pre-COBRA era, he knew that I would lose my insurance. I'm not sure how he convinced the higher-ups to allow me to keep my insurance, but somehow he did. In exchange I had to agree to give up the two weeks' severance pay that I otherwise would have received. The decision was a no-brainer for me. How Frank and I would pull off the feat of paying our bills during that period was unimaginable, but keeping my doctor and my ability to deliver Amber under his care was my priority.

And then, at seven months pregnant, I applied for and began receiving unemployment. In order to qualify for the unemployment benefits, I had to demonstrate that I was putting in a legitimate effort to find a new job. And though I got a fair amount of interviews, one look at my ever-expanding belly meant a polite "We'll be in touch," a follow-up that didn't occur. To say that things became unsustainable financially for Frank and me during that time would be an understatement. We rationed gas. We rationed food. We rationed electricity—no easy feat for someone in her final trimester of pregnancy during the hottest Texas summer months.

I will never forget the unexpected blessing that arrived right after Amber was born. Though my boss at Dresser had brokered a deal with me to give up severance in favor of insurance, he continued to press my case, unbeknownst to me. And the fruits of his efforts appeared not long after Amber Nicole Underwood came into the world. I remember that day so vividly, my palms sweaty as I stood beside our mailbox, holding a check in the amount of two weeks' pay from

Dresser. That letter had been preceded by an electricity cutoff notice. A bill we could now pay. Another answered prayer from God. Another angel to my rescue. With tears streaming down my face, I fell to my knees right then and there and said a prayer of gratitude.

And so it was that I was able to deliver Amber with the doctor of my choice at the hospital of my choice and to bring her home to a place where cool air could chill her room from a small window A/C unit that we'd bought used. We were surviving. If only for the short term, I knew how great my blessings were.

Amber was born that August, by cesarean section. She was healthy, six pounds, thirteen ounces, with beautiful dark skin and dark hair and dark eyes. Both Frank's family and my family were there, and my dad instantly and proudly pronounced Amber the most beautiful baby in the nursery. She was born into a world where she had grandparents and parents who were excited to greet her and to do our best to try to provide a good life for her.

We were excited about our baby, and I was lucky enough to regain my job at the pediatricians' office so we could have free pediatric care for Amber and as many free samples of medicine and formula as I needed. It got us through another rough financial spot, but even that couldn't save my relationship with Frank. More from financial pressures than anything else, Frank and I struggled to maintain some semblance of cohesion. Eventually the tensions grew to a degree where we couldn't look at each other without harboring unspoken resentment for the circumstances we were now in. We were young, overwhelmed kids in a situation that neither of us should have been in, and we weren't handling it very well.

We were broke. We were just always broke.

During that period, Frank and I ceased living together. He was working out of town—I don't even remember where now. I think he wanted to be free of me, of our fights grown out of the tensions we blamed each other for. For my part, I felt the same. It's hard when people are that young—or even when they're older—to cope with the burden of financial challenges, and rather than being able to find within each other an escape from that difficult storm, we instead thought, *Had I not met you, I wouldn't be suffering with this.*

I withdrew from him completely during that time, and we no longer had anything in the way of a physical relationship. I think he was happy for the opportunity to go to work far away and to be living separately. I know he always loved Amber, but I believe he came to feel that she honestly might be better off not being exposed to the difficulties we were facing as a couple.

For a very brief time we attempted to make it work again. We celebrated Amber's first birthday together at his parents' home, but we couldn't fix what was broken.

One day not long after that, on our way to my mom's house, Frank and I got into a terrible fight in the car. When we pulled over, we were screaming at each other, and we became explosive—it reached the point where we were physically fighting, each of us taking out our frustrations on the other. For me, that was the absolute end. That's when I knew there was no way we could possibly create a healthy relationship in which to raise our child.

That was the day I took Amber in my arms, went to my mother's house, and never returned to that mobile home. After a year and a half of our marriage, and a year and a half of living removed from the safety net of the community I'd grown up in while in that trailer, I was determined to put that part of my life behind me. Frank and I were now officially on the path to a divorce. Though we had lived apart, we both knew this was really the end. Neither of us looked back or ever second-guessed our decision. I think for both of us it felt easier to be responsible only for ourselves, not each other.

I filed for divorce from Frank in December of 1983. In the divorce, which would become final about six months later, in May of 1984, Frank got the trailer. I, believe it or not, was given possession of the 1971 Pontiac Trans Am and the other dead car that Frank was always fixing. I can't imagine what I would have done with either of them, so I left them behind.

The only real asset I cared about—the most precious one of all— Amber—I took with me.

With the benefit of hindsight, I can see that history was repeating itself: I was moving home after my separation from Frank the same way my mother had moved home to Muleshoe after she divorced my dad. With two jobs and a very young child, I was unable to make it completely on my own. Though the circumstances of our situations were very different, the broad strokes were the same. I, too, was a single mother with a one-step plan. But I had a port in the storm: my mom, who took Amber and me into her home until I could get on my feet again. Which I did, though those feet were wobbly, the following spring.

Plans are hard to make when you're struggling, and there wasn't a time in my life after my parents' divorce and after my dad left his job when I wasn't struggling. That just seemed to be where I was. Stuck— paycheck to paycheck. If I had a flat tire, there was never an extra twenty dollars to fix it. During our marriage and while I was living in the trailer on my own, I'd made several visits to pawnshops, first with my clarinet from high school and later with some of Frank's car parts, just to turn the phone or electricity back on. I struggled to pay my bills, without any help. Neither my mom nor my dad had resources, not even in the most basic way of being able to slip you twenty bucks every now and then just to help you get through the month— they simply did not have the means.

It took me a while, but eventually, working two jobs as I always had—as a receptionist at the pediatricians' office during the day and waiting tables at my dad's theater at night—I scraped together enough money to get an apartment for Amber and me, and we moved out of my mother's. Once again, my plan started with a single step, but it was a step toward a new beginning.

And sometimes one step is all you need.

TEN

Nothing will work unless you do.

—MAYA ANGELOU

WHEN I WAS ON MY OWN with Amber after my separation from Frank, all my energy was focused on trying to stay ahead of our bills, and a deep disappointment settled in. To say that I felt a sense of shame would not be an overstatement. I knew I was possessed with the blessing of a good intellect. And I was angry and frustrated at myself for allowing my life to get so off track.

Since high school my dream had been to become a doctor—a pediatrician. It's why I'd gone to work in the doctors' office through my high school's vocational program, and it's why I'd enrolled at UTA. I'd had a plan. I was going to go to college for four years, and then I was going to go to medical school. And even though a chemistry course I took in my one semester at UTA made it clear that I probably wasn't cut out for that particular career, I still had a dream for myself: to get an education and to do something meaningful with my life.

Most people from my high-school class didn't go on to college— Richland Hills was a middle-income town, and while some families had a generational history of college, many more did not. My family didn't have that history, but I still thought I was going to be one of the people who went to college. I thought I was going to excel. I'd grown accustomed to achieving in school and had come to expect something of myself because of it.

Part of the confidence I had about learning is something I can trace to my earliest years in elementary school. When I was reading through the color-coded boxes of materials in that experimental school in Chula Vista, I began to understand for the first time that I was smart. Self-motivation was clearly part of the purposeful design of the box—working your way up through the colors meant you were advancing to higher-level reading material. But it also showed each child his or her reading progress as it compared to that of others; some kids were back in the yellow category while other kids were up in the red, or the purple, or the olive category. We all knew, if only subtly, who was going forward and who was falling behind. That was my first experience of comparing myself to others, but when we moved to Texas, the schools did that in a much more formal way. Students were put into tracked math and reading groups, always organized by color or by letter in a halfhearted attempt to disguise the true meaning of the divisions.

Because I was always in the top groups, I was learning, in those very formative years, something even more important than academics: that I was a person who had abilities and potential. It never occurred to me until years later that the children in the Orange Group or the C Group were learning a very different lesson: that they weren't as academically capable. I began to see that a system that was labeling me as smart or gifted was also one that was labeling other kids as below par. And as I realized that, I became concerned about a system that locked kids into categories at such an early age, categories we would probably view ourselves through forever, whether the categorization was fair or not. For every child who grew self-confident about his or her capacities in such a system, there was another child who was being told that he or she wasn't making the cut. This "tracking" of students, I believe, is one of the greatest challenges we face in a public-school system. And it is furthered by the road to ruin that high-stakes tests put our children on. It seems such an ineffective way of helping all children reach their potential. Labels can be powerful. But they can be damaging as well. Having been on the upside of that labeling, I am grateful for the benefit of growing up believing that I was smart. And I am committed to making sure all children have the benefit of seeing that potential in themselves.

Recognizing that reality, I fortunately had always believed I would make something of my life. But when my dream of getting a higher education and becoming a doctor was interrupted, I'd very quickly gotten to a place where I didn't see how I was going to put it back on track. Responsible for a child and so strapped for money, it was all I could do to just work the hours I was working and take care of the duties of a young parent. The idea of somehow fitting school into the existing mix of work and child care was unfathomable.

B ut one fateful day during 1984, after I had moved out of my mom's house and into my own apartment, a nurse in the doctors' office where I worked came in with a brochure from Tarrant County Junior College (now called Tarrant County College). She'd stopped by there on her way to work because she was thinking about taking a few business classes and had picked up some information about the vocational programs they offered. She just happened to put the brochure down on my desk, and, curious, I began to read it. I took it home with me that night. And back to the office with me the next day. And I began to let myself dream of college once again. The two-year paralegal degree program offered there seemed like a good fit for me. I loved English, was fairly decent at written communication, and a job in that field would pay twice what I was currently making.

Ever since that neighbor knocked on the door when my mother put us all in the trunk of her car in the garage in Rhode Island, I've believed in angels. That first angel saved my brothers and my mom and me, a second one made sure I had health care during my pregnancy with Amber, and now a third angel had placed that brochure on my desk. I honestly do not believe I ever would have taken the initiative myself to stop by the school and inquire about vocational classes. And I often wonder how different my life would be today had it not been for that one moment. Ironically, the nurse who had gone by the campus to pick up the brochure never signed up to take any classes. But her action led to a dramatic change in my life. Having left UTA after only one semester when I became pregnant with Amber, I didn't think I'd ever get a second chance. I didn't think it was ever going to happen for me. More than that, I had lost something that I'd always had. No matter how hard things had been, and through all the ups and downs, I'd always possessed my dad's optimism and a belief in myself. I believed in my potential. But that self-assuredness had turned to defeatism. And that brochure was a light breaking through.

Fear is a great motivator, and the intense desperation I felt as a young single parent who couldn't pay my bills—who sometimes couldn't keep the electricity turned on despite not spending a dime on anything that wasn't an absolute necessity—turned my fear from something that had frozen me in place to something that propelled me into action. The mere act of picking up that brochure was all the impetus I needed to find my way back to my dream.

There were many times I had pushed through fear prior to my re-entry into the college arena, many times when I knew there was no easy escape hatch and that I would have to just put my head down against the wind and push through. I couldn't afford to let myself fail again. My fear was met with a newfound resoluteness that I had not possessed before. I knew it would be really challenging to keep working two jobs and also take on the responsibility of school, but I was bound and determined. And once I enrolled in the paralegal program at TCC's Northeast Campus in Hurst, all I had to do was push myself harder than I'd ever pushed before. And from the moment I resolved to do that, I didn't look up again until I had fully forged that path.

I am forever grateful to the doctors I worked for—Dr. Julian Haber and Dr. Barry Bzostek—who allowed me to come in a bit later so that I could take early-morning classes several days a week and who let me off early enough to take evening classes as well. With my new school schedule, I was still able to wait tables three nights a week at my dad's theater.

But it was the logistics of child care for Amber that made the schedule truly grueling for both of us. Lisa, one of the nurses I'd become friends with at the office, had just started staying home with her little boy. To earn money she began caring for a few children in her home, and she agreed to keep Amber for me during the day. Knowing that Amber was in the care of someone loving and kind was a huge relief and help. But Lisa lived in the neighboring town of Watauga, and it was a haul to get there each morning. More difficult was the fact that I also had to find child care in the evenings when I was at school or waiting tables at Stage West. I had no consistent help in that regard. I still feel the pangs of guilt that came from shuffling

Amber from place to place. Each evening as I would finish my day-time job, I would make the drive back to Watauga to collect Amber, drop her off around 6:30 p.m. at her second sitter for the day (which sometimes, thankfully, was my mom). Then it was on to school or to Stage West, which was downtown. And often it was ten o'clock at night before I could pick her up, bathe her, and put her to bed. After which I would try to focus on studying until I fell asleep, exhausted. Only to start the whole thing over again the next day.

I think about it now and don't know how I did it. I honestly don't. There was never a moment to rest, for either of us, and the worst part of it for me by far—even more than the exhaustion and stress—was feeling such guilt about what that kind of schedule was doing to Amber. I wish more than anything that I could have spared her such a difficult infancy, prevented her from being flung here and there every day. There was no downtime for the two of us, no quiet mornings or evenings when we could hang out with each other, or do things together, or just relax. We were always moving. Always, always, always on the go. Always driving in my little red Mazda pickup truck (by then I'd traded in my Grand Prix for something more affordable). Occasionally we'd have a little quiet time on the weekends, but I was still waiting tables every Saturday night, so even those days weren't sacred.

Amber deserved something so much better than I was able to provide for her back then, and I will forever wish that I could have given it to her. But I did the best I could. The only way for the two of us to make it out of the quicksand we were in was to move directly through it to the other side.

And ultimately we did, because I knew I couldn't not try to go to school and get that done, and I also knew I couldn't afford not to wait tables or work at the doctors' office. Once I'd fought back the initial fear of taking those first classes, I don't remember feeling afraid. In fact, I became pretty fearless. I was tired and overwhelmed from time to time, but my drive was strong, and I pushed through the stress every day: getting up to study at four o'clock in the morning on the days I had exams and sometimes not getting into bed until well after midnight.

Worrying about money would often keep me awake into the wee hours. I had a car payment, I had my rent payment, and I had child-care costs, and on my little ledger there was not a dime to spare. I had to be so disciplined about what I could buy at the grocery store. And like many people in a tough financial spot, I came to know the embarrassment of standing at the checkout counter, realizing there wasn't enough money to pay for what I had in my cart and the humiliation of selecting items to put back so that I could pay the cashier and leave. I had to be disciplined about everything, from how high I set the thermostat to rationing gasoline and driving only for absolute necessity. Every dollar was sacred, every dollar spent a choice between priorities. Never a choice between luxuries, like a new top for me or a new toy for Amber.

By this time Frank's presence in our lives had slowly but surely receded. Occasionally he would make a child-support payment. And he tried to help take care of Amber on his designated visitation days. But ultimately, and especially after I started dating Jeff Davis, who would become my second husband, Frank disappeared from Amber's life altogether for a while. His parents, however, continued to consistently be there for us, and they were a real stabilizing force for me and for Amber. At least twice a month, they would keep her overnight on a Saturday night when I was waiting tables. It was a great comfort to know she was with them. They were and still are kind and loving grandparents who cared for her and who showed me tenderness as well. I vividly recall Stan (Frank's father) slipping a twenty-dollar bill into my jacket pocket as I left their house one Sunday morning when

I came to collect Amber. Reaching into my pocket after getting into my truck and discovering the money there literally brought me to tears. I sat there crying, so grateful for the gesture and so appreciative of the gift of money that I desperately needed. To this day, every Thanksgiving and Christmas, Amber spends time with her paternal grandparents, and through them she has rekindled a relationship with Frank as well. He loves and is proud of her; they have forged a special bond.

These periods in my life helped me become the person I am today. I wouldn't trade a moment of them, even the hardest of hard days. I know my story is not unique. It's the story of millions of women who know the strength it takes as young single mothers to survive and improve their circumstances. Like so many other women, I knew I was going to have to work to get us out of where we'd been stuck if I was to give my daughter a better future.

And through the grace of God and a few angels along the way, I was on the path to do it.

ELEVEN

A single rose can be my garden . . .
a single friend, my world.

—ATTRIBUTED TO LEO BUSCAGLIA

I T WASN'T EASY going back to school while working two jobs and always making sure I had child care for Amber, but once I enrolled and got into a routine and started advancing through the paralegal program, my confidence grew. College wasn't only for other people anymore, and in time I allowed myself the luxury of believing that I could become a lawyer, rather than a lawyer's assistant. That important turning point set me on a path that changed my life in ways so profound I could not have possibly anticipated it at the time. Education would come to make all the difference in my life.

I was about to start my second semester at TCC when I met Jeff Davis. I had dated a couple of guys following my separation and divorce from Frank, but no one who made much of an impression on me. Jeff was different. Not only was he one of the patrons of Stage West, my father's theater, he was also on its board of directors, and I'd seen him there on many occasions, either attending a play or attending a board meeting. He was significantly older than me and well established in his career. He was a lawyer, and when he was twenty-seven he'd been the youngest person ever elected to the city council in Fort Worth, a record he still holds. He was self-confident and self-possessed, and whenever I'd waited on him at my dad's theater, he'd always treated me with kindness and respect. That, plus his support of the theater as a board member, was something that made a significant impression on me, made me want to get to know him better. Shy as always, I'd asked my father to make an introduction, and before I knew it, he'd cast himself in the role of the least subtle matchmaker imaginable:

"How do you feel about younger women, Jeff? Because my daughter would really like to go out with you."

I suppose he felt okay about younger women—I was just twenty-one, and he was thirty-five—because eventually he called and asked me out. Jeff wasn't like anyone I'd ever dated before. He was worldly, sophisticated, and college-educated. And he hadn't gone to just any college—he'd gone to Princeton. *Princeton University.* He'd majored in religion and played three sports there, then gone on to law school at Southern Methodist University. He had a stable life—he was well-educated and had a reliable income—and was in the process of buying an actual house with an actual yard in a neighborhood near downtown Fort Worth, called Mistletoe Heights. One of the things that struck me about him was that he owned two cars—one a showy red Porsche, the other an old two-door Mustang. It was the Mustang he preferred to drive, and I thought that said a great deal about him. He liked to have fun, but there was something so centered, so grounded about him, too. I was impressed by him, not by what he owned but by the confidence he portrayed and the commitment he gave to things he believed in, my dad's theater being one of those things. Anyone who supported and believed in helping advance my dad's dream of delivering quality live theater to our community immediately scored a checkmark in the "pro" column of my book.

From the outside looking in, we probably could not have appeared more different. But despite the gap in our ages and accomplishments, we did share common ground: we'd both had to get where we were on our own. Jeff didn't have a whole lot growing up either, and while his family certainly didn't have the kind of fracture running through it that mine did, his trajectory from a fairly ordinary military family to Princeton and beyond was, I thought, remarkable. Though he wasn't a first-generation college student and though both of his older brothers had also attended and ultimately graduated from college, Jeff, like me, was the kind of person who set his sights high and was competitive in a healthy, productive way that pushed him to maximize his opportunities. He was smart and driven, and when we started dating, I believe he saw those similar qualities in me and understood how hard I was trying to improve my life. Had I not been on my own journey of self-improvement, I have no doubt that Jeff wouldn't have given me a second glance. But he understood something about me, he "saw" me, in a way that most people wouldn't have noticed. He took the time to get to know who I was, deep inside, who I was becoming. Like me, he was also divorced and had a child from his first marriage—a son, Erik, who was a few years older than Amber and who lived with his mother in Louisiana.

Our first social outing occurred at a Christmas party in 1984. The host, also a board member at Stage West, had invited us both, deciding it would be the perfect setting for us to get to know each other. I was nervous but excited about the opportunity to get to talk to him. And talk we did. We sat down facing each other and didn't stop talking for hours. Not long after, our courtship began.

Dating someone like Jeff was a whole new experience for me—a very positive one—and I got caught up in it quickly: in his intelligence, in his professional achievements, and in his level of social so-phistication, so far beyond my own. Our first date was at Sardine's restaurant in Fort Worth, something of an institution at the time that is sadly no longer in business. But it was *the* place to go back then. There was always a great band, usually jazz, playing extremely loudly, so it wasn't a place that lent itself to much in the way of conversation. It was dimly lit, had a menu with items I'd never heard of before, and I thought it was the most romantic setting I'd ever been in. I spent the evening brushing imaginary bread crumbs off the red-and-white checkered tablecloth on the table as Jeff inquired about my journey and my dreams. I don't think I've ever been as nervous on a date be-fore or since. And from that point forward, I was completely smitten.

Following that date, Jeff took me to restaurants where they had multiple pieces of silverware on either side of and above the place set-tings and menus that mystified me—I recall watching his every move and mimicking each one. I had no idea which fork to use when. I would wait for him to pick up his utensils so I'd know which ones to use and take my cues from him on what to order. On one occasion, not long after we started dating, we drove past a store in downtown Fort Worth that had a beautiful lace dress in the window, which I'd remarked on. On our next date, Jeff showed up with a big box when he picked me up—inside was the dress from the store window. No one had ever shown me such tenderness before.

In fact, it was his kindness and generosity that struck me most about Jeff. He was kind not only to me but to Amber, who could be quite a handful at two years old. Jeff's most admirable quality re-mains his desire to lift people up. It's what he does. Some people take in and give shelter to animals in need. Jeff likes to rescue people. And I certainly fit the archetypal mold of a person he could rescue. I was Galatea to his Pygmalion, or, in more modern-day literature, I was Eliza Doolittle to his Henry Higgins. A perfect example of that came not long after we started dating. My phone had been turned off because I was unable to pay the bill. I had resigned myself to doing without it until I could afford the balance and the new deposit it would take to have it turned on, but, to my surprise, one evening the phone rang. It was Jeff. Cool and casual. Not mentioning a word of what he'd done. But I understood. He'd paid to have it turned back on, and I was simultaneously grateful and humiliated.

What I appreciated most about Jeff was that he could see beyond the shy, uneducated girl I looked like to most of the outside world. He saw my drive, and he admired it. It was what attracted him to me.

And so it was with us in those early years. Jeff was my greatest cheerleader, and he took pride in watching me do well. With his support I thrived. But I also had a nagging sense that I was somehow lesser than him. Where Jeff was sophisticated about politics, about law, about travel and dining, I was always intimidated. Our footing felt uneven, and for a long time I suffered an insecurity that was hard for me to overcome. When he was with peers, talking politics particularly, I felt unable to join the conversation. But that insecurity, ultimately coupled with my innate drive, became a motivator for me. I was determined that I would prove to myself, and to others, that I could hold my own. And with Jeff patiently at my side, I did.

B efore I met Jeff, I had already reset and redefined my goal to become a lawyer rather than the assistant to one. But now, watching the example of Jeff in his circle of friends, I also set my sights on attending a top-tier law school. I had lost ground to cover and something to prove to myself. I was determined not to be defined by the paths that had previously taken me off course, but instead to correct them.

With all that in mind, I began taking general-studies courses at

TCC rather than paralegal ones, so that I could position myself for the next step—a four-year university. Dreams didn't get much bigger than that from where I stood.

And so, in the fall of 1986, after two years of part-time classes at TCC, I was accepted into the honors program at Texas Christian University, which I'd chosen for its high-caliber academics and proximity, paying my tuition through a combination of need-based and academic-based scholarships. After my acceptance at TCU, Jeff helped me get a job as a legal assistant at a nearby real-estate firm. A new chapter was opening for me. I had a decent-paying job that I would go to after morning classes, I continued to wait tables at my father's theater, and I rented a student-housing-quality duplex near the campus for Amber and me to live in. And though I was not the typical TCU coed—I wore dresses and heels to school so that I could go straight to work after my morning of classes ended—I felt solid there, too. I felt that I belonged. It was a renewed dream to once again find myself walking through the campus of a four-year university on my way to who I hoped to become.

As I've said, I had transferred to TCU with the intention of preparing to go to law school. For that reason I purposely chose to major in English with a writing emphasis. Literature was my passion, and learning to write well, I felt, would help me ultimately in law school. I chose my minor in philosophy specifically to equip me to do well on the Law School Admission Test (LSAT). Through its philosophy department, TCU offered classes in symbolic logic and critical reasoning, a crucial part of the standardized LSAT. I became completely focused on my new goal: excelling in college and on the LSAT in order to gain entry into a top-notch law school. Unlike my first experience at UTA, when my dream of going to medical school ended before it even really began, this was going to be different: I was not going to give up on myself this time.

But with a renewed focus and commitment came a whole new level of fear. The more pressure I put on myself to excel, the higher the stakes became and the more anxious I felt about not doing well. Doing less than perfectly was not an option, and I became hyper-focused on performing to this new bar I had set for myself—no more last-minute preparation for exams and winging it with the assumption that I would ace them. I had made straight A's at TCC, and I was determined that I would do the same at TCU.

Aside from Amber and my job, keeping my grade-point average up became an all-consuming goal. After a time, I realized that as devoted as I was to order in my mother's home and later in my own home, my dedication to academic excellence was another way for me to find a sense of order, to feel in control of my life. There was a peace that came from that. A sense that I could make everything all right.

Jeff asked me to marry him about two years after we started dating. We'd gone to Cozumel, and on the way there I'd hinted at the question of our making a marital commitment to each other. "What makes you think that's ever going to happen?" he'd teased, and I'd started crying. That evening, after we checked in to the hotel and with my feelings still bruised from our conversation on the plane and a terrible migraine, Jeff took me for a late-night stroll along the beach. Then he got down on one knee and placed a beautiful ring on my finger. It was a princess-cut diamond in a modern setting that was far too big for my finger. For the rest of our trip, I had to wrap the band with toilet paper so it would stay on. We were in love and each of us was filled with happiness about what the future would hold for us as a married couple.

In May of 1987, we got married. Because we both loved Fort Worth and all its history, we were wed in a historic chapel set in a graveyard. Yes, in a graveyard. Jeff rather enjoyed doing something quirky like that.

His son, Erik, who was almost ten, stood as Jeff's best man. Amber, at almost five, was my maid of honor. It was a small and graceful ceremony, with our closest friends and family in attendance. Afterward we hosted a reception at our home on Mistletoe Drive, in one of Fort Worth's oldest and loveliest neighborhoods, the second home that Jeff had purchased on Mistletoe Drive, having sold the first to make more room for our expanding family.

I was twenty-four when we got married. And for the first time since the age of fourteen, I no longer needed to work while going to school. I could focus solely on that, which I did. Jeff, Amber, and I moved into *a home*, a ranch home that had a swimming pool in the backyard. Even though the mortgage was a stretch for us and we had little disposable income because of it, compared to the financially precarious way I'd lived since my parents' divorce, the stability and security of my new life was a blissful relief.

One of the most poignant things Jeff ever said to me came during that time just a few weeks prior to our wedding.

"I almost hate to do it."

"Do what?" I asked.

"Marry you," he'd said. "Because I don't ever want to take away from you the fact that you did this on your own."

He was referring to my schooling. It struck me as such a beautiful thing for him to say, to show that he recognized my mettle, to acknowledge to me that while we were partners going forward, he knew that I had forged my own path. That he put voice to that meant the world to me.

I have no doubt in my mind that whether I'd married Jeff or not, I would still have gone to law school. My head was down. I was working hard to put myself on that path. Through my efforts and grades,

I had made it possible to affordably attend TCU through a combination of financial aid grants and an academic scholarship. The fact that I was already on my own trajectory and that I'd already come as far as I had on my own before we'd married was something Jeff himself was extremely sensitive to. And I loved him all the more for it.

I settled back into attending TCU that fall to continue my undergraduate work, my first time to attend school without also suffering the stresses of a workaday job. It was a wonderful period in all our lives.

I was able to spend quality time with Amber in a way that I hadn't been able to before. She now had a routine that gave her a security she'd never known. She had parents who were reliably home with her, meals at a fairly routine hour. Bath and bedtime stories. This was the kind of stability I'd wanted so much to give to her but had not been able to because of the work and school schedule I'd been keeping throughout her early life. No longer was she shuttled from sitter to sitter. She had her first real home, plus an extended family with whom we spent a great deal of time.

Jeff's parents lived in Fort Worth then. His father, Bev, a retired air force colonel, and his mother, Doris, a stay-at-home mom who brought a beautiful artistic flair to homemaking, were with us often. Bev—or "Daddy-Bev," as his grandchildren called him—was a force to be reckoned with. About six-two and with a bark of a voice, he was an intimidating presence. He had a temper that would exhibit itself from time to time—more bark than bite. Amber was simultaneously afraid of him and drawn to him. Behind his gruffness he had a tender heart. And he and Doris—"Mama Doris," as her grandchildren called her—treated Amber, always, as if she were their own flesh and blood.

Getting to know Doris Davis was one of the most precious privileges I have ever experienced. She was loving and kind to everyone, and she showed me a particular amount of her nurturing attention, teaching me some of her homemaking skills that hadn't been a part of my household growing up. She taught me so much about cooking, gardening, and decor. Everything she did, she did with a special flair. And she graciously met my desire to learn with an enthusiasm to share her skills with me.

My mother was also able to spend more relaxed time with us during this period. She had remarried and was no longer working night and day. She, too, loved Doris and enjoyed being around her. And, like me, my mom learned a thing or two from Doris about the art of taking care of family and home.

Immediately, Jeff's and my home on Mistletoe Drive became the center of both of our families. Thanksgiving and Christmas traditions were celebrated there, our extended families gathering in our ranch house—a perfect open setting for large groups. Built in the late forties, the house was set atop a hill with an expanse of glass across the back that looked out over a spacious back lawn, with a pool and a guesthouse down below. It was in need of a great deal of upkeep and repair, but we resolved to try to bring it up to our standards bit by bit. The yard, both front and back, was filled with enormous live and red oaks, pecans, and a few hackberries (weed trees, as we call them in Texas).

These were precious years. We brought two dogs into our family— shelties, Chrissy and Lily. Erik came for summers and for extended weekends. And it wasn't long before Jeff raised the question about whether I would be open to having a baby. I remember it as if it were yesterday. If I would consider having a baby, he'd said, he would promise to do 50 percent of the caretaking—diapers, midnight feedings, the whole bit. "Mr. Fifty Percent," I would teasingly call him when things got off balance in that regard. With little effort I was soon excited to find that I was expecting. And I had a perfect pregnancy with Dru. I felt wonderful, ate well, and was happier than I'd ever been in my life.

Dru took the LSAT with me. In a sense anyway. I was seven months pregnant with her when I sat for the test. As usual, in my type-A way, I'd studied hard in advance by doing the practice tests in those big, thick prep books; my goal going into it wasn't just to score well but to score top-level-law-school well. And I did. The test was given in one of the big science lecture halls at TCU, a familiar setting to me, and except for the fact that I got incredibly hungry by the end of it—you weren't allowed to take a break of any kind, even if you were seven months pregnant—it went well. At some point I realized that as scared as I was to take the test, the second I put my pencil to paper, fear had fallen away and all my years of hard work had taken over.

Weighing in at nine pounds, twelve and a half ounces, Dru Amelia Davis came into the world on September 27, 1988, in the way that every child should—adored by her parents, grandparents, and siblings and surrounded by love and care. Coincidentally, she shared her birthday with Jeff, and her initials, we realized as we settled on her middle name, would spell "DAD." A perfect choice, we decided. As a nineteen-year-old mom, I had tried, unsuccessfully, to breast-feed Amber, giving it up after only a few weeks when I returned to my job full-time. But with Dru I was determined to make it work. Along with our Lamaze classes, Jeff and I also took classes on breast-feeding in preparation for her arrival. For nine precious months, I nursed her. It was such a privilege, such a joyful experience for me. I was determined that for the first six months she would have nothing other than breast milk to sustain her, and I stuck with it, my mother and mother-in-law gently chiding me along the way. They could not wrap their heads around the idea that a baby shouldn't be on cereal by three months. "Better to fill their tummies and keep them asleep through the night," they would say.

Dru didn't sleep through the night until she was ten months old. And though I longed for a full night's sleep, I loved our quiet time together those many nights. Mr. Fifty Percent was very helpful. When she would awaken, Jeff was usually the one who would rise to retrieve her from her crib and bring her to me in our bed to nurse.

In January I returned to TCU, completing my degree in May of 1990. Earlier that year, while Dru was a toddler and Amber was settling into the elementary school near our home, I was in the process of applying to law schools. I applied to a few "reach" schools and a few "safety" schools as well. Graduating with a perfect 4.0 GPA and scoring well on the LSAT had positioned me to hope that one of my "reach" schools, one of my dreams, would come true. One of my top choices was the University of Texas, at the time a Top 10 law school, so when I was accepted there I was thrilled, and excitedly began making plans to attend. Jeff's brother and his family lived in Austin, and I felt good knowing I would have family there. Jeff and I had even driven down to begin the process of looking for a place where the girls and I would live. The plan was that we would see Jeff most weekends.

But then the "big envelope" came from the school of my dreams, and everything about our lives changed.

TWELVE

The future belongs to those who believe
in the beauty of their dreams.

—ELEANOR ROOSEVELT

HARVARD LAW SCHOOL was offering me admission.
It is hard to describe what that moment was like for me.
Seeing the envelope as I drove up and got out of my car, walking nervously up our porch steps toward the big envelope that our postal carrier had clothespinned to the outside of our bronze mailbox because it wouldn't fit inside, was one of the most thrilling moments of my life. My hands shook as I grasped the envelope, ripped it open, and read these words:

"It gives me great pleasure to report . . ."

I reached for one of our wicker porch chairs and sat for a moment, the envelope in my lap, the letter in my hands, and I read it over and over and over again, tears streaming down my face.

I had been accepted to my dream school, and I was overcome with emotion. All that work. Those many hours of sacrifice that all of us had made—Amber most particularly. They really had meant something. I was about to become not only the first person in my family to graduate from college, I had been accepted by the best law school in the country. For me, going to an Ivy League school was a dream, a fantasy that was about to come true. Like a character in one of those motion-picture moments when they see their entire lives pass rapid-fire through their brains, I sat there and soaked it all in. Not cutting it in college when I first tried. The blessing and responsibility of Amber. That moment when I stood outside our trailer with a two-week severance check in my hand and cried, motivated by an over-whelming sense of gratitude at that particular blessing. All those miles that Amber and I had logged in my little red Mazda pickup truck. The blessing of all the people who nurtured me along the way—from the pediatricians and nurses I worked with; to my dear friend Lisa, who had taken Amber into her home and cared for her while I was at work; to my mother, who gave as much as she could in the way of help and support; to my ex-in-laws, who had played such an important role in providing Amber with stability when they could; to my dad—always my greatest teacher, and whom I still called to report my grades every time I received them at semester's end; to Jeff, who had cheered and supported and encouraged me when I wasn't sure I could manage. Angels, every one of them.

The religious beliefs I'd come to hold after being exposed to differing perspectives about God's direct role in each of our lives had morphed together into a personal belief that God does provide us a path. He asks only that we look for it, that we see his hand in it, and that we do our part to take advantage of opportunities he lays before us.

That day, sitting on my porch with the big envelope from Harvard, I couldn't help but see his hand in all the dips and curves and highs and lows I'd come through. That experience provided me a moment to stop and take measure of it all. And to receive it, to own it, as the incredible blessing it was.

"It gives me great pleasure to report . . ."

Jeff was the first person I called. And then my dad (who cried). And then my mom. Each greeted the news with much excitement and happiness. It felt like such an incredible achievement, not just for me but for our family as well. I knew that my dad felt that way. He was so, so proud. I would be living a dream, not just for me but for him, too. And wonderfully, without skipping a beat, Jeff began planning with me how we were going to pull this thing off. There was never any doubt in either of our minds that I would go. It was an absolute dream come true to have gotten accepted into what was considered to be the number-one law school in the country, and we both decided, without any hesitation, that we would figure out how to make it work. We immediately dismissed the idea of our entire family moving up to Boston, since Jeff needed to stay in Texas—his work was in the title-insurance arena, which is all about relationships and not the kind of job you can just pick up and move somewhere else. And we also dismissed it because Fort Worth was our home. It was the place we wanted to raise our family, and we weren't going to give up on that. Fort Worth was our long-term future; my semesters in Cambridge would be for the short term only. With that in mind, Jeff and I flew to Boston in the midsummer of 1990, not long after I walked across the stage at TCU and accepted my diploma bearing the words "summa cum laude," and began looking for a place where the girls and I would live.

We settled upon the historic town of Lexington, just under ten miles west of Cambridge but always a twenty- to thirty-minute commute. It had an exceptional public elementary school for Amber and a quality day-care center for Dru. And to lock in the rental rate, we signed a three-year lease with the landlord. We were confident that this setting would be most comfortable for Dru and Amber. But for me it meant a commute that became more of a challenge than I had anticipated.

Pushing aside doubts about how difficult these next three years would prove to be, Jeff and I loaded up a U-Haul truck with some of our furnishings to set up a new home for me and the girls in Lexington. It took us about four days to make the drive (unlike my dad, Jeff and I believed in stopping and resting along the way!). To pass the time, I read a mystery novel to Jeff as he drove. We talked with excitement and a bit of trepidation about what this part of our life's journey would hold.

Upon our arrival in Cambridge, we quickly realized the challenge that traffic there would present when we entered the ramp onto Storrow Drive, only to discover our U-Haul wasn't going to clear the overpass. This required pulling over and waiting for a policeman to stop traffic and allow us to back our way up the same ramp we'd used to enter the roadway. Other drivers were not amused.

Finally making our way to what would serve as my temporary new home, we unloaded the U-Haul and made my new place feel as much like home as possible. Then we flew back to Texas. A few days later, I flew back to Boston with the girls. Amber was eight and Dru was almost two when my first semester at HLS began. Amber greeted the whole thing as an adventure. Dru seemed more confused than anything. The day-care center I enrolled her in would be her first experience being cared for outside the only home she'd ever known. I feared that it would be hard on her. And it was.

In order to make it all work, I had to seek permission from Harvard to reconfigure my class schedule. At Harvard Law School, the incoming class of approximately five hundred people is broken into four sections. The one to which I was assigned was not feasible. It included 8:00 a.m. classes, which presented me with the impossibility of getting Amber to school, Dru to day care, and me into my classroom seat by eight. So, nervously, I went to a dean of students and asked if I could be moved into another section. Thankfully, I was switched to Section 3, a fateful turning point in my experience at HLS, because in that section I would meet and befriend Patti Lipoma, to this day one of the dearest friends I've ever had. Not only was Patti in my section, she was also in my orientation group—or "O group," as they were referred to. She, too, was from Texas—Dickinson, a small town outside Houston. Under any other circumstance, Patti and I would not have been put into the same orientation group. Harvard worked very hard at assembling a diverse selection of people within orientation groups, and putting two Texans together was not something they would have otherwise done. But my last-minute change into Section 3 and into that particular O group was a blessing. In addition to Patti, that whole group of around a dozen people would become dear friends, not only during law school but all these years later as well. I love them like family. And just as I'd always relied on Joey for companionship and moral support, the friends I would make in my O group became my touchstones while at Harvard.

Patti grew up in a stable, loving, two-parent home, quite different from mine. But we both had tremendous drive and focus. Most of the people in our group were coming straight out of college and were closer to twenty-two years old, but she and I were both a little bit older—I was twenty-seven and she was twenty-five, and because her mom had passed away a few years prior and because I'd never really had a best girlfriend as an adult, we became a female support system for each other. Later I'd be a bridesmaid at her wedding to her husband, Jonathan, and I would stay with her after the birth of her first baby, helping out the way her mom would have wanted to and as my mom did for me. Patti and I and our children remain as much a family to one another as our own flesh and blood, and I am the god-mother to her daughter, Sadie.

With my base of friendship support established, Amber, Dru, and I settled into a daily routine. Just as it had been in Texas, driving around for hours in my little red truck, going to work and school and getting Amber to and from child care, navigating the logistics of each day—instantly, all proved to be complicated and frenzied. Each week-day morning I would first drop Dru at her day care and then take Amber to school or to the school bus stop, depending on what time my day would begin in Cambridge; then I'd drive to the Red Line T station at Alewife, not far from Harvard Square (I'd been unable to get a coveted campus parking permit); then I'd take the train into Harvard Square and walk to the law-school campus to be in my seat by 8:30 a.m. At one point I even started taking a bus to Alewife in-stead of driving there and spending money on parking. Even though Jeff had been making a comfortable income for us when we'd all been living together as a family in Texas, paying for the cost of my school-ing, another place for me and the girls to live, and day care for Dru was a pretty significant strain on our family budget. It was a real stretch for us; I did my best to help keep my costs down, but eventu-ally in my third year we had to take out a student loan and cash in Jeff's 401(k) in order to pay the tuition.

Whereas my fellow students would essentially stroll across cam-pus from their dorms and come into the classrooms to begin the day, by the time *I* sat down at *my* desk, my day would already have in-cluded getting two girls up, fed, dressed, and off to school and then a commute into Harvard Square. Thinking that living in Lexington would somehow make life better for me and the girls was proving to have been a misjudgment on my part, but it was too late to change course. We were locked into that long-term lease.

I started law school on September 4, 1990. There are precious few dates that I have committed to memory, but that is one of them. It's hard to describe what those first days were like—the stress and determination and excitement I felt at what I knew was going to be one of the most amazing experiences of my life. That first semester of my first year was, not surprisingly, a very challenging time, one filled with the fear of failing: I was living in a strange city where I didn't know a single human being outside my O group, I had my girls with me, and I was trying to set up a household there and be a good mom to them—all while engaging in the most hypercompetitive academic experience I'd ever known.

I wasn't unique in sensing those academic pressures. Just about all the students who ended up at Harvard Law School went from feeling like one of the ablest people on their college campuses to suddenly being in an environment where others were leaps and bounds ahead of them. I was simultaneously fascinated by the intellectual capacities of my fellow students and intimidated by them; ultimately I came to embrace the opportunity to be surrounded by such extraordinary people. One of the things I realized pretty quickly at HLS was that while the teachers there are top-notch, an equal or even greater benefit comes from what is learned from the observations and perspectives of your peers as part of classroom discussions. I can recall many instances of being awestruck by a particular light shed or an opinion voiced by classmates on many difficult and complicated issues— deeply nuanced perspectives from which I learned so much. I give tremendous credit for my acquired ability to see and appreciate differing opinions to the three years I spent at Harvard, and I will forever be grateful for the gift of learning that came from my peers there. Developing the ability to respect other people's opinions, similar to or divergent from one's own, was one of the most valuable take-aways I gained there. I truly believe that I became a better person, a fuller, deeper person, as a result of my time and experiences at Harvard.

Those observations are formed with the benefit of hindsight, of course. But even if I had known that at the time, even if I hadn't read *One L*, Scott Turow's classic tale of surviving his first year at Harvard Law, and even if I hadn't seen *The Paper Chase*, where Professor Kingsfield, played by John Houseman, tortures his poor first-year students with the Socratic method of teaching law, I still would have been filled with fear on my first day of class. Everyone is. Every first-year student is terrified that he or she will be the one to get called on that first day of class, and we shared a common fear of making complete and utter fools of ourselves in front of a roomful of ridiculously brilliant people. And we're all afraid of how we're going to perform on the high-stakes exams—exams upon which our entire grade is based—which are given at the end of the semester and on which we have to prove that we've got what it takes.

My first class that first day of school was Civil Procedure, a required course for all first-year students. Our Civ Pro class was taught by Professor David Wilkins, now one of the vice deans and the Lester Kissel Professor of Law. He and I are still friends today. Back then, in 1990, Wilkins was a young, dynamic, newly tenured African-American professor who'd been a Harvard Law School student himself. I found that former HLS students who had become law professors could go one of two ways. Either they could torture you so that, like them, you would have to endure the same trauma they once had. Or they could go out of their way to put you at ease and treat you with a softer approach. Thankfully, Professor Wilkins fell into the latter of those two categories. Instead of the stiff, formal, and intimidating Kingsfield-like demeanor we were all expecting, Wilkins asked us questions in a gentle manner and reassured us with his warmth and humor. "Just relax," he'd said. "You've done the hard part. You're here. You earned a seat in this classroom. It's all downhill from here!"

The first time I was called on in class was in Contracts. I can't recall what the case was about, but I do remember that our professor was at least kind enough to give us a day or two's fair warning that our turn was coming. Like Professor Wilkins, Professor David Charny was a Harvard Law School alum, and he fell into the softer, gentler category. He was young and brilliant and filled with a frenetic energy that kept us rapt with attention in every one of his classes. You could almost hear his mind racing from whatever point he was making to a series of fascinating tangents it would lead him to. He'd write all over the board, his chalk hitting hard at every stroke and often breaking. He was always moving, pulling at his hair and pacing back and forth in front of the chalkboard as he followed the trail down which his brilliant mind would take him; by the time class was over, he would literally be spent, his hair on end in several places, sweat soaking through his button-up shirt, which would have come untucked, and covered in chalk from head to toe as though he had just lain down and rolled around in chalk dust. We all loved him and were very sad to learn a few years later that he had passed away after a brief illness.

For all my anxiety, I don't remember ever completely embarrassing myself in class. Unless you count the sort of embarrassment that comes from your friends making fun of you for always raising your hand and trying to get called on to give the answer. *I know! I know! I know!* they'd imitate me, hands comically in the air while calling me Horshack, my apparent doppelgänger character from *Welcome Back, Kotter.*

———

With my dual role as parent and student, and with never enough
hours to execute either role as fully as I would have liked, I
tried to approach school as if it were a job, studying in the library as
late as I possibly could in the afternoon before it was time to pick up
Amber from school and Dru from day care. Sometimes Amber would
have to ride the school bus home and latchkey it with the help of my
landlady, who would look out for her until I could make it home with
Dru in tow. In the evenings I tried to be as disciplined as possible
about getting them fed and bathed and read to, checking in with Jeff
to share stories of our day before I could turn to my studies for the
evening. And just as it had been during those years prior when I was
at TCC, I would get very little sleep before having to wake up and do
the whole thing all over again the next morning.

At the end of the first semester, right before we went home for
Christmas break, the months of stress had finally taken their toll. I
was nervous about exams—first-year exams at Harvard are given after
you come back from break, not before, which prolongs the anxiety
even more—and then I got the flu. I paid a visit to a doctor in Lexington, who, after taking my blood pressure and checking my heart rate,
took my hands in his, looked me in the eye, and gently asked what was
going on in my life. My blood pressure and heart rate were both very
high, extremely abnormal for me. He could see instantly what I had
been in denial about as the semester wore on—the stress of it all was
really getting to me. With no support network—no mom, no sitters,
no Jeff close by—it was as if I were inside the *hiss, hiss, hiss* of my
maternal grandmother's old pressure cooker. So it was with tremendous relief that I boarded the plane home for Christmas, to study for
my first exams and to do so with my support network all around me

and the girls, who had also begun to show the signs of what our schedule was doing to them.

Especially Dru, who had always been the calmest, happiest, and most easygoing child but who now was acting out and crying a lot. Her asthma, which she'd begun suffering from around the time she turned a year old, had gotten significantly worse with the thick, damp air of the New England fall. That's when I was told that acid rain in the Northeast—precipitation that contains higher acidity levels—can aggravate asthma, which it clearly did, since Dru frequently used a nebulizer then. But once we finally returned to Texas at Christmas, the girls and I settled into our more relaxed selves again in the brief three weeks we were home. Seeing that transformation made Jeff and me do a lot of soul-searching about it, and ultimately we decided that for all of our sakes it would be best if the girls were back in their childhood home in Texas, around extended family and their friends and attending their regular school and part-time day-care program. My mom, as she had numerous times for me in the past, came to our rescue, agreeing that she would help care for the girls while I was away.

I would become a long-distance commuter student.

So once I returned to HLS, our new arrangement started. Every morning, my mom would come over to our house in Mistletoe Heights and get the girls ready for school. She cared for Dru in our home, did the grocery shopping, and made dinner every night for Jeff and the girls. Once Jeff got home and was with the girls, she'd go back to her own house and spend the night. Almost instantly the steam in the pressure cooker released for both girls. Instead of going to day care for a full day every day, Dru was now on a much more relaxed schedule, a half day of day care three days a week—giving her an opportunity to be in a social setting those three mornings without the stress of a full-time day-care environment. Amber was in elementary school and doing well. My mom did an amazing job, and I'm so deeply grateful for her help. Without her, such an unusual arrangement would never have been possible. She and Jeff were both extraordinary in making it all work.

For the rest of that first year at Harvard, I flew back and forth from Boston to Fort Worth, coming home as often as I could throughout the spring semester. Usually that meant that I'd go to school for ten days and then come home for five. Commuting like that meant I was missing three days of classes every other week (Thursdays, Fridays, and Mondays). Harvard's lack of a mandatory attendance policy made it possible for me to miss classes, but I still bore the responsibility of trying to keep pace with my studies while missing so many lectures. It wasn't the easiest way to go through law school, and I never would have been able to do it without the help of my friends, who were so generous about sharing their notes with me so that I could keep up with what they were learning when I was gone.

That summer and the next, I did clerkships at local law firms in Fort Worth and Dallas. And during my second year of school, I continued my habit of commuting back and forth, trying to make it home every other weekend. Despite the grueling flying and commuting schedule, not to mention the intense and crushing workload of law school, the arrangement worked really well for me. The added expense of the air travel wasn't ideal, but in my third year I was able to get out of the Lexington lease and cut costs significantly by moving into a tiny dorm room on campus. Those weeks at school became the first time in my adult life that I had the opportunity to experience what it was like to create close friendships and have normal everyday moments with friends over lunch and coffee. In my second year, I even started working out for the first time in my life, because one of my core group of friends, Andrew, got five or six of us to start working out with him. We all became completely obsessed: three days a week, we'd work out for two hours at a time doing weight training in a tiny, sweaty little gym room in the basement of one of the law-school buildings. And, while I was home, I would keep it up at a nearby gym.

In spite of the privilege I felt at being a Harvard Law School student, in the spring of my second year, I made arrangements with HLS to do a visiting year, my third year, at Southern Methodist Law School in Dallas: Harvard allows students to do a visiting year at another school and still graduate with a Harvard Law School diploma—it's just another example of how they will literally do anything to make things work for the students they accept. After thinking about the toll the commuting was taking on me, on our family, and on our finances, Jeff and I decided that I would go to SMU for my third year of law school, to eliminate the commute and still get my diploma from Harvard. We'd put everything in place to make that happen—I'd gotten permission from Harvard, I'd registered with SMU, and I'd even had a big good-bye party with all my friends at the end of my second year—but just a few weeks before my third year of law school was supposed to start, I found that giving up that final year at HLS was not going to be as easy as I'd thought. I'd gone to orientation at SMU Law School for transferring and visiting students, and as I sat in an auditorium full of people I didn't know on an unfamiliar campus, I felt a mix of emotions, not the least of which was that I wasn't finishing something I had started. I worried that when my Harvard diploma hung on the wall, I would know I hadn't entirely earned it from HLS. And I was very sad about not finishing out my last year among the friends who had come to be my family there. The third year of law school is usually considered the best one of all—the point at which you've finally gotten comfortable enough so that you're not scared to death every day. Leaving to spend my third year at SMU would mean missing out on that part of the experience and becoming a commuter student at a school where I knew no one. I couldn't help but be reminded of all the lonely first days at new schools I'd gone through as a child, and I wanted to spare myself another such experience.

That night when I came home from SMU's orientation, I sat down with Jeff and we struck a deal: I would go to Harvard two weeks at a time and come home for two weeks at a time. And so for my entire third year, with a few exceptions, that is what I did. Once again I had to be very diligent about keeping up with my studies, getting all my friends' notes from class lectures, so I made sure that every class I took always aligned with someone from my core group whose notes I could share. Just as in the previous year and a half, my friends continued to be amazingly generous in that way. I'm so thankful to those friends who made it possible for me. And though I wasn't quite the student I wanted to be, given that schedule, it all worked out in the end.

That third and final year at Harvard gave me the best of both worlds: when I was at school in Cambridge I was able to be fully present there, and when I was home in Fort Worth I was able to be fully present with Jeff and our girls. I'd never had the experience of being a young person without responsibility, and now, for the first time, I had segmented periods of time when I could focus on my studies with the freedom of being a normal law-school student. I'd never had the luxury of socializing with friends during the years before and after Amber was born in Fort Worth, when I'd had to be so careful about every precious minute of my time and every precious drop of gas. But now I'd left my rental in Lexington and moved to campus, into a tiny dorm room just big enough for a futon and a desk. And for two weeks of every month, I was a student much like my other classmates. Sharing shower space in the a.m., eating breakfast in the student center, and getting more involved in campus life. I continued working out

Little Frank Gets A 'Generation' Haircut

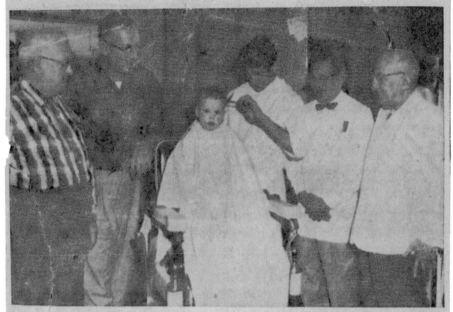

LITTLE FRANK R. KERSHAW III wonders what is going on as he gets his first haircut at age 16 months. Unique angle is that three generations of barbers in Russell family are cutting hair of three generations of Kershaw family. Group (l-r) include grandfather, Frank R. Kershaw, Frank R. Kershaw Jr. and little Frank. Snipping away is Jerry Russell, and watching are his father, Gerard Russell and his grandfather, Joseph Russell. Scene is at Russell shop in Anthony. —Times Photo

Frank R. Kershaw, of Anthony, began getting his haircuts in 1912 from Joseph Russell, venerable Pawtuxet Valley barber.

Today, 48 years later, he still goes to the same barber and his son, Patrolman Frank R. ("Doc") Kershaw, of Coventry police and his grandson, Frank R. Kershaw III get their haircuts from the three - generation Russell family of barbers.

Saturday marked a memorable occasion for both the Kershaw and Russell families. Frank R. III, at 16 months, got his first haircut from the youngest members of the Russell family, Jerry Russell, who operates a three-chair shop on Washington St., Anthony, with his father, Gerard, and his grandfather, Joseph Russell.

And little Frank, sensing the import of the occasion, sat quietly in the high chair while his daddy and grandfather stood by proudly and watched. And equally proud on the other side were Gerard and Joseph Russell.

My dad, his dad, and Pepé—three generations of barbers.

My paternal grandparents, Doris and Gerard Russell.

My maternal grandparents, Lela and Nealy Stovall.

My parents, young and in love.

My parents and Grandma Russell, Ensenada, Mexico, 1971.

Me when we lived in Muleshoe,
before my parents reunited.

At my grandparents' in Muleshoe.

After a trip across the border to Juárez.

In Muleshoe—just before my mother
drove us to reunite with our dad.

Chris (seven), Joey (six), Jennifer,
and me in El Paso. I was five.

My mom, in El Paso.

Our family in
El Paso, reunited
after Jennifer was born.

With my Grandmother
Russell. I was probably
around seven.

My first-grade class, with Mrs. Gary.
I'm in the second row from the back in the blue shirt, second from the right.

Third grade.

My parents in our
Chula Vista backyard.

With Jennifer in
Chula Vista.

TOP: Buddy Boy and
Buddy Girl, ages
eight and seven.

RIGHT: Buddy Boy and
Buddy Girl, cleaning
fish in New York.

At home with Joey in New York after our confirmation.
Notice the *Music Man* photo on the wall, with my dad as
Professor Harold Hill, Chris as Winthrop Paroo.

The long driveway in Pearl River that we had to shovel when it snowed.
This was taken when I went back to visit in 1985.

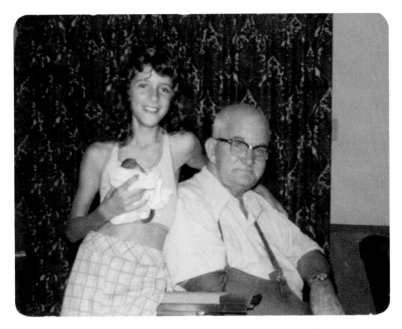

My Granddad Stovall and me (and my pet squirrel, Barney). I was ten.

O Holy Night solo, fifth grade.

Ten or eleven years old,
outside my house in Richland Hills.

At Six Flags with my Grandma Russell, my Great-aunt Bea, Jennifer, and Joey.
Note that I'm wearing the hip-hugger jeans with the *Peanuts* appliqués!

Another amusement
park visit…

High-school graduation, 1981.

Amber at ten months, in our trailer.

With Amber, 1983.

With Jeff on one of our first dates—I had to watch him for clues on which utensils to use.

Our wedding reception, held at our Mistletoe Drive home.

Precious Dru, 1988.

Proud big sister Amber, right after Dru was born.

On one of our traditional summer trips to Breckenridge, Colorado.

One summer at our home in Fort Worth, probably 1993.
FROM LEFT: Erik, Big Drew, Amber, me, Jeff, and Little Dru.
Our complete family always included Big Drew.

Texas Christian University graduation day, 1990, in my Mistletoe home.

My acceptance letter to Harvard.

HARVARD LAW SCHOOL
CAMBRIDGE · MASSACHUSETTS · 02138
(617) 495-3109

ADMISSIONS

June 12, 1990

Ms. Wendy U. Davis
2325 Mistletoe Drive
Fort Worth, TX 76110

Dear Ms. Davis:

It gives me great pleasure to report that your application for admission to the Harvard Law School has been accepted. You have been given a place with the class beginning its work in September, 1990. Please accept my warmest congratulations.

We would appreciate hearing from you as soon as possible whether or not you intend to be with us in the fall. Full information about the process for letting us know your decision is enclosed. Although we hope that your response to our offer is positive, we realise that you must satisfy yourself that this school is the best place for you both personally and academically. Please feel free to call us to discuss any questions that you have. We will be as helpful as possible, but you must also understand why we must impose certain deadlines on your decision-making process. There are many highly qualified applicants anxiously waiting to hear from us, and your early decision will expedite our notification of those applicants.

We have enclosed a handbook for entering students and other information about the school. We hope that you will visit the school and avail yourself of opportunities to learn more about us.

You should mail your $250 acceptance deposit to the Admissions office together with the acceptance materials and the two photographs no later than June 26, 1990. We hope that you will decide to accept our offer of admission, and we are delighted that you may be with us at Harvard Law School next fall.

Very truly yours,

Joyce P. Curll
Assistant Dean for Admissions
and Financial Aid

JPC/kem
Enclosures

Amber in our Lexington, Massachusetts, apartment.

My dorm room at Harvard, third year.

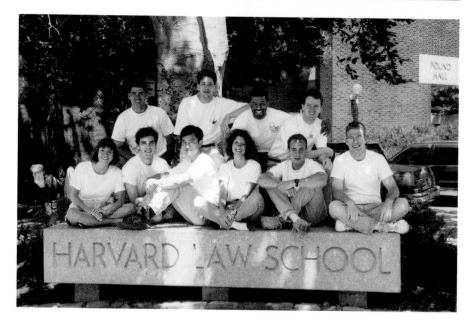

My best friends at Harvard Law School—most of whom were from my "O" group. Taken right before we graduated in spring 1993.

My dearest friend, Patti.
Graduation party, 1993.

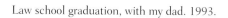

Law school graduation, with my dad. 1993.

With Amber, age eleven,
at my graduation from Harvard.

Meg, Judge Buchmeyer, and me at our swearing-in ceremony in 1994. Judge B. swore us in to the Texas Bar.

My first city council race, 1996.

Campaigning old-fashioned style for city council.

Amber and Dru with Moots (our Labrador)
and Charlie (our Yorkie-poo) at my post-divorce home.

Swearing-in at the eighty-first session of the Texas senate, 2009.

Wearing a TCU helmet at the eighty-first session. The helmet was to protect me from the traditional "hazing" I had to go through as a first-time senator laying out a piece of legislation.

With Amber and Dru at the start of the eighty-second session, January 2011.

In 2011, with J. D. Angle, Joel Burns, and Lisa Lowry.

Filibuster of proposed cuts to public-education budget. Eighty-second session, 2011.

With my family at my second swearing-in, January 2013 (eighty-third legislative session). I had to survive a redistricting battle and a tough 2012 reelection to get back there, so it was particularly gratifying. FROM LEFT TO RIGHT: Amber, my mom, Suzi (my stepmom), me, my dad, and Will Wynn.

Talking with Senator Ellis. Eighty-third session, 2013.

Waiting on a point-of-order ruling during the June 25, 2013, filibuster.

Finally sitting down after my historic nearly thirteen-hour filibuster, surrounded by the Texas Senate Democratic Caucus.

Post-filibuster, arguing about the fate of SB 5 at the Lieutenant Governor/President of the Senate's desk.

With Republican Senator Dan Patrick after I quietly worked the senate floor and killed his bill that I felt would have harmed municipalities.

like crazy, which became a lifelong habit for me and which not only got me into the best shape of my life but remains my most effective stress reducer and mood lifter. And I came into my own, figuring out what I liked to do and learning how it felt to be truly comfortable in my own skin. I've always considered those years at Harvard as a gift from Jeff and my mom, a gift that was more precious than anything anyone could have ever given me: the gift of time to be a young adult without a tremendous amount of everyday responsibility and with an incredible education and all the privilege and possibility that came with it.

There were moments, though, like those Sunday nights, when it was almost too painful to bear—I can remember sitting in the airport on more than one occasion, crying at having to leave Jeff and the girls behind. It made me question everything I was doing. Reentry wasn't easy either: I have a clear memory, in my second year, of landing at Logan late at night in the dead of winter and getting yelled at by a cabdriver for slamming his door too hard when I got in. Tears rolling down my cheeks in the backseat, I couldn't help but ache for my family. And for home.

When I would come home to Texas, I'd get to devote myself to being a mom to my girls, taking them to school and being involved in their activities—playdates and schoolwork and errands and sitting down to dinner as a family—all the normal parts of motherhood that I'd missed when Amber was young and we'd had such a chaotic schedule. In the end, it all worked. And as a family we came through it intact.

After three years of exhausting travel, crazy logistics, and hard work, I graduated with my friends and with honors, in May of 1993. Harvard graduations are major events—Harvard College and all the Harvard graduate schools (including the law school, the medical school, and the divinity school, among others) are graduated together in one huge ceremony in Harvard Yard; afterward each school heads over to its particular campus for a smaller ceremony in which graduates walk across a stage and receive their diploma. Each graduate gets only two tickets to the big ceremony, so my parents were my guests for that; everyone else—Jeff and the girls; Jeff's son, Erik, and Erik's friend, Drew; and my stepmother, Suzi—waited over at the law-school campus for us to arrive after the combined ceremony ended.

But at some point during the all-school graduation, I looked up to find a Harvard security officer standing at the end of one of the aisles of rows and rows of white-slat folding chairs. Amber and Dru, ages ten and four, were standing there with him. I'd later learn that Amber had gotten mad at Erik while waiting at the law-school campus with him, his friend Drew, and Jeff, and had grabbed Dru's hand and marched off to find me. She'd walked across the entire law-school campus and the main campus, asking adults all along the way for directions to the big graduation. She was mad—*she wanted to see her mommy graduate*—and so she did. She and Dru joined me at my seat, each sitting on my lap for the remainder of the ceremony, and at the point in the ceremony when the members of the law-school class were asked to stand up and be graduated, we all stood up together—Amber and Dru and me—and we were "graduated" from Harvard Law School. It was an incredibly sweet and meaningful moment for me. We'd all three been through that journey together; it was only fitting that we would graduate together as well.

Later, at our smaller law-school graduation where we walked the stage and were handed our diplomas one by one, I walked across the stage alone, accepted my diploma, and walked off the stage into the arms of my father. We stood there wordless, both of us crying for a time. I know that my dad felt as I did that day, that my graduation belonged to him as much as it did to me. That I was who I became because he made me believe I could be. He was so, so proud. My mother was proud, too, of course, but in a different way than my dad. For him, what I'd been able to do was an extension of ambitions and goals he'd set for himself. We all live vicariously through our children, and because he was so gifted and smart and could have done anything he wanted to, having one of his children do something like that for him made him feel that perhaps he hadn't failed me after all. It had been an amazing experience. Jeff, who'd been my most important partner on that journey, could not have been more proud of what we had accomplished together. Being there, in that moment, with the whole world in front of me, my whole future in front of me, standing among my family and with the best friends I was ever going to have for the rest of my life, it was an unimaginable privilege.

Now I would need to determine how I was going to put meaning to that privilege.

THIRTEEN

Doing justice is like a love affair:
If it's easy, it's sleazy.

—U.S. DISTRICT COURT JUDGE
JERRY BUCHMEYER

WHEN JEFF AND I were first dating, we'd often end up talking about politics. With his city council background, it was a passion for him, but at the time I found it all pretty boring. As I got older, though, I began to really take an interest. By then our home on Mistletoe Drive had become the logistical hub of our social network—people came over to watch presidential debates on television, to discuss the uproar surrounding our local zoo's controversial proposed expansion, and soon I became more and more interested in how things worked and how individuals and communities could organize to try to make things better. Jeff had a true devotion to doing what was right, even if it meant going up against the powerful status quo. He was every inch an idealist, which is one of the qualities that really drew me to him.

Though I never expected to follow his path into public service, I see now that Jeff's influence and the important and formative experiences in and around law school laid the groundwork for me to enter that arena. Together with my struggles and hardships, these experiences gave me what I believe to be one of the most important skills a person can possess, not only in general but particularly in public service: the ability to compassionately understand another person's point of view, even—and especially—if it differs from your own.

The most inspiring course I took at Harvard Law was called the Warren Court. Professor Morton J. Horwitz taught the class as a sociologist might have; we weren't to approach the material in the way we usually did in our typical classes, which was to think in terms of case law and how it builds to set precedent. Instead we were asked to reflect on the individuals who were deciding those cases—the nine white male justices of the Earl Warren Supreme Court, who, against the backdrop of a country that was not yet ready to accept the desegregation of public schools, decided unanimously in favor of the plaintiffs in *Brown v. Board of Education* (1954) to do exactly that. *Brown* was the seminal case of Warren's tenure and one of the most important civil rights cases ever heard by the U.S. Supreme Court. While Chief Justice Warren probably could have passed the decision down fairly quickly, 5–4, it was crucial to him that it be unanimous; he understood that without a unanimous court, implementing its ruling against the resistance of many Southern states would be nearly impossible.

During the course we read biographies and autobiographies of the justices, talked a great deal about the social context and the civil unrest around the issue of desegregation, and read a beautiful book, *Simple Justice,* by Richard Kluger, which captured the courage and tenacity of the people who fought to bring equality to our nation's education system. It remains one of the most influential books I have ever read. It was fascinating material, and through Professor Horwitz's gentle urgings, the book made me think for the first time in law school not about the decisions that were being made but about the *people* who were making them—how their own human failings and achievements had shaped them. To borrow a word from George W. Bush, I started thinking about these "deciders": who these justices were, how their experiences could be understood and therefore made a part of finding a path to common ground, to bringing people to a consensus. More than that, it made me think about this concept much more broadly and how it could be applied in everyday situations: finding respect for where individuals come from, not just where they are today, and how their journeys shaped their beliefs and thinking. That's what Earl Warren was able to do with each justice: draw upon something from each one's personal experiences, tap into that place, and guide them all to arrive at making a very courageous decision— that "separate" could never be "equal" and that only desegregation of our schools could lead us to being a land of equality.

The question that Professor Horwitz invited us to consider was this: What was it about Earl Warren that made him so personally committed to desegregation, and why was it so important to him that the decision be unanimous? Reading about his life provided a fascinating insight into his experiences prior to serving on the Supreme Court and how those experiences affected who he became as chief justice.

Earl Warren's appointment as chief justice was made by President Dwight D. Eisenhower in 1953. Talk at the time was that the appointment had come about because of a commitment Eisenhower made to Warren in exchange for the latter's backing down from his own desire to become the Republican nominee for president. Eisenhower had promised Warren a Supreme Court appointment. He intended to make Warren solicitor general until the first opening on the Supreme Court occurred. But before the appointment of Warren as solicitor general was finalized, something unexpected happened—Chief

Justice Fred Vinson died in his sleep. As the story goes, Eisenhower immediately reached out to Warren and informed him that he would be nominated to the Supreme Court. Warren insisted not only that he be appointed but that he be appointed chief justice. Eisenhower resisted, claiming that he had never promised Warren that position. But Warren pushed back, reminding Eisenhower that he had promised Warren the "first" opening on the Court. That opening, he argued, was the position of chief justice, and he demanded that it be given to him. As the saying goes, the rest is history. Earl Warren was nominated and approved for appointment as chief justice. He had never held a position on the bench before, but he would become one of the great jurists in our country's history.

Before he was made chief justice by President Eisenhower, he'd been both attorney general and then governor of the state of California. In those positions he'd been the driving force behind the internment of people of Japanese descent in camps during World War II, and it was his experience with the internment camps and the deep scar he would bear as a consequence of his role in the creation of those camps that shaped him most powerfully as a jurist. Warren had visited the camps that Japanese-American families had been sent to, and he saw how wives had been separated from husbands, children from their mothers. And he witnessed the pain that the stroke of his pen had imposed. He had signed an order that would stigmatize us as a nation that let our fears trump our better selves, resulting in racial profiling at its worst. In his memoirs Warren wrote that he "deeply regretted" his actions and the internment that followed: "Whenever I thought of the innocent little children who were torn from home, school friends, and congenial surroundings, I was conscience-stricken. It was wrong to react so impulsively, without positive evidence of disloyalty."

I've thought about that many times in my public and my private life, how we become who we are and how understanding the experiences that have formed others helps us find common ground with them. And I have drawn upon the lessons I learned in that class many times in my public-service career.

I've never forgotten what the Warren Court class taught me: to really think about my own perspectives and to question where they come from and whether they are objectively fair or just the product of a personal experience clouding objective decision making. I've also learned to trust my voice, to trust the myriad experiences that shaped who I am, that equipped me with the fire in my belly to stand strong for the things I believe in, for the values I hold dear.

Long before my tenure on the Fort Worth City Council, my first real experience with public service came during my second year of law school, when I worked as an intern for the Legal Services Center in Boston's Jamaica Plain neighborhood. The center did all manner of work, from civil to criminal, for its low-income clients unable to pay private lawyers. We were mentored in our work by several attorneys who were committed to providing needed legal services to the poor. I was assigned to the civil side, helping clients who'd been diagnosed with HIV or AIDS. It was 1991, and back then the diagnosis meant that people suffering from the disease needed to get their affairs in order. Living wills, powers of attorney, estate planning—these were my routine tasks.

But sometimes the tasks were more urgent and the stakes higher. I recall vividly my first day in a courtroom, arguing before a judge on behalf of my client, whose partner of many years had died of AIDS. The decedent's family was fighting against the wishes that their son had expressed in his will—he wanted to be cremated and for his remains to be kept by his partner, the love of his life. He wanted his modest estate of belongings to be given to his partner as well. His family wanted him buried in their family burial plot in another state, far from Massachusetts. I had come to work that day with no expectation that I would be standing in a courtroom that afternoon. And I was terrified. Thankfully, Patti lived close to the courthouse, and I was able to run by her place and assemble an outfit appropriate for appearing before a judge. And there I was, an intern, trying to win on an issue that was deeply personal and important to my client. He had just lost the love of his life. And now he was possibly going to lose him again.

Looking back, I can't say I'm exactly proud of the tactic I employed to win the hearing for my client, but it worked. It quickly became clear to me that the decedent's family was ashamed that their son was gay. As soon as I understood that, I made sure to include a statement to that effect in just about every sentence I uttered. Every time I did, I could see the decedent's parents bristle. And I knew then that we would win. As their awareness grew that their son's sexuality would be a very public part of the argument I would make before the court, they ultimately decided to withdraw their attempt to block the wishes he had expressed in his will. Keeping him closeted, even after his death, was more important to them than prevailing. I walked out of the courtroom that day a winner. My client was tearful in his gratitude and relief. Yet I couldn't help but feel some pangs of guilt for the strategy I'd had to use to win.

However, I also first felt what it meant in the legal arena to provide a voice for someone who could no longer express his own. And I was reminded of those times with my grandfather, after his stroke, when he tried so hard to dictate letters to me. I hadn't been conscious of why I'd chosen that work at the Legal Services Center, but in that moment I saw clearly that I was helping people who were facing severe discrimination and that it was deeply meaningful work. For them, their final voice could be expressed only through the signing of a last will and testament. For me, giving expression to that voice would come in the form of fighting to make sure their wishes were honored.

During my internship at the center, I had many clients who would come to mean a great deal to me, but one of the most memorable was a quiet, shy, but emotionally strong woman from Haiti who was dying of AIDS. She lived in the projects in South Boston, and she desperately needed someone to help her obtain access to adequate health care. Working through her immigration issues in order to achieve that access was a great challenge, to say the least. While I represented her, I spent a great deal of time with her, always going to her apartment for our meetings because she was too frail to come to the center. I'd pick her up and take her to the only clinic we could find, and I'd take her to appointments with the immigration officials who were working with me to help her obtain the legal status she needed for better health care.

She died late in my internship year, which devastated me. She died completely alone. No family to memorialize her. No friends. I was all she had, and my co-workers and I held a brief "ceremony" in her honor, the Polaroid that she'd given me of herself on prominent display as we each said a few words to honor her life and loss. I remember thinking as she was dying that I was one of the only people in the world she had any connection with. It was very powerful to realize that and to fully understand the sacredness of that role. The center was the place where I found an understanding of what it means to be a public servant. To put others before self. And to be reminded of my tremendous blessings relative to the struggles of so many.

Despite the deep connection I had to the work I did there, or perhaps because of it—it certainly was profoundly difficult to work with people who were so ill, knowing you couldn't take away their illness or their pain and that the best you could do was to try to ease their minds and provide comfort in any way you could—it wasn't the kind of work I planned on doing as a career. Since starting law school I believed that I would become a high-powered litigator. That I'd earn a fine paycheck, wear nice clothes, and carry a briefcase. The work in the Legal Services Center was emotionally wrenching and not in keeping with the vision I'd set for myself.

At the end of that next year, when I left the center for the last time, two of the supervising lawyers I worked with sat me down for my exit interview.

"We've got you," they'd said, meaning they felt as though they had brought me into the arena of public service as the career path I would follow.

I smiled at them but shook my head no. "I loved my time here, but I'm off to practice law soon, for a big firm, getting paid to do work for paying clients."

Years later I would come to understand that they saw in me what I had not yet seen for myself. They had indeed "gotten" me. I just didn't realize it yet.

It wouldn't take me very long practicing law before I decided that it wasn't at all what I'd hoped it would be. I went to work for a fairly large Dallas-based firm, in their Fort Worth office, assigned to the "specialized litigation section," which sounded intriguing but in reality was not. Working as one lawyer of many on really big antitrust cases that take years from start to finish felt meaningless to me. Rather than having the capacity to stand back each day with the satisfaction of saying to myself, *I did good in the world today,* I found myself sifting through mounds and mounds of discovery materials looking for a lead to crack open a case or traveling to city after city taking what felt like the same deposition over and over again. The paychecks were nice. But the work offered little in the way of personal reward. Fortunately, prior to entering work in the private arena, my first year out of law school offered me another tremendous learning experience and made another profound impact on shaping the adult I was still to become.

B esides my father and Jeff, perhaps no other person has had a greater impact shaping me than Judge Jerry Buchmeyer. He was a United States judge for the Northern District of Texas in Dallas for whom I was lucky enough to clerk the year after I graduated law school. He possessed a wisdom and a sense of justice and fairness that suited him perfectly for his judicial role. Whenever I think of Judge Buchmeyer, who passed away in 2009, I can't help but smile. He was soft-spoken, with a keen sense of humor; to spend time with him was a real joy. A modern-day Solomon, he was the essence of what every judge should be.

I'd learned quite a bit about Judge Buchmeyer in law school during a mock trial that involved applying constitutional equal protection to a lesbian police officer who'd been fired from her job after her employer learned that she was homosexual. Back then, in the early 1990s, there was no real protection for people who'd been discriminated against based on sexual orientation. But Judge Buchmeyer, as I was later to learn, true to form for him, had written a landmark opinion in *Baker v. Wade* (1982) striking down Texas's sodomy law, which would have the effect of decriminalizing homosexuality. Buchmeyer's decision was published in 1984 and it stood for just three years before the Court of Appeals for the Fifth Circuit overturned his decision. I was quickly intrigued by this judge from Dallas who'd done something so bold. And as I began reading about him, I discovered that he was also incredibly funny and that he would assemble humorous vignettes from courtroom settings or depositions to be published each month in the *Texas Bar Journal*. His column, called "et cetera," was widely read, and Judge Buchmeyer was therefore widely known in Texas legal circles, not only as a fair and good judge but as someone possessing a profound wit.

I'd clerked with about six different law firms during the summers of my law-school years—in the early 1990s there was no shortage of firms vying for students, particularly those from the top law schools. It was a seller's market for students at schools like HLS, and we were courted fairly heavily by the firms we clerked for. I accepted an offer to go to work for a Fort Worth firm, but first I wanted to take a deferral year and work as a judicial clerk. I applied for several judicial clerkships and was invited to interview for three of them, two in Dallas and one in Fort Worth. One of my Dallas interviews was with Judge Buchmeyer. And it was the clerkship I wanted most of all. Even the recruitment notice he'd placed in the huge HLS jobs book (as I said, it was a sellers' market back then) to entice students to apply for the position was unusual and intriguing. After listing the qualities one might expect a judge to say he wanted in a clerk, Judge Buchmeyer had written that he was looking for someone who "collects kitsch." Collects kitsch?! Ha! If I hadn't already been smitten, now I most certainly was. Even in that recruitment notice he was demonstrating the tongue-in-cheek nature he brought to everything he did.

But his quirky humor belied his brilliance. Buchmeyer had graduated from U.T. Law School in 1957 with the highest GPA in the school's history—an honor he held for fifteen years. When President Jimmy Carter appointed Buchmeyer, then forty-six years old, to the federal bench in Dallas in 1979, he left a highly paid partnership as an acclaimed litigator in a large Dallas firm to take the lower-paying appointment because he believed in the value of the work he'd be doing there.

Every federal judge receives thousands of applications from young lawyers who want the experience and résumé credential of having done a judicial clerkship. But each judge, unless he or she is the chief, typically hires only two clerks each year. It's such a competitive field, in fact, that even to be granted an interview is rare. When I showed up to Judge Buchmeyer's office for my interview, I was more nervous than I'd ever been for any previous job interview. I recall that he spoke so very softly I had to lean quite close to hear the questions he was asking me. A technique, I would come to learn, that he employed to focus people's attention entirely upon him. Later I would watch him use this technique from the bench to tremendous effect. A few days after our interview, when he called to offer me the job, I jumped sky-high with excitement. Judge Buchmeyer—I was going to work for the great Judge Buchmeyer. *What a treat,* I told myself. And indeed it was.

Most federal clerkships last a year, and while each judge takes a different approach to the tasks assigned to his or her clerks, a clerk's primary duties include drafting orders and opinions, preparing bench memos for the judge, and reading and making determinations on procedural filings by the parties in the lawsuits before the court. Typically these duties are in the form of recommendations that the judges would use as a starting point and take a heavy editing pen to before signing their names. But not Judge Buchmeyer. Instead we wrote orders and opinions, and if he agreed with them, he simply signed them. No edits! Which created a sense of responsibility that was pretty overwhelming for a brand-new baby lawyer. He would literally read them and sign them. He never changed a word. With Judge Buchmeyer we would do our research and then just go talk to him about our findings: *Here's what the issue is, here's what we're being asked to decide, here's what my recommendation is.* And nine times out of ten, he would agree. Sometimes he would ask you to go do a little more work or challenge you to think about it a bit differently, so the decision, in the end, was always a collective one. But he was deferential to us and had so much respect for our intellectual capacity that it was truly an incredible experience to clerk in his court.

My co-clerk was a woman named Meg who had grown up in a very conservative family—so conservative, in fact, that I was really surprised that Judge Buchmeyer had paired us. In addition to all the other important qualifications they're looking for, judges try to find two clerks who they think will get along and work well with each other in such an intense environment. Meg and I were clearly opposites, down to the law schools we'd attended—she had gone to Pepperdine Law School, arguably the most conservative law school in the country, while Harvard is considered to be one of the most liberal.

On our very first day, Meg and I were at lunch in one of the tunnel restaurants under the streets of Dallas when she looked me straight in the eye and said, "I don't think that women who have children have any business being in the workplace." I was completely stunned. From that moment forward, we disagreed on absolutely everything. In fact, our perspectives were so diametrically opposed that for a while I admit I was truly miserable and wondered why the judge ever would have thought we'd be a good match. But as the year progressed, an amazing thing began to happen: Meg started reconsidering her perspectives on many different issues, and ultimately, toward the end of the year of our clerkship, she came out to herself and to us that she was gay. I realized that Judge Buchmeyer must have seen something in her and somehow understood that underneath all her rhetoric was a person struggling to find her true identity. The clerkship helped her get there, and I often wondered what would have happened if she hadn't spent that year under the wisdom and guidance of Judge

Buchmeyer, and if she hadn't been exposed to so many of the people to whom we were exposed. Would it have taken her much longer to evolve to where she could allow herself to be truly who she was and have the courage to say it?

One of the first memorable experiences I had during that clerkship was getting to know two men who'd been found guilty of a federal environmental offense, some sort of illegal dumping that their company was engaged in. In addition to their sentence and fine, Judge Buchmeyer had added a public-service component to their sentence: an order to create an environmental learning center for the schoolchildren of the Dallas Independent School District. It was intriguing to watch these two men morph from the shame of a guilty verdict to the pride they took in creating the center. When I met them, the verdict had long since been handed down and the finishing touches were being put on the center. They came to collect the judge one day to show him their progress, and he invited me to come, saying only that he wanted to show me something he thought I'd be interested in seeing. Not long after we pulled away from the courthouse, Judge Buchmeyer turned to me.

"By the way," he said, "the two gentlemen in the front seat are convicted felons."

At my reaction, which must have been written very clearly on my face, he began laughing, as did the two gentlemen themselves. They laughed and laughed but never really would tell me the details of their case. Instead they wanted to talk about how excited they were to be opening the center. And as they gave us a tour of the facility, I could see the impact my wise and good judge had had. Time and time and time again, he knew what he was doing. I can't imagine a person more aptly suited to be a judge.

Judge Buchmeyer was well known not only for the opinion he'd written decriminalizing homosexuality but also for another progressive opinion on a case brought by a group of African-American women living in housing projects in West Dallas, *Walker v. U.S. Dept. of Housing & Urban Development*. In 1987 Buchmeyer ruled that the Dallas Housing Authority (DHA) was providing substandard housing for its residents and ordered that most of its almost thirty-five hundred units, built in the 1950s next to a toxic lead smelter, be torn down. But his plan wasn't just to move the entire population of residents wholesale to another location. It was his belief that keeping low-income families in concentrated communities with only other low-income residents fostered a cycle of generational poverty without giving the children of those communities an awareness and experience of something different and better. So instead of ordering the mass move of all of the residents to a newly built project, Judge Buchmeyer ordered that they be dispersed into housing in middle- and higher-income areas of the city. It was an incredibly controversial decision, and the process, which took years to be put into action, was already under way when I came to work for him.

He'd received a tremendous amount of criticism and even death threats over that decision, for a time having to have security protection assigned to him. But he put his head down and forged on, appointing a special managing conservator to oversee and manage the day-to-day work of the housing authority and assure that the relocations were carried out in accordance with his order. During my time clerking for him, the judge would hold occasional briefings to the court, hearing from the managing conservator, the housing authority, and the plaintiff residents. And what was remarkable was that while the housing authority had initially resisted his order, they had come to embrace it and were carrying it out with pride for the impact they were having on the lives of their residents. It was an inspiring and incredible thing to see.

Like Solomon himself, he was a judge for all the right reasons, and he was always willing to do brave and hard things because he believed them to be the right things, and I learned so much from the great example he set. I remember how we would watch him preside over very complex trials and how eminently fair he was—always so sensitive not to color the jury's perspective in any way with either his words or his body language as some judges do—interrupting counsel and asking questions of the witnesses themselves, thereby transmitting to a jury what their perspectives are. Often, the lawyers before him requested bench trials rather than jury ones, so trusted were his judgments and his ability to treat defendants, whether civil or criminal, with fairness.

During one such bench trial that I observed, a criminal case, a defendant was telling his version of events on the stand. It was a long story that his lawyer was walking him all the way through. I watched as Judge Buchmeyer sat quietly listening, not a sign of what he was thinking conveyed on his face. And then he employed that soft-spoken technique of his to great effect. At the end of the witness's testimony, the judge leaned over to him and ever so quietly, in almost a grandfatherly way, started to ask him some very simple questions about the veracity of the testimony he'd just given.

"And you didn't really do such and such, did you?"

"No, I didn't."

"And when you said such and such, that wasn't true, was it?"

"No. It wasn't."

And just like that he elicited the truth from the witness. Ever gentle. Ever effective.

Another very poignant memory I have of serving with him came in the wake of new federal sentencing guidelines that dictated and constrained what a federal judge's subjective decision making in sentencing could now be. At the federal level, Congress had adopted these guidelines that set forth minimum and maximum sentences, and judges were not allowed to order any sentencing outside this framework. It was what the public came to know, in layman's terms, as the "tough on crime" movement, which included stricter and mandatory sentencing laws such as the "Three Strikes" rule.

The judge's inability to mete out what he believed to be a just sentence under the constraints of these new guidelines came into full relief during my clerkship year. The defendant was a young man, seventeen or eighteen. He had gotten caught up in a gang that had robbed several convenience stores at gunpoint. The case had been tried, and guilt was determined. He was the driver of the getaway car, and it was the third in a string of robberies in which he'd been convicted. Under the Three Strikes rule, the penalties for each incident compounded greatly. Accordingly, the sentence this young man was facing was one that would put him behind bars for the rest of his life.

In the days that led up to his sentencing, I watched the judge, always very studious and quiet at his work, become even more so. No breaks to tease and joke with us. In fact, we barely saw him. Always in the habit of arriving at the courthouse around five-thirty or six in the morning, now he holed up in his office, poring over legal materials, books stacked up all around him, trying to determine whether there was any way around the mandatory sentence that would put the defendant away forever.

Did the judge believe that the defendant should serve time?
Absolutely.
But spend the rest of his life in prison?
No.

On sentencing day a judge hears from the defendant, from the defendant's family and other character witnesses, as well as from the victims, should they choose to testify. The hearing of these witnesses on this particular day would be perfunctory. The judge had determined that he was hamstrung. There was no way that he could hand down a less severe sentence under the law. He came to the court very somber that day, donned his robe, and took the bench. He listened as the young man described, through tears, having been caught up with the wrong people and spoke of his heartfelt regrets. He listened as the young man's mother, a single mom who had raised him in a housing project, described that she'd done her best, that they'd struggled through many hardships, that her son was truly a good man at heart, that he'd lost his way.

And then the judge, soft-spoken as ever, rendered his decision:

A lengthy sentence, long enough to put the young man in prison for the remainder of his life.

He showed not a hint of emotion as he spoke, nor as he watched the young man's mother cry out in agony.

But when he retired to his office afterward, we could hear his soft sobs.

I could have asked for no better teacher, no better mentor than him.

Judge Buchmeyer died fifteen years after my clerkship with him ended. He had been struggling with dementia. On the morning of his death, the staff at the facility where he was living reported that he'd risen in a spry mood, dressed himself in business attire, and declared that he was going to work. And then, just like that, he was gone. I like to think that that's exactly what happened. That he's at work today, speaking to those of us he influenced during his life's journey. I know he speaks—quietly, of course—to me, and I pray that I give honor to his voice in some small measure through my actions as a public servant today.

FOURTEEN

There is no greater agony than bearing
an untold story inside of you.

—MAYA ANGELOU

MEMORIES LIVE IN THE BODY, and in the mind, but some of my most precious and sacred ones live also in a small wooden box: a memory box for a very much loved and very much wanted child, Tate Elise, the daughter we lost before memories of her could even be made.

In the fall of 1996, Jeff and I were greeted with welcome news. I was pregnant, for the fourth time.

My third pregnancy, in 1994 during my first year of practicing law after my yearlong clerkship for Judge Buchmeyer, had ended very sadly. Neither Jeff nor I had thought about or planned on having another child. Dru was six and Amber was twelve, and we had moved into that phase beyond the complications of toddlerhood and into the complexities of Amber's approaching adolescence. But I'd always wanted another baby after we'd had Dru—it had been such a joy to raise her in a stable environment and to be able to give her the kind of home life and childhood I'd been unable to give Amber, and I so wanted that experience again. Though it was a surprise, I was very excited and sure that I was carrying a boy; almost immediately Jeff and I began referring to "him" as "Baby Lucas."

But problems began to arise sometime just past the midway mark of my first trimester, when a sonogram revealed that the placental sac had collapsed. That day in our doctor's office, Jeff holding my hand as we looked at the sonogram screen, searching for our baby and seeing only the odd-shaped sac with no sign of life there, was a devastating one. Our "Lucas" had implanted in a fallopian tube, rather than in my uterus. Fallopian pregnancies, also known as ectopic pregnancies, are unsustainable and not viable. My doctor advised us that it would be dangerous to my health to continue the pregnancy. To do so would result in the rupturing of my fallopian tube. The only medical option was to have surgery to terminate the pregnancy and remove the affected fallopian tube—which in Texas is technically considered an abortion, and doctors have to report it as such. I was heartbroken. Within the next forty-eight hours, I was scheduled for surgery to remove the tube; all our dreams—mine, Jeff's, Amber's and Dru's—of an addition to our family were brought to a close.

We all grieved the loss, but I grieved most deeply—a sadness and an emptiness took root in me where Baby Lucas had been. In time I returned to the demands of my law practice and lost myself in the daily joys and distractions of raising our two girls, but my renewed hopes and desires for another child never diminished. Soon Jeff and I made a conscious decision to let nature determine if we might once again receive such a blessing. We stopped taking any measures to prevent a pregnancy, and, knowing that with only one fallopian tube our chances were greatly compromised, I secretly prayed that were it God's plan for us we would find ourselves expecting again.

In the fall of 1996, I learned that I was pregnant again, a pregnancy that brought immediate joy to our entire family. Dru would be almost nine when this baby was born, and Amber would be almost fifteen. All three of us were excited about becoming "mamas" to this baby. But we were more cautious with our happiness this time. It wasn't until my first routine sonogram that we fully exhaled. When the sonogram revealed that I was expecting a girl, we were elated. We would have three wonderful girls. We picked out her name, Tate Elise, and bought a few items for her layette.

I continued practicing law and actually did a fair amount of traveling for work. I was working on a large antitrust case that required numerous depositions in various areas of the country. While my boss enjoyed a glass of wine at dinner, I drank skim milk. I wanted to be so careful to do everything just right. When I'd been pregnant with Amber, I gained forty-seven pounds, mostly due to the fatty, high-sodium fast-food diet that was my staple, given my financial challenges and basic lack of understanding about how to eat well. With Dru I'd gained less weight—thirty-two pounds—though her birth weight was much higher than Amber's had been. At twenty-five I had a much better understanding about how to take care of myself and my pregnancy than I had at eighteen with Amber. Now I was thirty-three and completely dedicated to having the healthiest pregnancy possible, reading every book on the subject that I could get my hands on.

Because I was in my thirties and Jeff was in his late forties, our doctor suggested in my second trimester that we have a Tri-Screen done, a blood test that would determine whether my pregnancy showed the possibility of a risk of chromosomal or neural defects. When the doctor called a week or so later and left a message for us to call him back after the results had come in, I immediately grew worried, but when I reached him, his tone was reassuring.

"Nothing to be too concerned about," he said. "One of the indicators was a bit off. Following up with a specialist would be a good idea, just to make sure."

I don't recall understanding what was "off," but I do recall that first wave of sinking fear.

The specialist we were referred to practiced in an obstetric group that dealt with high-risk pregnancies and he was a social acquaintance, more a friend of Jeff's than of mine—a member of his Friday-afternoon wine club. We'd scheduled the appointment with him, and now, in his office, I was full of anxiety. He took a detailed family medical history from both of us and performed a targeted ultrasound. As I lay on the table with cold gel on my enlarged belly, I watched nervously as he began to move the wand, getting just the right angles and taking measurements of Tate's physical development—the length of her leg and arm bones, the circumference of her head. Afterward, when I was dressed, he met us in his office, and his tone was reassuring.

"Everything looks good," he told us. "Her head is slightly enlarged, but not enough to cause me any sort of real alarm. Come back in a few weeks and we'll take another look."

Jeff and I left his office relieved. And I went back to planning for Tate's arrival, her place in our lives.

A few weeks later, I returned for my second high-resolution ultrasound, which I was sure would confirm what we'd been told only a few weeks before. I was so unconcerned that I hadn't thought it necessary to have Jeff come with me, though he'd offered. This time I went alone.

As I had on my prior visit, I lay back in the exam chair, awaiting the cold gel and the wand, anxious to see my baby girl on the screen. Quietly, too quietly, our doctor moved the specialized wand over my belly. Once again he took measurement after measurement, but this time he didn't offer commentary along the way. Instead, when he finished, he repositioned my chair to its upright position and reached for a box of Kleenex, his hand actually shaking. I remember it like it was yesterday. I was immediately filled with dread. I could see in his eyes the news even before he opened his mouth to speak.

I don't recall exactly what he said at that point. But I do remember the words "Dandy-Walker syndrome."

An acute brain abnormality.

The right and left sides of her brain had developed in complete separation, without the normal cerebral connector between the two. And it looked as though she had the most severe consequences associated with the syndrome's abnormalities.

I couldn't breathe. I literally couldn't catch my breath. My baby. My precious baby Tate. I don't remember much else about that day other than calling Jeff, trying to contain my hysterical crying. The rest of it is a shocked, haze-filled blur.

Jeff's friend, our doctor, believed that it would be best if he turned us over to one of his partners in the practice. He felt too close to the situation, he said. It was too personal, too hard for him. It would be too hard on all of us. That day when I cried in his office, he cried with me and held my hands. His hands shaking. That's the visual I recall most about that day. Even as he tried to hold mine, to soothe me, his hands continued to tremble.

His partner met with us the following day, reviewed the sonogram results, and confirmed the sad prognosis. Her condition, extremely rare, fell on the most severe end of the syndrome's spectrum. Terminating our pregnancy was gently suggested as an option. It was likely, he told us, that she wouldn't survive to full term, and if she did, that she would suffer and likely not survive delivery.

Perhaps out of shock and denial and a longing to believe that there could still be hope, I wanted yet another opinion. We were referred to a doctor in Austin who specialized in obstetric neurological diagnoses. Once again we received grim news. "Likely incompatible with life" were some of the words that hung in the air like a thick fog that I could not see through, that I could barely hear through.

Back home I did as much research as I could to find some shred of hope that even in the severest cases and the grimmest scenarios we'd been presented with, there was still a chance she could have some semblance of a sustainable existence. We had been told that even if she did survive, she would probably be deaf, blind, and in a permanent vegetative state.

When I was alone, with time ticking away and the urgency of making a decision pressing down upon me, I would talk to her. I spoke in the most reassuring way I could. I promised I would not let her suffer. But I needed more information. To make such an impossibly awful decision, I needed to feel surer.

And so we went for yet another opinion. This time at a teaching hospital in Dallas. Our specialist there was a woman whose manner combined a detached professionalism with a measure of warmth. After confirming what we had already been told by three other doctors, she respectfully asked whether she could record film of Tate, in the womb, to use as a teaching tool. "Yes," we said. "Yes." *Let Tate's life mean something,* Jeff and I each thought, though neither of us said the words out loud.

At some point in the almost two weeks of second and third and fourth opinions and tortured decision making, I could feel her little body tremble violently, as if someone were applying an electric shock to her, and I knew then what we needed to do. She was suffering. I'd finally caught up to where Jeff had already resigned himself, though he'd patiently waited for me to find my own way of getting there. It was time to accept the grim prognosis shared by those four physicians.

With the heaviest of hearts, we let our doctor know of our decision: that we would terminate our pregnancy, that it was the most humane and compassionate thing we could do to spare Tate the further pain and suffering that would surely follow if we decided otherwise. In his office, we talked through our options; later that day I called him and asked whether he could please help us. And he agreed.

The following morning, after spending my last night with Tate, talking to her, sobbing as I felt her tiny body tremble inside mine, I managed to rise, to dress, to take Jeff's hand as he helped me into the car and drove me to the doctor's office. The previous night, as I lay awake, I was unsure if I would be able to muster the strength to make my body move toward the inevitability of what would follow from each of those movements. But somehow, and with Jeff's support, I did.

In our doctor's office, with tears flowing down both our faces, Jeff and I looked at our baby daughter's beating heart on the sonogram screen for the last time. And we watched as our doctor quieted it. It was over. She was gone. Our much-loved baby was gone.

Afterward I accompanied my doctor to the hospital and delivered Tate Elise Davis by cesarean section, just as I had when Amber and Dru were born. The following day a dear friend who was a nurse in the unit where I delivered Tate brought her to me. She had dressed her in a tiny pink dress and placed a knit cap on her enlarged head. On her feet were crocheted booties, and next to her was a small crocheted pink bunny. Jeff and I spent the better part of the day holding her, crying for her and for us. We asked an associate minister from our church who was a trusted friend to come and baptize her. We took photographs of her. And we said our good-byes. The next day, as I lay in the hospital sobbing, my hand over my now-empty womb, Tate's lifeless body was taken away and cremated.

An indescribable blackness followed. It was a deep, dark despair and grief, a heavy wave that crushed me, that made me wonder if I would ever surface. It would take me the better part of a year to ultimately make my way up and out of it. And when I finally did come through it, I emerged a different person. Changed. Forever changed.

The staff at our doctor's office had done a commendable job of counseling us through the initial days of the tragic decision with which we were faced and the resulting loss. It was through the literature that they provided us, stories recounted by other couples who had endured a similar experience, that we decided we wanted to see Tate after her delivery. I am so grateful for those stories, for the willingness of other couples to share how they handled their loss and grief. It was because of them that we have the precious memories of seeing Tate, of holding her, of baptizing her, of photographing her. And I am so very thankful for those memories, as bittersweet as they are. In a wooden memory box given to me by Patti, with Tate's name carved on its top, mementos of her are stored: the photographs, the program from a private memorial service we held for her at our home surrounded by a small group of our closest family and friends, cards sent by people who reached out to us to provide comfort, and that little crocheted bunny. Each year, on the anniversary of that terrible spring day, I take them out and open myself to the grief and the comfort they bring.

It was a time of great sorrow for our family, and in the weeks that followed, we went through group grief counseling with other couples who had experienced similar losses. Our girls, Amber and Dru, grieved along with us, and we did our best to soothe them. Patti flew in from Boston while I was still in the hospital and stayed for almost two weeks, cooking for us, taking the girls to and from school, shopping for loose, post-pregnancy clothes for me to wear, but mostly caring for and helping to hold me together during the darkest initial stages of my grief.

The following fall we participated as a family in a "Walk to Remember," writing Tate's name and the date of her birth and death on a small card that we attached to a tree in Trinity Park. It was important to all of us to memorialize her, to recognize that she *was*. That she was loved, and is still loved, and always will be loved by us.

FIFTEEN

All politics is local.

E ARLY IN 1996, before my heartbreaking pregnancy with Tate, my entry into politics began. Fort Worth's mayor, Kay Granger, decided she would run for Congress, creating a cascading effect that set me up for my first run for public office. The councilman for the district I lived in, Ken Barr, announced immediately that he would run for mayor, leaving our district's seat open. I jumped into the void and filed my candidacy in the special election that would be held to replace him.

I wish I could say that I had been planning a run for public office for some time, but honestly, I had not. I even took Jeff by surprise when I told him that I wanted to run. But I was at a place in my life and in my career where I felt like I needed something more. I needed to feel that I was making an impact, and my law practice wasn't providing me that kind of fulfillment.

I suppose it wasn't entirely unexpected. After all, I had literally "grown up" from my very early twenties with an admiration for Jeff's service, for his ideals, and for his interest in local politics. Viewing it through his world-lens, I believed it would be something I would enjoy. And that I would be good at. My experiences at the Legal Services Center during law school and clerking for Judge Buchmeyer had taught me the value of working for others above self. And, given my own life experiences, I knew I could relate to and connect with the people in my diverse district who faced many challenges similar to my own. I had the blessing of having moved from a place of struggle to a place of opportunity. And I had the benefit of the analytic training that law school had provided me. Both, I believed, would serve me well as someone who wanted to and could make a difference.

District 9 was a place I'd called home ever since I had enrolled at TCU in 1986. I felt I understood the needs of the district—from building upon the work to improve its declining commercial corridors, to protecting its historic neighborhoods from unnecessary encroachment, to improving its declining neighborhood parks and working to add additional community centers. And I was committed to improving the quality of life of all who lived in the district—whether in its affluent or economically distressed neighborhoods. District 9 also included all of downtown Fort Worth, which was experiencing a rebirth, thanks to the efforts and resources that the Bass family had committed to it. Partnering on these efforts was intriguing and exciting to me. I believed strongly in the work they were doing and I wanted to help. I wanted to be a part of that. I wanted to work on something that I could stand back with pride and say, "I helped do that. I helped do something tangible, something that matters." The job paid $75 a week, so anyone asking to be elected certainly needed to be committed to the work, rather than having a desire, or the need, to be financially compensated.

Trouble is, I hadn't exactly laid the groundwork for establishing myself in the community. To most folks in the district, particularly those activists who had been working long and hard in the trenches to make positive changes, I was an unknown and an unproven quantity.

Except for getting involved in my neighborhood association to fight the expansion of a zoo parking lot behind my home—the one and only time I'd ever seen the inside of the Fort Worth City Council chambers—I wasn't someone who was very well known in town. That issue had grabbed me, not just because I was concerned about its impact to my own quality of life and the value of my home, but because I was deeply concerned about the loss of park space that had continued to occur with the zoo's expansion. What had once been an area with baseball diamonds, soccer fields, an archery range, and a small amusement park that my family and families from all over the city, particularly from the minority community, had enjoyed, was now being gobbled up bit by bit by the zoo's expansion.

But in spite of my limited experience inside the walls of city hall, I believed I could prove myself worthy, and I worked hard to quickly get up to speed on budget and long-term planning issues. With Jeff's guidance I began meeting with smart, thoughtful city staffers who helped me see the landscape of both the opportunities and the challenges that the district faced. Jeff also helped me strategize about what the campaign would look like, and soon we hired a firm owned by one of our neighbors to help us. It was through that firm that I met and first worked with J. D. Angle, who is now a partner in a political consulting and call center firm that he and two friends created. J.D. has gone on to work in presidential races, helping to model likely voter targets and design strategic outreach. But back then, his experiences had been limited to working for the local Democratic Party, staffing a state senator, and now, working as an employee for the Tyson Group, whom I hired. Like me, he had been raised in difficult circumstances, the youngest of eight, raised by a single mother after his parents divorced, and had taken on a high level of responsibility of helping to care for his family at a very young age. We were both young and hungry to grow our impact on the world, to make a difference in the lives of people who had struggled as we both had. From those early days of fighting for that city council seat together, J.D. and I built a friendship that lasts, strong and deep, to this day, and J.D. continues to be a valuable and vital resource in my campaigns.

Cathy Hirt, a very capable lawyer who lived in a neighborhood not far from mine, had also decided to run. Two other people got into the race as well—a Hispanic man, Lee Saldivar, and another Anglo woman, Judy Phillipson—bringing the count to three Anglo women and one Hispanic man. Lee and Judy had much stronger résumés when it came to community work, but what Cathy and I both lacked in that regard we made up for in other ways. We each had the benefit of a law-school education and an ability to absorb and strategize effective policy positions. And we could also raise money and put together sophisticated and effective campaigns. All four of us worked hard and brought passion to the table in that election, but Cathy and I ran very aggressive campaigns from the start and were quickly considered the front-runners.

Jeff had always told me that he'd won his city council race at age twenty-seven by sneaking up on his opponent, a longtime incumbent who believed that this upstart kid had no chance of beating him. But Jeff did it by knocking on doors and talking to voters for hours every single day. Before his opponent knew what was happening, Jeff had gained a significant following in the district, and by the time his opponent tried to mount an offense of his own, it was too late. So I set about trying to do the same thing in my campaign. I would knock on doors for several hours a day—as soon as I got home from work, I'd go out for a couple of hours, and on Saturdays and Sundays I would knock for four or five hours each day, sometimes with Jeff and the girls alongside me, sometimes alone.

As I talked to people at their door, I'd ask about issues that were important to them and I would do my best to convince them that I was the best person for the job. I also tried to distinguish myself from Cathy on the basis of having lived in the district for ten years while Cathy had lived in Fort Worth for only about two years. To her credit, though, she had quickly emerged as a neighborhood leader in her own neighborhood and had forged alliances with some of the strongest community leaders in the south side of Fort Worth, who pulled together an active volunteer organization to help her. And Cathy was much better at selling herself than I was. In fact, I found that aspect of campaigning the hardest. I'd always been very modest by nature, and shy. Whether at someone's door or standing before a group of people, I was extremely uncomfortable—I wanted to talk issues and debate differing perspectives, not talk about myself. That necessary quality for an effective politician to possess was one I had to learn over time—it didn't, and still doesn't, come naturally to me.

It was a tough race, and the debates, which took place at several different arenas with all four of us, were nerve-racking. It was all totally new to me, and despite my legal experience and being thoroughly prepared for the events, again, I was still at my core a very shy person, and being in the spotlight wasn't something I was comfortable with. The degree of scrutiny, even in entry-level local politics, is intense, as is the near-constant feeling of rejection. It's hard not to take everything personally when you're in the middle of a campaign and struggling to convince people that you're the right one to do the job. But I truly felt I was the right person for the job and I was deeply committed to playing a role in shaping and improving my community. Challenging that discomfort and anxiety gave me a newfound respect for people willing to put their name on the line and endure judgment, scorn, and criticism. Now, whenever I meet someone who has mustered the courage to put his or her name on a ballot and run for office, whether for constable, school board, or Congress, I tell them that I admire their willingness. It's hard to describe the exposure you leave yourself open to unless you've run for office. It is not for the faint of heart. And in that first city council race, I often wondered whether I really had the mettle to get through it. Nervous anxiety left me with little appetite and I lost quite a bit of weight, something I could hardly afford at the time. By the end, my mouth had broken out in blisters from the stress. Looking back on that, as hard as it was, I'm grateful for it. I see the blessing I was given through it. Because it toughened me for the journey I had ahead. A journey I could never have predicted at the time.

After several months of a grueling campaign, election day arrived. I waited nervously with family and supporters in my headquarters. When the final votes were counted, there was no winner. No candidate had received more than 50 percent of the vote. Cathy Hirt and I would meet again in a runoff. The two of us would be left to debate our positions on a variety of issues—from the planned construction of a major toll road, to improving the quality of life for the people in our district. Cathy went into the runoff just slightly ahead of me in terms of the number of votes received. So now we were really scrambling. And she continued to prove her capacity as a worthy adversary. Until that point I'd run a very positive campaign—we both had. But Jeff had a different, more aggressive campaigning style, and during that runoff period he convinced me to be much more aggressive than I probably would have been if left to my own devices—particularly back then when I was such a novice. But the buck stopped with me, to paraphrase the old saying. And I must own the actions taken in each and every one of the campaigns I have run. It was my call on whether to send out a negative mail piece on my opponent—one that pointed out her failure to initially pass her state's bar and to work as an attorney prior to becoming licensed. In other words, it called her qualifications into question. To this day I regret it. The mailer was mean-spirited and it hit below the belt. It wasn't in keeping with the tone that either Cathy or I had set in our campaigns. And she certainly had proven her credentials to be a worthy representative of the district. At the end of the day, I believe that sending it out did me much more harm than good. I am absolutely certain it cost me support. Most certainly, it cost me self-respect and a feeling of pride about how I had run my campaign.

What hurt me even more than that, though, was an extremely negative editorial that the *Fort Worth Star-Telegram* ran about me on the day of the election. Their normal policy, and the policy of most newspapers, is not to run an editorial about a candidate on election day, because it leaves no possibility for the candidate to respond before voters go to the polls. But on the day of our runoff election, almost the entire left-hand column of the newspaper's editorial page was taken up with a very strong and very ugly editorial about me, making what I believed to be purposely false—and therefore libelous—statements about my position regarding the Fort Worth Zoo expansion that I'd opposed as a concerned citizen and the circumstances of my departure from Kelly Hart, a law firm I'd worked for. I believed that editorial, and the fact that I didn't have a chance to respond to it, contributed to my loss of the election.

By ninety votes.

The publisher of the *Fort Worth Star-Telegram* at the time, Richard L. Connor, was very close to the major financial patrons of the zoo, Lee and Ramona Bass, people who had done a great community benefit by investing in dramatic improvements to that institution. But my neighborhood and the adjacent neighborhood had been very heavily affected by the loss of park space and by the threatened expansion of a parking lot into some of the park space that remained. As I said earlier, this was an issue I had previously gotten involved in. I had spoken out about it at a city council meeting. But the issue had long since been decided, and it was one we had accepted and from which we had moved on. Though it had not been an issue in the race, the newspaper worked to resurrect it, I believed to sully my name. I was repeatedly asked about it by a reporter from the newspaper during the course of the campaign, though neither I nor anyone else in the district was raising it as an issue, and it was never discussed as an issue in any of the debates. I tried to provide responses to the reporter's questions, indicating that the issue was behind us and that I looked forward to working with the zoo's benefactors if elected. Both Jeff and I were concerned, though. We saw a strategy at work and believed that the resurrection of the issue was purposeful and that the publisher was directing its coverage on the news side so that the paper could use it as a jumping-off point from which to editorialize against me—which is exactly what happened on the day of the election:

"Given the plethora of vital issues that cry out for the immediate attention of the next council member from District 9, it is surprising and disappointing that some of the candidates have chosen to try to open an old, healed wound. Making the zoo a political football in this race can serve no useful purpose. But it could provoke another round of detrimental community divisiveness . . . Any candidate who seeks to stir up unwarranted hysteria about the zoo instead of concentrating on existing issues does a disservice to the community and deserves rejection by the voters of District 9."

Of course, I will never fully know how much impact the articles and the editorial had. Nor will I ever know how much impact my own actions in sending out a negative mail piece had on the outcome of the election. But I had lost. And I was devastated.

Not long after the election, a top female editor at the *Star-Telegram* left the paper in a highly publicized resignation or firing, depending on whose version you believed. She left on terms that were not good, and eventually she filed suit against the newspaper, agreeing to a settlement with a confidentiality provision in it, but eventually, through other sources, information came to us that shed some light on what had gone on at the paper during the election, including her overruled objections about running the editorial about me, which we outlined in the suit we filed:

"An example of the malicious conduct is as follows: Before being interviewed for the story that ran on May 1, 1996, concerning the resurgence of the zoo as an issue in the race for the District 9 seat, Davis questioned the reporter's reasons for wanting to write a story on this issue since it had been a non-issue for over a year. The reporter, Kristin N. Sullivan, indicated that she had 'been told' to cover the issue. Careful not to make the zoo an issue in her campaign, Davis offered several positive viewpoints regarding the zoo. Despite her efforts, however, Davis was later told by Ms. Sullivan that she would not be happy with the way the story was going to run the next day. Sullivan informed Davis that the story she had originally written, which reflected the positive nature of the interview, was edited in a manner that would cause Davis to be unhappy with the story. Ms. Sullivan apologized and said she was powerless to do anything about the article as 'things are very political around here [at the *Fort Worth Star-Telegram*].' . . .

"The Star-Telegram intentionally wrote and published this news article so as to purposefully avoid the truth . . . To Plaintiff's knowledge, only former Star-Telegram executive editor Ms. Debbie Price attempted to prevent the publication of such malicious stories and editorials.

"On the morning after the May 1, 1996, story ran, Davis, at the suggestion of Ms. Sullivan, contacted Ms. Price to express her displeasure with the paper's stories on her candidacy. Davis indicated to Price that she felt that certain stories had been purposefully edited to create a false impression in the minds of the readers. Price indicated that she had not been involved in the editing process and that if the paper were to cover the zoo issue again, it would include Davis' positive statements. Subsequent to this conversation, the Star-Telegram ran three defamatory editorials about Davis, one of them specifically addressing the maliciously fabricated zoo issue. Within a few days after the publication of the May 25th editorial and run-off election, Price was terminated. A Wall Street Journal article covering the disappearance of Price stated that she was fired for refusing to go along with 'unethical editorial policies.'"

And that's why we decided to file a libel suit against the paper and its parent companies: in order to find out, through the power of legal discovery, what had really happened. In order to determine that, we'd have to legally pierce the terminated editorialist's confidentiality agreement, and the only way we could do *that* was by filing our own suit in the hopes of being given the opportunity for discovery. We'd been told that we had a good chance at a compensable claim, but that truly was the least of my concerns and my interest. All I really wanted was a chance to get to the bottom of things.

At almost the exact same time that we were going through our decision-making process about whether to file the libel suit against the *Star-Telegram*, the law firm I worked for, Haynes and Boone, had hired a partner from another firm. The *Star-Telegram* was one of his clients, which meant that the *Star-Telegram* had now become a client of my firm, and what that meant was that if I attempted to file suit, it would be a conflict of interest and I would have to leave the firm. We waited right up until the one-year statute of limitations to file the suit had almost run out before making the decision on whether to file. It was 1997. And my firm tried hard to encourage me not to file—telling me that I had an incredibly bright future there; that I'd not only be a partner but was considered one of their rising stars. They wanted me to stay, but I decided to file the suit, which would come to be my second regret from that first campaign. Though I sincerely wanted to get to the bottom of what had happened in the editorial decision-making process to determine whether something untoward had occurred, there was little to really gain from it other than looking through the rearview mirror. Leaving the firm, though, in spite of the possibility of a very bright future there, turned out to be a move in the right direction in my life's journey. My heart was not in it. My heart had already set its sights on public service and the kind of personal fulfillment that I believed it would bring.

Ultimately, Jeff and I filed the suit on April 18, 1997. Neither of us liked the idea of being litigious, but we felt wronged, and we wanted to know why. It wasn't something I did lightly. I wanted the truth, though. Libel cases are notoriously difficult for public figures to win. In order to succeed, a public figure (and all candidates are considered public figures in the eyes of the law) must prove not only that a published statement was false but that the speaker knew it to be false at the time. In the end, our case was dismissed without any discovery being granted, because we couldn't sufficiently clear that hurdle. And my quest to find out what had gone on in that editorial office went nowhere.

Looking back on it now, after years of experience in the political arena, I've learned that having a newspaper say ugly things about you when you're running for office is just part of the deal, even if you feel it's gotten the story entirely wrong. And in today's social media environment, the terrain for that sort of vitriol has grown exponentially. It comes with the territory. And as a candidate, you accept that that's just how things are when you decide to run. I've trained myself to tune it out, put my head down and move forward. It's noise. Only noise.

I know that much can be said about living life looking in the rearview mirror and second-guessing our actions, but I can say with all candor that I regret some of my actions—both in filing that suit and choosing to tarnish my opponent—during that first race. Did I learn from them and become a better person as a consequence? I would like to think so. Would I go back and do things differently if given the chance? Yes. But life brings no do-overs. Only opportunities to learn and grow from and act accordingly when the next bend in the road comes.

I am pleased to say that after all the drama, my nemeses during that time period later proved to be friends. It says far more about their capacities for forgiveness and grace than about my own. Cathy Hirt, as a city councilwoman, eventually gave me an appointment to a citizens' committee on a highway expansion that would affect my neighborhood and proved herself a person who took the high road. I will forever be indebted to her for that. It was my role on that committee that helped establish my credibility in a way that set me up for a successful city council run three years later when Cathy decided not to stand for reelection. The zoo patrons I had tangled with became people I worked closely with as a councilperson, and they supported me in many races after that first one. Even my very first opponents, Lee and Judy, came to be two of the people I would rely on to partner with me on projects to benefit the district during my years on the city council. And the newspaper publisher? He and I found our way to a peaceful accord when I dated his nephew, some time after Jeff and I divorced. Making peace, I have found, even with once-sworn enemies, is powerful and can help soothe those recesses in our lives, those voids created when living with regret.

T hat first city council election was the first thing I'd ever put my whole heart and energy into that I hadn't succeeded at—and in the days and weeks following, I had a hard time dealing with the loss. It felt like an enormous personal rejection, and that, coupled with the unease I still felt about the negative mailer we'd sent out and how unjustly I felt the *Star-Telegram* had behaved, made the whole situation difficult to get past. I'd gone into the process understanding that I might lose, but accepting the reality of it was a much more painful and complex process than I ever could have anticipated.

After a lot of soul-searching, I unpacked my disappointment and my crushed ego from the reasons that the voters had not chosen me. I reexamined some of the decisions I had made. And I resolved to learn from the experience—especially that a run for office must reflect more closely the values you hold dear. For me, that means standing strong for the things I believe in to my core—no matter what. I've learned that I'm at my best when I'm fighting for people, for the cause of equality and justness. In pursuit of that, I've also learned that sometimes, punching my opponent—*above* the belt—is necessary to ensure that people are informed about who will best serve their interests.

I also learned that losing doesn't actually kill you. That may sound trite, but I'm a deeply competitive person, made that way in large part thanks to my father, and that was a concept I'd never truly understood. He had always taught me, through his own example, to work as hard as you could at winning but that, win or lose, you should do so gracefully. I didn't bring the right measure of grace to my city council loss, and I learned and grew from that. It gave me a new perspective on how I would process the torments of a future campaign and how I would respond to them.

Integrity is in the record of work a public servant leaves behind. A record of work made up of everyday deeds, of acts of compassion, and of simple human connection with those whose trust you hold. After I lost that first race, I began to lay the foundation of my record. And the first brick of that foundation was proving myself to the community whose support I hoped to ask for again one day.

What I realized in time was that, in that first race, I hadn't done the community building necessary for me to deserve to be elected. In my first campaign, people would say to me, "Well, what have you done? We don't know you. We haven't seen you working on this issue or that issue." Most people who get elected to local offices do so by proving themselves, creating reputations as community leaders. I had not done that. I'd just rushed into it and tried to get people to see how much I wanted to do the work to make Fort Worth a better place. But it's not that simple. You have to give people a reason to trust that you're going to fight for them, and my lack of experience in the community had not achieved that. It drove me to get more involved in my neighborhood in a substantive way.

First, I became president of the Mistletoe Heights neighborhood association and joined a group devoted to the revitalization of a commercial corridor in our community, the Berry Street Initiative. Together with a group of local residents, volunteers, and private investors, we worked hard to transform an area in decline near TCU into an appealing pedestrian environment for students and residents.

Then came the appointment by Cathy Hirt that I mentioned; my work on that committee helped me to be seen as someone who could work constructively, even on controversial issues. I will always be grateful to Cathy for giving me the chance to be involved at that level.

Never a quitter, and emerging from the many months of darkness that followed the loss of Tate, I decided to try again for a city council seat in 1999. This time there were three people in the race: Dan Roberts, a public-affairs consultant, and David Minor, a successful businessman who had started mowing lawns as a teenager and built an incredibly successful landscaping operation. David was young and good-looking, charming and smart, with a very compelling personal story of bootstrapping his way up in the world. While he'd been hand-picked by the business community as their candidate of choice, he didn't have the connection to the grassroots community that I now had after the several years of relationship building I'd done.

I knew it would be tough to get a pure majority of the vote with three of us in the race. Dan ran a positive campaign, but David and I ran better-financed strategic campaigns. I braced myself for a runoff but worked really hard to avoid one—aggressively knocking on doors again—until I ended up winning the election with just over 50 percent. It was a narrow win, one I felt grateful for and proud of. I'd been bound and determined to stay absolutely positive, and to his credit, David Minor did, too. I know that we both came out of the race feeling proud of the campaigns we had run. No regrets. I had resolved that no matter how things turned out, this time I would have no regrets.

The evening of the election, my supporters and I had gathered at one of my favorite Mexican restaurants on the city's south side— Benito's. While everyone else congregated in the main area of the restaurant, I was off in the back hall with Jeff and J.D., on the phone with someone that we had placed at the election administrator's office so that we could hear the results of each precinct's box as soon as it had come in. Because the vote margins were so tight, it literally came down to the last one—a box I felt sure would be good for me because I was strongly supported in that neighborhood. When it came in, I'd avoided a runoff. I had won.

I was so proud and so happy. I had run a race I felt good about, and the people of the district had placed their trust in me. I was bound and determined to hold that trust, to show them that they'd been right. And, a few weeks later, joined by my family and friends, as I raised my hand at my first city council meeting to be sworn into office, I made a silent promise to myself—that I would always vote my conscience, no matter how hard. And that I would always choose what was right for the people I represented, even if that meant choosing the harder route.

When I first started serving on the Fort Worth City Council, I was certainly well outside my comfort zone. I was still that painfully shy little girl, so doing a launch at a groundbreaking or taking my turn to speak at the council table always made me feel a bit nervous. But I actually think that's a good thing; it's a sign that you respect the people who are your audience, that you want to make a good impression on them, that it matters to you what they think.

Working on the city council quickly took me far beyond where I expected it would in terms of my personal growth. I was now coming to understand the true meaning of being a public "servant." I felt, to my core, the tremendous privilege of service above self and the incomparable satisfaction that comes from helping to make your community better for the people who live there. Real people were relying on me for things big and small, and I saw, close-up, that small things are big things when it comes to improving the quality of life for hard-working families. Tremendous sacrifices are required of people who answer the calling of being a servant—the biggest and most painful of which is the fact that attending to the needs of the people you represent can often trump the needs of people who are personally dear and who need you as well: family and friends. Public service is nothing less than a family affair, and there's no question that my daughters have had to make sacrifices of their own because of my years of service.

When people have a day-to-day connection with the person who represents them, they feel they can be heard. They believe they can come to meetings and be part of the process and part of the solution regardless of the issue being addressed, and it's that connection that's at the very heart of what it means to be an elected official. You're making a promise to people. Every day. And when you look people in the eye, people you represent, people who have voted for you and trusted you with what they treasure most—their family and their future—and you promise you're going to do your best to help them with something they need—it's real. And it's sacred. Maybe it's helping to install a pocket park in a neighborhood that has no open space, or getting lights for a Little League field, or putting sidewalks in a neighborhood so that kids can walk to school safely instead of having to walk in the middle of the street. Every single thing my constituents needed and asked my help with touched upon their daily quality of life and their greatest investment and what they valued most: their homes and their children's well-being.

There was hardly an evening when I wasn't attending a neighborhood meeting or a small gathering of community leaders to work on projects important to them. Things like code enforcement issues, which sound small in the grand scheme of things, were actually very important. As the "broken windows" theory goes, code violations within a community can begin to degrade it bit by bit, contributing to an environment of disinvestment and crime. Cleaning up declining commercial corridors and encouraging reinvestment was a key collective goal. So was improving parks and funding and building community centers where they were needed—especially in some of the economically distressed neighborhoods that I represented. To anyone who asked me for help, I always made the very same promise:

I'm going to help you with that.

I'm going to do my very best.

And I did. I was tenacious. Joined by the help of extraordinary council aides, first Vonciel Buchanan and then Kristi Wiseman, I developed strong and respectful relationships with city staff people in the parks department and the public-works department, so that if someone in my community needed something, I knew how to go about getting it done and whom to ask to help me get it done. Those positive working relationships made all the difference.

The district I was elected to serve also included all of downtown and was therefore considered one of the most influential seats. In the morning I might find myself in a meeting with downtown power brokers, working to make continued improvements to the investment and job creation there, while in the afternoon I might find myself at a kitchen table in one of the Latino neighborhoods in my district, helping to plan a way to get more streetlights to make the community safer. I represented some of the most affluent neighborhoods in the city and some of the least affluent. And I loved them all. Every bit of what I had the privilege of working on, I enjoyed and took tremendous pride in. But I found the most satisfaction in working with my constituents living in impoverished neighborhoods. Sometimes fulfilling the simplest of needs brought the greatest rewards.

One of my favorite things to do was to meet in someone's kitchen and talk over something that was very important to them. Many of those kitchen conversations helped me actively partner with them and fight to receive federal Community Development Block Grants for streetlights, street improvements, and other crucial basics that lifted up their neighborhoods.

One of the kitchen conversations I remember vividly was with the Florez family; they lived in one of the most economically challenged multigenerational Hispanic areas in my district. They'd lived there long enough to see things go downhill, especially when the commercial corridors that abutted their neighborhood had become crime-ridden, full of seedy bars and hourly motels. They were watching other parts of the city grow and thrive, and they wanted that for their neighborhood, too.

When I met with them, we focused on how we could redevelop that area—the Hemphill Corridor Task Force was formed by Fernando Florez, who served as its chair for many years. He helped me to see that one of the things that built integrity in neighborhoods was assuring compliance with city codes—mowed yards, porches free of debris, lighting in good repair. One ramshackle, unattended house can bring down the next house and the next, until a whole street is suffering. Likewise, improving a neighborhood one house at a time, one street at a time, can make a tremendous positive impact. Neighborhood leaders like Fernando and so many others were people who loved their communities and were willing to do the hard work to turn them around. And I came to love these people as though they were my own family.

Fernando's wife, Roberta, was equally committed—her passion was helping kids whose parents worked and couldn't afford adequate daytime care for their children during summer vacation months. Through her commitment to the children of her community, she had started the Mobile Recreation Summer Day Camp, a program that moved around and wasn't housed in a permanent facility—therefore the "Mobile" part of its title. Instead she'd arranged with the parks department to let kids gather at a local park in the morning for constructive recreational outdoor time and then, in the afternoon when it got really hot, to go to a church-annex building nearby and use their gymnasium. That first summer Mobile Summer Rec started with around seventy kids.

After she invited me to help so that I could bring in additional resources, we worked to gradually grow the program to the point that it is now serving approximately seven hundred kids at no cost to their parents. It partners for facility space with the Fort Worth school district, which provides the use of school buildings and helps, along with the parks department, to staff the program with trained child-development folks who work to provide a summer program of learning enrichment as well as recreation. My most important role was to secure city funding for the program, and I proudly succeeded and also secured Mobile Summer Rec as sacred ground; even when the budget would ebb and flow, even when times were tight, Mobile Summer Rec always got what it needed. We, along with Roberta, Fernando, and the committed staff of our parks department, made sure of it. It remains one of my proudest shared accomplishments during the time I served on the city council.

One of the most poignant experiences with the program came very early in its development. Roberta had arranged for field trips to occur on most Fridays. But the trip costs would have to be borne by the parents. I had come, at Roberta's invitation, to welcome the parents and kids to the first day of the camp that year, and I will never forget watching a mother have to explain to her two children, who'd been jumping up and down with excitement as they read off the field-trip opportunities from the flyer, that they would not be able to participate. She couldn't afford the costs for zoo admission, museum admission, or admission to the public swimming pool. I could see the crushing disappointment in her face, and I left the park that day determined to do something about it.

As soon as I was back in my council office, I got on the phone, calling generous community leaders who I knew would be willing to make donations to the field-trip program. I raised enough money to fund the field trips for every child who wanted to participate. And every year after that, two months before camp started, I'd send out fund-raising letters and manage to get the field trips underwritten. I'm proud to say that the person who won election to that seat after I stepped down, Joel Burns, continued to work to keep the program funded and raise money for the field trips. And he's taken it to a whole new level of success.

I also had the privilege of working on big-picture things—in my second term in office, Mayor Kenneth Barr appointed me the chair of the powerful Housing and Economic Development Committee, and I became part of the team to pitch companies to move to Fort Worth. I learned a great deal in the role, about the power of public-private partnerships and the ability to stimulate job creation and investment through public participation. I was also proud to work with our able and talented economic development staff to structure the agreements so that companies that failed to hold up their end of the bargain in exchange for the public dollars they'd received to fund a project—creating a certain number of jobs; using local companies and minority- and women-owned businesses during and after construction, among other things—would lose their public funding through "claw back" mechanisms we would employ to reduce their funding in proportion to their failures. Through that role I was able to play a vital part in shaping the growth of my community. Today, there are many projects I can look at with pride, knowing I helped to make them happen. It felt just like the end of a long day in my grandma's garden, when we sat on the porch and surveyed our handiwork—economic development gave me the opportunity to experience that same satisfaction of the benefit of hard work well done.

———

I t was never easy, though. Guided by what I'd learned in the Warren Court class, I worked to understand why people believed what they believed, especially within the council itself—and especially when dealing with one of our brashest and most conservative members, Chuck Silcox. Chuck had been on the council for many years and used his overbearing size and loud voice to intimidate his way to getting what he wanted. Needless to say, he and I butted heads quite a bit. I believed in development standards—meaning I believed in sustainable building standards for commercial and residential development, he did not; I believed in the use of public-private partnerships to stimulate investment and job creation, he did not; I believed in zoning standards that would concentrate mixed-use developments into our urban core, he did not. Time and again, I would find myself on the receiving end of his booming voice and his imposing stature. But I never backed down.

Later I discovered that behind Chuck's brusque exterior, he had a soft heart for animals and for people struggling to make ends meet. In other words, he had a soft spot for the vulnerable, and eventually I would learn why: a close family member of his was homeless and an alcoholic. Understanding that he could be reasoned with when talking about how people could fall victim to the harsh actions of others, I was proud to work with him on expanding our anti-discrimination ordinance and to join him one evening on the council dais in doing so. Chuck had come so far on the issue of adding sexual orientation to the ordinance that he was not only the last vote and therefore the deciding vote, but he actually made the motion for passage we needed, which was hugely significant. Though he and I continued to oppose each other on a variety of issues, and though we could still have some good old-fashioned knock-down, drag-out fights, we became friends.

True friends with a real respect for each other. I was deeply saddened when he succumbed to illness and passed away in 2008. And I was proud to attend the grand opening the following year of a new animal shelter, named, appropriately, in honor of Chuck.

I was also guided by what I'd learned from Judge Buchmeyer about the importance of deconcentrating public housing. It helped me through a tremendously contentious time involving the relocation of residents from the Ripley Arnold public housing projects downtown to free up the property for Radio Shack's corporate headquarters. Just as had happened in West Dallas under Judge Buchmeyer's oversight, an agreement was reached (one I had helped to broker) with the residents of the housing authority that they would be moved into areas of the city that were not low-income ones. It would involve the purchase by the housing authority of an apartment complex in an affluent area of my district, which they intended to use for a mix of tenants, by income, some paying market rate as before, but with the intention of setting aside about 20 percent of the units to be used for relocated residents from Ripley Arnold. It was one of the true tests of my character while on the council. I had to face the wrath of a community that was angered and frightened by what the purchase of the apartment complex might mean to their neighboring homes and property values.

On the evening when the issue was first raised during a city council meeting, the council chamber was filled to overflowing and many people had to be moved to other areas of the building to watch remotely. People were angry, screaming, primarily at the mayor and me. In the following weeks, we held several town hall–style hearings in church auditoriums large enough to hold the hundreds of people who wanted to be heard. It was rough. My girls felt the impact at school, each coming home with stories of having heard criticisms of me from friends. For months, I had to stop going to my local haunts because I'd had several experiences, whether at the dry cleaner's or the grocery store or a local restaurant, of people angrily confronting me. It was one of my most challenging experiences in elected office. It brought into stark relief the fact that policy making has real-life impacts, and that our decisions as policy makers change people's lives in ways that won't always make them happy. Little did I know that the experience would serve as a precursor of, and preparation for, challenges that I would face during my time in the Texas senate and that it would help better prepare me for the fact that public service isn't always about doing what's popular. I'd seen Judge Buchmeyer do brave, hard things in the face of anger, and I knew I, too, could get through this by listening and being as responsive as possible to legitimate concerns. We set up a task force of representatives from the housing authority, the relocated residents, the residents of the surrounding community, and the police department to address problems, and ultimately the housing authority moved ahead with the purchase of the complex and the relocation. In time the anger subsided, and today it stands as a model of how mixed-income communities can benefit generations of children to come. In fact, one of my former senate staffers is now engaged to be married to someone who credits the move as something that changed his life for the better. By moving from Ripley Arnold, he had been able to attend a top-rated nearby elementary school, he came to aspire to be a college student like most of his classmates did, and he ultimately became a proud first-generation college graduate in his family.

These are the stories that make public service so worthwhile, and these are the ones I remind myself of on tough days, when the work can feel frustrating because achieving your desires for your constituents is harder than it should be. When politics gets in the way of doing the right thing—when people who are elected to serve their constituents instead serve a lobby interest or an ideological score card—those are the days that make me want to pound my desk and call it out for what it is. But working effectively in the political arena means keeping enough alliances to get things done. And so I take a deep breath and move on to the next challenge.

After my fifth election to serve District 9 on the Fort Worth City Council, I made a decision to step down from my seat about midway through the term to run for the Texas senate. In the nine wonderful years that I served my constituents in that local office, I am proud to say that I never took my district for granted, I never forgot that serving my constituents was a privilege, and I always viewed being in public office as I think it should be viewed: *that the job belongs to the people*. And while you're the person who's being honored with the seat, it's their seat, not yours, and you have to remember to respect that. For me, serving was the perfect marriage of all my life experiences, of all my education and my struggles. And that's why I think I could so comfortably move across the different environments of the people I represented. I felt just as comfortable sitting at the kitchen table in the humblest home, trying to work on a neighborhood issue, as I did sitting in a corporate boardroom. I had a foot in both of those worlds from my past and my present that helped me serve my community the best way possible.

It's my hope that the people in my beloved neighborhoods would tell you that they saw me as someone who genuinely cared, someone who went to bat for them over and over again, someone who worked really hard for them and who was a true partner. Someone who was willing to go the distance for them and fight when a fight was what it took. From the mall in the Latino area of my community that was saved through a public-private partnership (one of the ones I got Chuck Silcox to vote for!), to the new streets and streetlights in neighborhoods that needed them, to the summer day camp program that I helped grow, to the numerous new economic development projects throughout my district and the city as a whole that have provided thousands of jobs—these were the things I fought alongside my constituents to provide.

Through that service I gained something invaluable: clarity and certainty of my mission in life.

It was on the Fort Worth City Council that I figured out that public service was my calling. The compassion and the character that grew from the struggles I'd had in my life, coupled with the amazing education I'd had the great privilege of receiving, made me a true public servant. And I'm not embarrassed to say that. I'm a public servant in every sense of those words. I really am. Because I'm in public service for the right reason—to serve—and because I have a sense of justice that is my guiding light, my divining rod, my compass. It's the filter through which I determine everything I do. You can look through my legislative history during those years (and in the years that would follow in the state senate) and see that compass. It's in everything I do and in everything I fight for. Every person who is the victim of a predatory high-interest loan, each kid who isn't getting a good education, any woman who isn't being paid fairly, or every consumer being abused by an insurer or by a public utility is a personal affront to me.

W hen I left the city council, my loyal and wonderful aide Kristi and her son Todd put together a video for me, recording some of my most precious memories and friends from those council years. My dad narrated it. In it he describes me as a person who was always nurturing, even as a little girl. And he refers to me as the mediator of our family. I suppose that part is true. With two older brothers and a younger sister, you have to learn to mediate sibling spats—whether it was a war in the backyard, or a battle over G.I. Joes, I had to learn to hold my own with my brothers. I suppose that helped me navigate better in a world that is still dominated by men—whether in local, state, or federal offices. You have to learn how to play well with others and develop a skin as thick as rhinoceros hide. I think I've managed to do both.

The mediating part came fairly naturally. But when you're a girl as shy and fearful as I grew up being, the thick-skin part had to be learned. I think, were my dad alive today, he'd tell you I learned that part pretty damned well.

SIXTEEN

God made the world round so we would never
be able to see too far down the road.

—KAREN BLIXEN

THE YEARS THAT JEFF and I shared with our girls on Mistletoe
Drive were, for the most part, happy ones. They were punctuated
with the stresses of my time away in law school, my runs for public
office, and Jeff's move to the new title company of which he became
a part owner and the years spent building that company into a competitive, thriving one. The loss of our expected "Baby Lucas" through
an ectopic pregnancy took us off course and into a crevasse, but it
was one that we moved out of together and weathered as well as could
be expected. But it was the loss of Tate in the spring of 1997 that
nearly undid me, and therefore us. Both of us grieved deeply. But my
grief was so black, so incalculable, that I found it almost impossible
to climb out of the void I fell into. Jeff and I had been married for just
shy of ten years at that point, and our marriage had sustained many
stresses. Regaining a desire for intimacy after losing Tate was tremen-

dously hard for me, but Jeff was patient. He let me heal at my own pace and in my own time. And, eventually, our shared grief over Tate and our ability to respect each other's journey out of that grief helped us to survive the loss with our marriage intact.

We were partners. In all things, always partners. We cheered each other on and supported each other through disappointment and celebrations. Everyone who knew us during the seventeen years of married life that we shared together would likely tell you that ours was a marriage to be admired. And I would proudly say the same. During those years, as Dru grew older and witnessed some of her friends' parents divorcing, she would ask me for reassurance that this would not happen with her dad and me. And, with all honesty and candor, I would soothe her anxieties and assure her that, no, it would not.

Jeff and I built a family together that was filled with traditions, good humor, and fun. Our home, though by no means in perfect condition, was well laid out for social gatherings. And we loved to play host. Whether it was for neighborhood events, shared times with other couples who were our friends, or for extended family gatherings, our home was a hub of activity. And we both enjoyed and contributed to making these gatherings work. Jeff, the consummate host when it came to serving excellent wine. Me, the less-than-perfect, but decent host(ess) when it came to experimenting with cooking and serving a good meal.

The girls continued to grow with nothing more than the typical bumps and bruises that a growing girl in the world attracts. My dad's theater continued to succeed and gain tremendous respect in the live theater community. My brother Joey came to live with us for a few years following a difficult divorce from the marriage he had entered so very young; he stayed in our modest guesthouse and built a fairly thriving handyman business. And he and I had time together again. Often, we would sit down over the daily *New York Times* crossword

puzzle and, as a team, could do a good job of getting through it. Sometimes we played chess, but he, always the cleverest of my siblings,
could shut down just about any strategy I tried to employ. After Joey
moved on to Tennessee again to rebuild his life there, we took in Jeff's
sister and her children, who also lived in our guesthouse for a couple
of years. Family came first for us, and we shared a commitment to
taking care of them. We were blessed in so many ways and I felt lucky
and grateful for everything we had, and for the ability to extend our
blessings to the people that we loved.

Together, we created traditions for the girls and for Jeff's son,
Erik, who had moved from Louisiana to Virginia, and eventually to
Plano, Texas. During those times when he lived at a distance, Erik
would stay with us usually one weekend a month, or Jeff would go to
visit him. And during the summer, we would have him for at least a
month, and sometimes more. After some of his first visits to us, when
Jeff and I were only dating and had not yet married and begun living
together, Erik would often bring his best friend, Drew, from Louisiana on his visits. Drew eventually became as much a loved and cherished part of our family as our own children, ultimately coming to
stay with us almost as much as Erik did. When our own Dru was born
in 1988, we began referring to them as "Big Drew" and "Little Dru"
and they still refer to each other that way. Occasionally Amber and
Erik felt the typical strains that can occur between stepsiblings. But
for the most part, our time together as a complete family were filled
with fun. We had a pool for the kids to swim in and we played lots of
games, just as I had with my own dad growing up. We began taking
yearly vacations in the summer to Breckenridge, Colorado, where one
of Jeff's business partners had a condo, and we built traditions there—
competing with one another to see who could get through the "human
maze" the quickest, racing one another on sleds down the Alpine
SuperSlide, daring one another to climb the highest on the Rockpile

Climbing Wall, riding the ski lifts up to the top peaks and hiking (or once, unsuccessfully, mountain biking) down. We laughed so much when we had all the children with us. They were our strongest tether, our deepest connection to each other.

Jeff and I weathered many outside storms together and we were each other's closest friend. When Jeff began to become more interested in playing golf, he encouraged me to learn to play as well, signing me up for lessons from a former golf professional so that we could share in that hobby together. When time and our obligations to the children would allow it, Jeff and I would be on the golf course. He cheered my every good shot and soothed my angst when I would play poorly. We played in couples tournaments together, and when we would travel, we would always take our clubs and play while on vacation.

When I was elected to the Fort Worth City Council in 1999, and it would become a full-time job for me, we still made time for our rituals, our gatherings, our family time. When Dru was still in elementary school, I became her Girl Scout troop leader. Because I am not very good at arts and crafts, most of our time as a troop was spent picking areas where we could go and volunteer—from senior centers, singing and reading to the residents there, to homeless shelters, where we would help to serve food, or to a center for homeless children, where we would take crafts to work on with them. One year, I cochaired the big annual fund-raising event at Dru's school, giving me new admiration for the parents who had done it all those years before. And because Dru was always interested in playing sports, I signed her up for softball and basketball leagues and, along with Jeff and Amber, and Erik when he was in town, spent untold hours enjoying watching her as she participated in team sports. I worked to nurture Amber's artistic talents—she was always the "entertainer" of the family, having clearly inherited that characteristic from my dad, and I happily shuttled her to her various interests, from gymnastics to horseback riding.

As Jeff worked to grow his title company's share of business, I also began working to help in that regard, attending networking events as a representative of our company to help strengthen its presence. And Jeff gave me a formal role with the company as I came to do more of that.

We were, in all ways, a family.

But somewhere along the way, in the midst of all that we had going on, a fracture occurred. Watching the documentary on former Texas governor Ann Richards recently, I was struck when she talked about the fact that, though she and her husband, Dave, much like Jeff and I, had always been partners in all regards, it was her election to state treasurer that ultimately placed a strain on their marriage that it could not sustain. I suppose much of the same can be said of my time on the city council. Because somewhere in the midst of my service there, sadly, inexplicably, our marriage began to slowly unwind.

Even now, as hard as I try to put words to it, describing how our relationship came to fray is incredibly difficult. As I reflect over the unraveling of our marriage, I am reminded of something my dad said to me after my teenage breakup with my first real boyfriend. "As individuals," he'd said, "we continue to grow and evolve. The best couples, the ones who succeed," he added, "are the ones who evolve together." From his own experiences, my dad could certainly speak to the fractures that could come from an evolution that was not complementary. And, up until I was several terms deep into my city council service, Jeff and I had always grown in ways that continued to sustain us.

But at its most basic point, our relationship had begun and been built upon a power differential. Jeff was the mentor, and I his mentee. And I began struggling with that. I grew to resent more and more Jeff's well-meaning input on how I should handle issues that confronted me on the council. I had my own style, a style that better suited me in my public-service work. As I entered my late thirties, I could feel our roles shifting and I found myself trying to find my own footing outside his protective umbrella. I had begun to break from our long-shared pattern of mentor and mentee. I returned to the love of working out that I had discovered during law school, and through that, gained a new love of running and road-biking. These were hobbies that became more and more important to me, while Jeff's love and passion for collecting wine was becoming more and more important to him. We developed new, more separate circles of friends. We weren't communicating as we once had been.

And then I turned forty. As I faced the fact that I was likely at the midpoint of my life, what started as a quiet little voice in my subconscious became louder. I found myself longing to discover more about who I was capable of becoming. I had been with Jeff since I was twenty-one. I had, quite literally, grown up under his care and guidance. I was struggling with a need to forge my own way for a while, to get to know who I could be separate and apart from him. At some point during that year, we took a trip to Napa Valley, just the two of us. It was becoming painfully clear that, other than talking about our children, we had little to say to each other. I recall a particular evening at dinner at a very posh restaurant while on that trip where we barely spoke. Not because we were mad, but because we had become so disconnected.

Through months of counseling on my own, in hopes of quieting that inner voice that was speaking to me, it instead became louder, clearer. And, ultimately, I asked Jeff to join me in my counselor's office on the eve of Thanksgiving to talk constructively about how we might approach a separation. I had hoped we would jointly devise a plan about how to talk to the girls about it and that we would wait until their Christmas break to do so in order to give them time to process and to express their sadness outside the demands of being in school. Understandably upset, Jeff left the counseling session abruptly. And when I came home that evening, my hands full of bags of groceries for our Thanksgiving meal, he met me at the door with a document already in his hand. He had filed for divorce. Thus began a very painful chapter in our long shared history.

In the dark quiet of many nights, I have since visited and revisited my memories of that time. Both Jeff and I could likely tell stories about things we did during that journey that we look back on with remorse. For my part, I cannot escape the regrettable responsibility of having caused hurt to the people that I loved most in the world. But nor can I escape the understanding of a responsibility that I owed to be true to myself. As I came to adapt to the person I would become during the time and distance of my separation from Jeff, my life journey took an entirely different turn than it otherwise would have taken had we remained married. I feel sure that, had Jeff and I stayed together, I would have settled into the comfort of a life that was on its way to becoming easy. I would not have pushed myself into continuing on the path that became such an important part of defining who I have since become. As theater was to my father, public service has become my life's calling—a calling that, while arduous in contrast to the comfortable life I could have owned, has brought a personal fulfillment that has been worth the costs I've paid. And, like the traveler in my dad's riddle, I believe that my inner voice ultimately demanded of me that it be heard when the question was presented about which path was the right one for me to take, leading to the path I was meant to travel.

Ultimately, Jeff and the girls and I came through that very tough time relatively healthy and whole, though Jeff and I were not able to put the pieces of our relationship back together sufficiently to find a renewed bond. I still hold out hope that we will find our way to a true friendship again. But regardless of whether that happens, I am grateful to look back on the years that Jeff and I spent together as some of the happiest, most formative, and most fulfilling times of my life. I am grateful to have had Jeff as my partner, my invaluable friend, on my journey. Both of us grew, were shaped as people, as a result of the almost seventeen years that we lived together during our marriage. I know without question that I wouldn't be the person I am today without his influence, his help, and his love. And for that, I will always be indebted to him.

SEVENTEEN

Do right, and risk the consequences.

—SAM HOUSTON,
seventh governor of Texas

IN THE SUMMER OF 2007, the idea of running for a seat in the Texas state senate in the November 2008 election was first presented to me. Several minority community leaders approached me, and then political strategists Matt Angle and Lisa Turner, with the Lone Star Project, a Democratic political research and strategic communications organization, and J. D. Angle, Matt's brother, my longtime political strategist and friend, came to me with a road map for how we could win the race. They'd done a poll and felt that even though the district had just been redrawn a few years before to the advantage of Republicans and was represented by an entrenched Republican incumbent, minority growth in the district was robust enough that if we could capture that vote, we could win. They also believed, and presented me with information to back it up, that my would-be opponent was neither well known nor well liked in the district. And, they told me, he was ethically flawed—he'd used campaign money to buy a condominium in Austin and he'd done it by using a loophole in the law that he himself had created, by putting the property in his wife's name rather than his own.

My hackles were raised. I kept listening.

Next, a Texas organization committed to the elections of pro-choice, progressive female candidates came to call on me. Annie's List, founded in 2003 and named for Dr. Annie Webb Blanton, the first woman elected to statewide office in Texas, had been in existence for only four years, but had already successfully worked to elect twenty-two women to the Texas legislature by creating an infrastructure of donors whose resources they would draw upon to help fund competitive races and by inserting trained campaign staff into these campaigns to make them successful ones.

Even with all the encouragement, and my interest piqued, I was resistant. Besides, I'd already decided to serve my final term on the Fort Worth City Council. It was time for fresh representation, and I needed to find my next growth opportunity. I had not considered that running for a higher political office would be my next step. But taking on an entrenched Republican in a Republican district? I knew it would be a battle—and a bloody one. Was I up for that kind of fight? Would I be able to raise the $2–$2.5 million that J.D. and Matt were telling me I would need?

After a couple of months of thinking it over, I decided I would do it. My girls were supportive of the idea, though neither they nor I fully understood the battle that lay ahead. *What the hell?* I thought. *I'll give this my all.* The worst thing that could happen was that I would lose. But I'd already learned that I could survive losing a tough race. And I believed, deep in my heart, that this senate district needed representation that reflected the entirety of the district, not just the powers-that-be, which had been the case under the incumbent's tenure. He had settled into that comfortable place that a lot of longtime legislators do, where they believe the seat belongs to them and they forget it actually belongs to the people.

Big, cigar-smoking, with a full shock of white hair and an intimidating LBJ-like presence, Kenneth "Kim" Brimer had a reputation for being quite a bully in the legislature. I knew that the path to winning would involve getting people to understand that he wasn't doing a good job for them, which meant that we'd have to adopt an almost entirely negative strategy—I didn't have enough funding to paint a positive picture of myself *and* a negative picture of him. Given my unpleasant experience going negative in my first city council race, and the fact that I knew it would be a very tough battle to take on someone as established and feared as Brimer was, it took my team a lot of work to get me to come around and agree to enter the fray. They'd convinced me that Brimer was unacceptable and that the necessary task of educating voters about why he was unacceptable could be done in a way that hit above, not below, the belt. The negatives would deal directly with his actions as a state senator and his capacity to serve.

So, I took a deep breath. And dove in.

In August of 2007, as soon as I decided to run, I resigned my city council seat. I filed for the senate seat on the deadline day, and immediately there was talk that the county Democratic chair was going to find fault with—and possibly reject—my application to be on the ballot because he wasn't happy about my candidacy. Though he has long since become one of my biggest supporters, at the time he knew me only through my voting history and he wasn't exactly enamored of it. Because I'd voted in Republican primaries (as many Democratic lawyers do in Fort Worth because our judicial candidates are almost always all Republicans) and contributed to a Republican congressional candidate, he clearly felt I hadn't earned my stripes to become the

Democratic nominee. I remember making very sure that we dotted the i's and crossed the t's and submitted a perfect application to be on the ballot right before the deadline in order to prevent its rejection.

The application was accepted, but immediately afterward, I was sued by a group of firefighters for whom Brimer had helped pass a piece of legislation and who, as a result, were very loyal to him. They were trying to remove me from the ballot by claiming that when I'd filed my application, I wasn't qualified because I was technically still a city councilperson—that is, even though I had resigned, I had not yet been replaced. Therefore, they argued, I was in violation of a holdover provision in state law that required me to maintain the seat until I was replaced.

We won in district court, and then we won again in the appellate court, which ruled that the firefighters didn't have standing to bring their claim and that the only person who did have standing was Brimer himself. We all assumed that he wouldn't refile the suit, since trying to knock your opponent off the ballot on technicalities makes you look afraid and as if you're not playing fair—which voters never like—but sure enough he filed it, this time in his own name, involving us in more expensive and lengthy litigation. We won again in the district court—even though the front row of the courtroom was full of some of the leading Republican Party officials who were there to make sure that the Republican-elected judge knew they were watching what he was doing. That judge was strong enough to do the right thing and rule in my favor, but it took a lot of courage on his part.

Brimer appealed the decision to the circuit court of appeals in Tarrant County, and literally the day before we were supposed to have our hearing, the chief judge filed an application with the state supreme court, asking to have the case sent to another appeals court, in Dallas, because he felt that their judicial objectivity had been compromised. He wouldn't say why, but we could certainly imagine the reason. We believed that someone had tried to exert influence directly on at least one of those judges who were to be on our panel. Because of that, the supreme court granted them the right to transfer it to the Dallas court of appeals.

With all the delays, it wasn't until the spring of 2008 that I even knew for sure that I was on the ballot, but that purgatory hadn't stopped us. We'd ramped up our campaign in the meantime, put our heads down, and plotted our strategy. Again, because of our financial limitations, we would need to focus on our opponent's negative job performance, a plan I'd finally and reluctantly agreed to after hearing my team's convincing argument:

You're asking the voters to fire someone from his job, and they're not going to fire someone, no matter how great you are, unless they have a reason to do that. And you have to tell them what those reasons are.

I am not embarrassed to admit that I actually cried over that decision. It took my team a great deal of strong-arming to get me there. In the end, though, I trusted them. And my gut told me it was the right thing to do. The voters deserved to know, and this time, unlike in my first city council race, I knew that our negative attacks were justified. But not everyone agreed. My close friends were absolutely certain this was the wrong approach:

Why aren't you telling people about you?

Why aren't you telling people about all the things you've done and that you can do?

Their agony over our strategy made my own agony about it even worse, but I remain convinced that if we hadn't made voters understand why Brimer needed to go, he'd still be there and the district would continue to be woefully underserved because of it.

The other compelling reason for the strategy was money. We were in one of the most expensive media markets in the country. Senate districts are incredibly large in Texas, bigger even than our congressional districts: in a state of almost 270,000 square miles, there are only thirty-one of them. As our population has increased, they've gotten bigger and bigger—the number of people that candidates need to reach is huge. The Dallas–Fort Worth media market is also one of the most expensive ones in the country, in part because it requires advertisers to buy the whole market, not just segments of it.

Once again, as I'd seen happen before, my opponent didn't take us seriously until late into the campaign—too late for him to catch up. Like Jeff Davis did to his opponent in his first campaign, I snuck up on Brimer. I had spent hour upon hour knocking on doors in targeted swing neighborhoods in the district. And, like Jeff's opponent in that first campaign of his, by the time Brimer realized how much ground I was covering and decided he would really try to engage, our momentum had already gained too much steam. We built a strong ground game of getting base voters to turn out, and because of our financial limitations, we targeted only a small group of potential swing voters— about 40,000 people out of a district of about 750,000—with mail, and phone calling, and door-to-door knocking efforts. With the help of third parties and house races going on within the district, we were able to communicate with and turn out our base vote.

Throughout the race there was a consistent drumbeat of doubt from Austin insiders:

There's no way she can do this! This is ridiculous! She'll never raise the money!

The pundits, however, weren't taking me seriously enough to say much of anything.

Brimer had been endorsed by every mayor in the district. He'd been endorsed by the police and firefighter associations. He'd been endorsed by the *Fort Worth Star-Telegram*. He had the ability to raise money easily through political insiders, the lobby group, in Austin. Raising the amount I needed was much, much harder. I started out with less than a hundred thousand dollars in my campaign account. For more than a year, I traveled the state, introducing myself to would-be donors, trying to convince them that I was a wise investment—that I could win. It was tough going, with every insider in the state predicting that I'd lose. I worked fourteen-hour days from the moment I announced in August 2007 until the election in November 2008. I never stopped. I was either on the phone asking for donations, or meeting with people to do the same, or hosting fundraisers and giving speeches and knocking on doors in the district. My team was lean and mean. And they were smart as hell. By election day I'd raised around $1.8 million—only half of what Brimer had raised, but it was enough to enable me to do what I needed to do.

For my election night watch party, I had reserved the JFK suite at the Hilton Hotel in downtown Fort Worth, formerly the Hotel Texas, where President John F. Kennedy spent his very last night before being assassinated. My team and I, along with only very close friends and family, gathered there to watch the returns come in. In early voting, I had come in five points ahead, but as the election day boxes were reporting, we watched nervously as my lead began to slip. When all the boxes were in, I had won with 49.9 percent of the vote. A Libertarian candidate had claimed two points. It was quite late, close to 11:00 p.m., before we felt comfortable declaring victory and joining the Tarrant County Democratic watch party that was taking place in the ballroom of the hotel downstairs.

It was an amazing moment in the lives of my family and of my team who, through determination and a well-executed strategy, had pulled it off. Though most folks had written me off in that race, my team and I proved them wrong. Against all of their predictions, we had managed a win that some political commentators referred to as one of the biggest upsets in Texas political history. I had beaten an entrenched incumbent whom many thought was invincible. And I had done it in a district drawn to favor a Republican. After delivering celebratory remarks to a packed room of incredibly excited supporters and then doing a few press interviews, we returned to the JFK suite, where we celebrated our victory until the wee hours of the morning.

Giving meaning to the phrase "no rest for the weary," J.D. called me the next morning at around 7:30. I'd only been asleep a couple of hours. "Put your suit back on," he said. "We're heading to Austin to be a part of a press conference being held at the party headquarters." Still on an adrenaline high, I was up for it. And off we went. Within a few hours, I was in a press conference celebrating a number of successes that the Dems had had the prior evening. Things were looking up for us. We had gained enough seats in the state house to put us at an almost even split with the Republican majority—76 Republicans, 74 Democrats. And in the senate, gaining my seat meant a new momentum for our minority block and our ability to exercise a more balanced influence.

After leaving the press conference, J.D. and I drove over to the capitol, where, after conferring with a Department of Public Safety officer, we were granted access to park on the capitol drive (reserved for members and their staff only). Walking into the eastern door, the wing that contains the senate chamber, was such a magical moment. The Texas capitol is, I believe, the most beautiful capitol building in the country, built with Sunset Red granite donated to the state by the owners of Granite Mountain near Marble Falls, Texas, which gives it its distinctive pink hue. The dome is painted to match. Its terrazzo tile floors are intricately laid works of art, depicting a number of Texas symbols and traditions, and the huge wooden doors on the east, west, south, and north sides of the building are held in place by intricate metal hinges, each weighing seven pounds and inscribed with the words TEXAS CAPITOL. My first stop, of course, was a visit to the senate chambers. While I had been to the capitol on numerous occasions to lobby for our city's interests as a council member, I had never been in either of the two chambers where the legislators do their work.

The senate chamber is magnificent, with its soaring ceiling from which hung magnificent lanterns, each bearing on the points of our state star the letters "T-E-X-A-S." When the legislature is not in session, the public is allowed in and can wander the outer area of the senate floor, looking at paintings of historical figures, including that of the great Barbara Jordan, as well as two large paintings—*Dawn at the Alamo* and *Battle of San Jacinto*—depicting epic Texas battles. At the time, their foreboding symbolism about battles I would fight on the senate floor was lost on me.

A tour guide is typically seated there to answer questions that visitors might have. When I told him who I was, he greeted me enthusiastically, unlatched the green velvet rope that cordons off the area reserved for members of the senate, and waved me on through with the words "Welcome to the Texas senate." Welcome, indeed. I was awestruck. This would be my new home. I placed my hand on one of the thirty-one wooden desks there on the floor, wondering which would be mine. J.D. and I were in heaven. For him, it was a homecoming of sorts, having worked for a former Democratic senator from Fort Worth, Hugh Parmer. And it was his idea that we should go introduce ourselves to the secretary of the senate, Patsy Spaw, whose office is located off the back hall behind the chambers.

When I went in and put my hand out to shake Patsy's, her face lit up. Little did I realize at that moment how much I would come to respect and admire her. A lawyer herself, Patsy is the senate's rudder, steering us gently but with an assured calm. She knows the senate rules like the back of her hand, and when the senate is in session, she has a command of the room that is hard to describe. To the members, she shows the utmost respect and is very protective of each of us, rising above the partisan rancor that sometimes exists and holding us each in a place of esteem. As we do her.

On this day meeting her, though, I knew none of that yet. For that matter, I wasn't even sure what the secretary of the senate actually did! But as we said our polite hellos, I knew I liked her right away. She offered to show me the senate lounge, and then her eyes brightened as a realization came over her: the ladies' room in the senate lounge held only four lockers. There had never been the need for more! Because of my election and that of a newly elected Republican member, Joan Huffman, from Houston, new lockers would have to be built. We were making history—numbers five and six for the first time ever! *I'm a part of Texas history*, I thought with incredible pride.

In the following weeks, I began assembling my senate team. Going from a city council office with only one council aide to the state senate with a budget to build out a capitol and district staff was a big leap. I would need a chief of staff, a district director, at least one constituent services manager, several policy analysts, a legislative director, a communications person, and perhaps most important of all, a gatekeeper. The gatekeeper came to me via a senator who has become one of my closest friends, Senator Rodney Ellis from Houston. Unbelievably smart, filled with frenetic energy, and a true champion for people, he called me after my election and, before I had even met him, offered to send one of his staffers over to help me. I was still nervous when talking to fellow senators, not quite feeling like one of them yet. And I was a little taken aback by his offer. *Was he trying to unload a less than stellar staffer on me?* I wondered. But I took him up on his offer and hired Jean Dendy as our office manager and gatekeeper. A seasoned veteran in the Texas senate, Jean was a heavyset African-American woman who could strike fear where and when it was needed and could offer joy and love in equal measure. She turned out to be a godsend, literally showing me and the rest of my freshman staff how things were done. I honestly don't know what I would have done without her that first session.

When I told her on our first day working together that I wanted to meet with anyone and everyone who requested a meeting with me, she just looked at me, amused. "My door," I declared to her, "is an open one. I'll meet with anyone who requests that I do so." She just chuckled at me and shook her head. "Okay," she said, "if that's what you want." Of course, it didn't take me long to understand why she had laughed at that idea. It's an impossible task, I would soon learn, to do that and still get all your work done. So I relied instead on her gentle guidance about when and with whom I should meet. She knew how to sort the chaff from the wheat, as the saying goes, when it comes to the lobby. And she knew to show her greatest respect to people from my own district back home; they were our priority. We adored Jean, but sadly had the benefit of her magnificent light through only one session, losing her to a heart attack during the interim between the eighty-first and eighty-second sessions. At her funeral service, she was eulogized by the three senators for whom she had worked, each of us proud to share our stories of the extraordinary woman she was.

Assembling the rest of my team had to happen quickly. I brought over a trusted friend, Hector Nieto, who had been doing communications work for the state party, to manage things for the first session until I could get my sea legs. And I brought along some of my most loyal, hardworking young staffers from the campaign to help in the policy and administrative arenas as well: Sonya Grogg, Graham Stadler, and Bernie Scheffler. The rest I built by going through résumés. Other than Jean, we were all new to the senate, so we knew we had our work cut out for us. I have to say, looking back, that we managed really well for a freshman team and I am proud of the things we were able to accomplish.

I was sworn in to the Texas senate on January 13, 2009. It was a joyful day. One of my dear friends, Chris Turner (who would ultimately become the manager of my gubernatorial race), had been newly elected to the state house (also unseating a Republican incumbent) in a seat that was contained almost entirely in my senate district, and we, along with our house colleague from Fort Worth, State Representative Marc Veasey (now a congressman), brought in busloads of folks from back home who had manned the phones, knocked on doors, and made our victories possible. All day, as I sat in my new senate office in the below-ground extension of the capitol, I was greeted and congratulated by a steady stream of people who were sharing in the heady exuberance of all that we had accomplished together. But before all the meeting and greeting was to take place, I took my oath.

How to describe that moment? I felt like I was living in a dream. There I was, about to be ensconced in one of the most powerful legislative bodies in the country. I would be one of only thirty-one, each of whom represents districts larger than congressional ones, and in a state legislative body where the legislature, rather than the governor, holds the real seat of power. I was joined on the floor that day by my girls and by my mom, dad, stepmom, and my then boyfriend, Hugh, and his precious daughter, Brailey. On swearing-in day, the normal rule that only members are allowed "inside the rail" where our desks are placed is lifted and our families are seated right beside us on folding chairs. So there I was, surrounded by the people I loved most in the world, celebrating an incredibly important moment in our family's history. My dad was literally about to bust, he was so proud. And, perhaps more than any of us that day, he was relishing in the pomp and ceremony of it all. You could not have wiped the smile off his face if you tried. When I rose from my desk to join the other senators in raising our hand to swear our oath of office, I looked back at all of them there. Only my dad and mom could appreciate with full measure the journey our family had been on to see this day. How fortunate I was to have them both there with me to share that moment.

I joined fifteen other senators to be sworn in that day. (Texas senators run on staggered terms.) Only Joan Huffman and I were new. I wore a yellow rose on my lapel that someone had given me when I arrived on the floor. And I raised my hand and promised out loud to my state that I would be loyal to it, that I would vow to uphold our constitution. And, to myself, I repeated the silent promise I had made on that day that I was sworn in to the Fort Worth City Council—that I would never hesitate to take a hard vote if I knew it was the right vote for the people who had entrusted me with the privilege of serving them.

I was struck by the deference I was shown as I would walk the halls of the capitol. Literally every person there would greet me as "Senator." I considered myself Wendy, not "Senator." And I pushed back on it for a while, insisting that people call me by name. But I soon gave up on that, because no one would. Over the years, though I love for people to call me Wendy, and in fact still prefer it, I have come to own the honor of what it means to hold the title of senator and what a privilege it is to have earned the vote of the folks I represent back home.

In the weeks that followed, I worked with legislative council and my policy staff to author or sponsor eighty-two bills, twenty-five of which were passed into law—an ambitious number for a freshman senator, especially a Democrat facing a Republican majority. The bills I filed centered primarily on consumer issues. I had come with an agenda on behalf of the people I represented and I was determined to bring fairness and opportunity back to those from whom I felt it had been taken. As I worked to learn and understand the rules by which law was made, I began to perceive which senators I could trust and which I couldn't. I observed members from both sides of the aisle whom I came to admire tremendously and who became the people I would go to in order to get things done.

Like all freshman senators, I was hazed (gently, thank goodness) when laying out my first bill on the senate floor. Knowing it was coming, I brought a deep purple TCU football helmet with me and playfully donned it as soon as my colleagues started in on me. Thereafter, I kept it handy in my office as a reminder to stay tough when things got truly rough.

And so it began.

As I said earlier, the senate district that I came to represent was drawn to favor a Republican candidate. In every other race, with the exception of both of my elections, the precincts within it had collectively voted Republican—even President Barack Obama lost the precincts that make up my district in 2008 and again in 2012—so winning that district was an extraordinary victory for all of us. But from the moment I came into the Texas senate, there were some Republican members who weren't happy with me. I'd just knocked off their buddy in a race that no one believed I could possibly win. Being a Democrat in the Texas senate meant that I was definitely in the minority, a fact that would soon become deeply frustrating to me. It was my first experience of functioning in a partisan environment, and I was learning a disappointing reality: instead of voting on what they believed to be right, I observed the sometimes members were setting personal beliefs aside to vote instead on party lines.

I came into the senate as the twelfth Democratic vote, which was very important, because our senate functions under a two-thirds-majority rule. Until I was elected, of those thirty-one senators, twenty were Republicans and eleven were Democrats. The eleven Democrats had constituted just enough in number to create a minority block, enough to stop a bill from coming to the floor if they all banded together. In order to bring a bill to the floor for debate, twenty-one votes are needed. With only eleven Democrats, all of them had to hold together in order to keep legislation that they were opposed to from coming to the senate floor, and that hadn't always been happening. Sometimes, the Republicans would succeed in picking a Democrat off.

With my election, Republicans were now going to have to pick off *two* Democrats in order to get a bill to the floor—meaning it would be much harder for them to move controversial items forward. That's why I was instantly viewed as a problem by some of the Republicans. We Democrats viewed their controversial issues—among them, redistricting efforts that would further disenfranchise minority voters and a sonogram bill that would require women seeking an abortion to undergo an invasive transvaginal sonogram twenty-four hours prior to their procedure—as unfair and discriminatory. And we were prepared to fight them with everything we had.

Each state senator is put on four committees, and I immediately asked to be put on committees dealing with issues I was most passionate about—Public Education and Transportation—both of which I was given. I was also put on the International Relations and Trade Committee, which dealt with community relations along the Mexican border, and on the Veteran Affairs and Military Installations Committee (VAMI). With Public Education, I had numerous meetings with education experts to learn how school finance works in Texas, which is extremely complex, and to figure out where we'd been, policy-wise, and where we were headed. I worked hard to push my ideas and perspectives in that committee, despite having a chair who was fairly restrictive of what she would let pass through her committee. She was strongly in favor of increasing accountability measures, while I was coming to learn that we actually needed to ease back on that gas pedal because high-stakes testing in Texas had become so stressful and counterproductive that administrators, teachers, and parents were crying out for relief. The chair did allow some of my bills to be heard and voted out, but nothing of significance was accomplished through them that session. Instead, I learned I would need to become a voice in shaping others.

I got thrown into things much more quickly than I'd expected to in that first session. The Republicans were attempting to pass a voter-ID bill, and while none of us took issue with people proving that they are who they say they are when they vote, the bill was designed in such a restrictive way that we truly felt it was discriminatory. And we knew it would have a discriminatory impact. Many voters, particularly low-income voters, who were predominantly minority, wouldn't be able to satisfy the photo requirements, because of the need for underlying documents—birth certificates and such. And they'd have to spend money to obtain them, making the voter IDs feel very much like the modern-day version of a poll tax. The Republicans knew this, which is why they were trying to pass it—it was another egregious attempt to suppress the minority vote.

I was just getting my sea legs, but because the voter-ID bill got fast-tracked through, we knew we'd have to have a big debate on it early in the session. I was one of the lawyers in the senate (the lawyers are usually relied upon to attack a bill that we are sure will pass in order to lay the appropriate predicate in court, where the law may ultimately be challenged), and because this bill was so important, the entire senate caucus agreed that we would hear it as a committee of the whole—meaning the full senate. This meant that every senator would hear witnesses testify in favor of and against the bill and would be able to ask questions as though each of us were a member of the committee the bill had been referred to. It was a long, laborious process that went on through the night—all of us dividing our roles and taking turns questioning the witnesses in an effort to get certain points into the record. We Democrats knew we were going to lose, but we needed to build a legal record of our case.

I'd had to really muster my courage during the debate that night, since it was just weeks into my first session and I had not yet spoken a word through the microphone from my desk on the floor, but ultimately I pushed through my nerves and did my best. I was new, but my constituents back home were depending on me. I didn't have the luxury of being quiet. They'd elected a senator to speak for them. And speak for them I did.

As part of the proceedings that night, I asked the bill's GOP author question after question about the bill as I tried to make points that I felt would help us build for the inevitable legal case. Every time I would ask him something really difficult, he would say, "I'm sorry. Could you repeat your question?"

So I would repeat it.

Sometimes he would ask me a third time: "Would you repeat your question?" And then, finally, at one point, he said, "I'm sorry, but I have trouble hearing women's voices."

Because the bill was of great importance—a constitutional issue—people were gathered in the gallery above the senate floor to hear it, many staying until the wee hours of the morning. They hissed at him. Ironically, he was actually being sincere—he really *did* have hearing issues, and whatever the pitch of my voice was, he truly was having a hard time hearing me. Later it would become a big joke among all the senators, and even to this day, if I'm making a good point and someone wants to tease me, they'll say, "I'm sorry, I have trouble hearing women's voices." The author of the bill caught all kinds of grief through social media and blogs, because people felt he was being sexist in his remarks. Though he and I would rarely see eye to eye on controversial bills, I knew he was not trying to show me disrespect. And to his credit, he takes my and other members' teasing him about it in stride.

The voter-ID bill ultimately passed the senate and was sent to the Texas house, where the Democrats managed to "chub" it—killing the bill by a procedural maneuver where each member basically talks a bill to death using the maximum time allowed each of them. This was successful because it was the deadline day for senate bills to be heard and passed on the house floor. But it also meant that many good pieces of legislation we'd sent over from the senate for passage in the house that were still awaiting consideration and were behind the voter-ID bill on their calendar were killed, too.

Struggling to bring our bills back to life on the last day of the eighty-first legislative session, after we agreed to employ a parliamentary workaround, by attaching our senate bills to house bills as amendments, we stopped the hands of the clock on the senate floor at 11:59 p.m. to allow us more time. In the interest of getting things done, we worked feverishly—and civilly—until the early hours of the next morning to get them passed as amendments on house bills. Ending my first session on this note struck a deep chord in me. I was proud to be part of a group that could work together like this, both Republicans and Democrats. It was in that moment that I came to truly appreciate and respect the body that is the Texas senate.

Every legislative session year, one of our statewide magazines, the *Texas Monthly*, writes a piece naming the ten best state legislators. Often, they also name a Rookie of the Year, choosing among the new house and senate members. I was thrilled to be awarded that honor in 2009. In awarding me the title, they said, "That old rule that fresh-men are supposed to stay quiet? She proved it can be ignored if you're smart, tough, and well prepared."

I was pleased, of course. But the best part was the fact that as a freshman senator I had managed to pass some significant bills: one to help our oil and gas industry transport natural gas more easily; one that helped electricity consumers have low-cost options by requiring providers to give thirty days' notice before their contracts expire; one to help children who were aging out of foster care to more easily ob-tain their personal records so they could apply for college entrance and jobs; and one, the Jamie Schanbaum Act, named for a young woman who had contracted bacterial meningitis while at college and who barely survived and had been left with amputations of parts of her legs and hands, which would require every Texas college student to be vaccinated against bacterial meningitis. Among other bills that I also passed, these were the ones I was proudest to have worked with my constituents to achieve. I was a Texas senator now. I had my foot-ing, and I anxiously looked forward to the next session, which would come a year and a half later, since our sessions occur only every two years and last only 140 days.

My second legislative session in 2011 was much more controver-sial: we had the voter-ID bill back, and this time it did pass because Governor Rick Perry placed it before us as an "emergency item," meaning that it would be considered within the first sixty days of a session and that it couldn't be chubbed in the house. Though it was signed into law, it's been wrapped up in litigation ever since under the available protections of the federal Voting Rights Act. There was also an attempt to pass an anti-immigration bill similar to one that had passed in Arizona. Our Republican members tried to make it sound like a kinder, gentler version of the Arizona bill, but despite its euphemistic name—the Anti–Sanctuary Cities Bill—it was essentially the same bill as the Arizona law allowing law-enforcement officers to ask anyone, anytime, for his or her citizenship status, based solely on a suspicion that someone had violated or been witness to a violation of the law. This thinly veiled attempt to legalize racial profiling was fought not only by members of the minority community who feared they would fall victim to it but also by law enforcement and members of the clergy from all over the state, including every Catholic bishop in Texas. Law enforcement was already concerned about the people in our undocumented community who were afraid to report a crime because they feared that their immigration status would be called into question—now the concern was that this bill would force people even further into the shadows. Fear of reporting crimes means that assailants and other criminals go free. In committee hearings, several undocumented members of the Texas community shared such stories with us, including one involving a woman who was being badly battered by her husband but was afraid to come forward because she was undocumented. In time the local police had built a strong relationship with her community, giving her the comfort level to report her husband and help put him away for attempting to kill her. But under this new law, she told us, she wouldn't have reported him, and she believed she would have eventually died by his hand.

The sentiment behind the law was very much an anti-immigrant one. It's the antithesis of where I hope the conversation will go at the federal level. We should be aspiring to create a path to citizenship, with appropriate conditions attached, for people who are law-abiding, hardworking, and an important part of the economy of our country already, and who desire to seek legal status. But the conservative side of the Republican party in Texas has displayed a harsh perspective about our immigrants, and they capitalize on the emotions of voters who have strong negative feelings about immigration. (The 2014 Republican primary in Texas drove that point home shamelessly.)

I and others in my delegation fought that piece of legislation very hard. But, in the end, it was not the Democrats who succeeded in killing it. Instead, it was Republican donors who stopped it by putting pressure on their own party members to kill the bill: they were afraid that the law would be used to round up and deport undocumented workers in Texas that form an important part of their economic bottom line, particularly in the home-building and agricultural arenas.

From the moment I decided to run for the senate, I fought many battles to get there and stay there. Some would say—and this is certainly *my* perspective—that the story behind those battles is that I have fought attempts by the Republican majority to pass laws that I felt would harm my constituents. And I've not been shy about that. Alongside my caucus, I was pushing against the tide and fighting against what had once been easier for them to accomplish.

For obvious reasons, education is one of the two arenas in which I've been most active. Education played such an important role in shaping the opportunities made available to me and in shaping who I am that paying it forward has become my passion. I feel it is my duty to make sure other children in Texas have the same opportunities I had. That's why I filibustered the $5.4 billion in proposed cuts to public-school funding in 2011, a decision that was very unpopular— even among a few of my own Democratic colleagues, not because they supported the cuts but because they believed the filibuster was futile and they feared what a special session might bring.

So there weren't too many of my colleagues who were happy with me on that late spring day in 2011. It had been a brutal session, and we were exhausted on that very last day, May 29, bringing bills up and voting on them at a fairly rapid-fire pace because we still had a huge docket of bills that needed to be passed. Whenever we would get a break on the floor, my Democratic Caucus and I would gather and debate whether we should filibuster the education-funding bill. Some of them did not want to do it because they felt it was futile. But I kept saying, "You know, even if it ultimately passes, I think it's important that we stand against this. And through a filibuster we can bring much greater attention to it, so people around the state will know what's happening in this capitol."

Most people, living their busy lives, don't have the time or luxury to notice what's going on in a legislative session in Austin, which meant that most people at the time probably had no idea that huge cuts in education funding were looming. Filibustering would help bring the issue to light for the public, and if we went into a special session during the summer, we'd have an opportunity for teachers and parents to come to the capitol and actually weigh in on the issue and participate in trying to save our schools from this massive blow. I felt that from a principled position we had to try. Our house members were telling us they felt they could get some funding added back, but they couldn't do it unless we could get them to a special session. I'd awakened that morning not having any clue I was going to filibuster a bill—I went to the capitol happy that the session was at an end and looking forward to the traditional adjournment *sine die* ("without day") party. But by midmorning a few of us from the Democratic Caucus were called over to a meeting with our house Democratic colleagues. They begged us to filibuster the bill, a power that their legislative body does not possess.

"We really think we can get some money added back," they'd said. "We have a plan, but we can't do it if you guys can't get the bill killed and get us into a special session."

When we went back to our side of the capitol, we were divided. I argued passionately in favor of the filibuster, understanding that if it were to happen, I would likely be the one to do it, because I was leading the argument in favor, though several others in our caucus were strongly in support of the idea. When we took a private vote among us, it was decided that we would filibuster the bill and that I would be the one to do it. We left our final caucus debate unified as a result of the vote, even though some among us still felt strongly that it was not a good idea.

We had such a long docket of bills—so many of them really important bills that members were trying to get passed—that as soon as I'd informed the lieutenant governor, as a courtesy, that I was going to filibuster the education-cuts bill, he made the correct decision to hear all the other bills and get them up on the floor first, before we brought up the education-cuts bill. Otherwise, if I'd filibustered the bill first, everything else behind it on the calendar would have died. Because there was such a full docket, the filibuster didn't even start until 10:44 p.m.

Up to the moment when I was about to rise and say, "I intend to speak for an extended period on this bill," which is the polite way of saying, "I'm about to filibuster this bill," I still had some of my Democratic and Republican colleagues coming up to me saying, "Please don't do this." The Democrats were worried about coming back into a special session; they worried that things would be put back on the call that we'd successfully killed in the regular session—which was a fair concern. But the fact of the matter was, we had not yet passed the congressional redistricting bill, which meant that we were going to be called into a special session no matter what. And the likelihood of having other matters added to the special-session call already existed, whether school funding was on the call or not. This was my only way to force the funding bill into the special session.

It certainly wasn't "the filibuster heard around the world"—there was no live streaming back then, and even if there had been, the filibuster lasted just a little over an hour—but it was definitely heard around the state. As punishment, and because he knew it would make me even more unpopular with my colleagues, Governor Perry called us back into special session at eight o'clock the following morning. So much for the late-night customary *sine die* parties that typically go on until the wee hours . . . Needless to say, I was not exactly the most popular person in the senate lounge when we gathered there the next day. Barely anyone there, or on the floor, spoke to me. And I was grateful when my Republican colleague Senator Deuell came up behind me as I sat at my desk, touched my shoulder, and said, "You look like you could use a friend." Tears welled up in my eyes. It meant a great deal to me.

On a more positive note, the filibuster did create a surge of people coming to Austin who rallied and spoke against the bill in the special session. And for a brief moment it looked as though the filibuster was going to pay off. We had ended the 2011 regular session with $5.1 billion in our Rainy Day Fund, and the comptroller's estimate was that the fund would grow to $9.1 billion over the next two years. One of our house members, Representative Donna Howard, had proposed an amendment to capture that growth and put it toward making up the shortfalls in the funding of our schools. Despite bipartisan support of the amendment, within twenty-four hours extreme conservative groups (and one in particular), started hammering at Republican members who were in favor of it and threatened to run candidates against them in their primaries if they voted to keep the amendment on the bill. It's hard to imagine people being hostile to education spending, but their perspective is that any shrinkage of government spending is a good shrinkage, *even* if it means dramatic cutbacks in basic and vital support of our children. And they successfully pressured enough Republican members to change their vote, killing the amendment in conference committee, and, with it, those resources that should have gone to deserving schools and students.

We came so close to actually making an impact by staging that filibuster, but in the end the bill passed—just as it had been intended to pass in the regular session—the $5.4 billion in cuts went through, and twenty-five thousand educators in Texas lost their jobs, eleven thousand of them teachers who were handed pink slips and the remainder through open teaching positions that went unfilled.

As a consequence the state received and granted an unprecedented number of classroom-size waiver requests—thousands and thousands of such requests to increase classroom sizes, because the state-mandated 22:1 student-to-teacher ratios could no longer be accommodated in elementary-school classrooms. Also gone were teacher aides who were helping struggling students to get on track with their reading skills by grade three (studies have proved that children who aren't on reading track by third grade will likely be lost forever in terms of educational success). And programs that were really working got cut:

We'd been moving toward full-day pre-K—which got cut.

We'd been moving toward a program called Student Success Initiative that was helping kids who were falling through the cracks in high school, getting more one-on-one attention to them, to help them get back on track in high school—and that got almost completely gutted.

Money toward science and technology grants was zeroed out. So was money for reading, science, and math course improvements. And seat belts in school buses. Money for advanced-placement courses was cut in half.

And those massive public-education cuts had a huge impact across the state on so many children. Texas was already ranked forty-sixth in per-pupil investment in the United States, and that $5.4 billion cut took us down to forty-ninth out of fifty-one (the District of Columbia is counted in the mix). For a state with one of the strongest economies in the entire country—*Forbes* magazine included Austin, Dallas, and Houston on its list of Best Big Cities for Jobs in 2014 and included four Texas cities (Austin, Dallas, Houston, and San Antonio) in its ranking of America's Twenty Fastest-Growing Cities—this kind of disinvestment in our people and in our future labor force creates a tremendous discrepancy between potential and reality. In fact, Rice University sociology professor and former state demographer of Texas Steve Murdock has cautioned policy makers about the trend line we're on: 18 percent of our adults don't have a high-school diploma or equivalent, and his prediction is that by 2040 that percentage will rise to 30 if we don't reverse course. What that says about the future workforce of Texas alarms me, and I agree with his strong recommendation to invest in full-day pre-kindergarten and other programs that keep students from falling through the cracks. And that advice comes from a former Republican appointee who served as director of the U.S. Census Bureau under President George W. Bush.

Of course, swimming against the tide, fighting against the status quo anywhere—let alone in the Texas senate—doesn't go unpunished. As a consequence of my 2011 filibuster, I was removed from the Senate Committee on Education when committee assignments were handed out by the lieutenant governor in 2013, after having served on it in 2009 and in 2011. Instead, I was put on the Economic Development Committee. After learning of my new assignment, I couldn't help hearing the Br'er Rabbit refrain, "Oh, please don't throw me into the briar patch!" Economic development was a forte and a passion of mine. But it was clear, and everyone understood, that my removal and reassignment was a punishment to me for having filibustered the education cuts.

That didn't stop me from being involved in a facet of our government that I felt was critical to all Texans. I continued to attend the education committee's meetings—in fact, I think I had better attendance than most of the actual committee members. I may have missed one or two. I sat at the dais as if I were a member; made my own nameplate, which I placed in front of me at my seat, asked questions of the witnesses as if I were a member, and weighed in on policy conversation as if I were a member—which the chair was gracious enough to allow. I refused to be forcibly divorced from the conversation. While I no longer had a committee vote, I could continue to be a voice for the people I represented, committee removal be damned.

But before I even had the chance to filibuster that bill, first I had to fight a redistricting bill that would have assured my demise. Like every legislature, we redistrict every ten years, after the results of the United States Census come out. We receive our new population numbers and redraw our lines to rebalance the population so that the districts we represent are similar in size. As is the case in other states, Texas is losing population in its rural areas and dramatically gaining population in its urban ones. Accordingly, district lines have to be redrawn so that each senator represents an approximately equal number of people. Our senate districts now contain an average of 830,000 people, having grown by about 100,000 people per district in the prior ten-year period, which means that a shifting of lines has to occur. There's a process that goes along with that, but in this particular instance it seemed to be quite focused on drawing my district— *only mine*—in such a way as to guarantee that I couldn't be elected again. But much more important, if the redistricting map were to pass as drawn, members of the minority community that I represented, who had coalesced with like-minded Anglo voters in electing me, would forever lose their voice in electing a member of the Texas senate. And that was precisely the point. The reason the Voting Rights Act was passed in 1965 was as a means of protection against pernicious efforts like these to silence minority voters at the ballot box and therefore in elected representative bodies. Despite my protest and after months of wrangling, all the other senators wound up with a district that would protect them, including all of my Democratic colleagues.

All except me. And the people I so proudly represented.

In the minds of many of my Republican colleagues, I had done the unforgivable—won as a Democrat in a district they had drawn during the last redistricting to favor a Republican. Perhaps worse, once elected, it was clear that I was not going to be of the "go along to get along" sort. Unbelievably, I was not shown the new map until about ten o'clock the night before it was going to be voted out of committee, and when I saw it projected onto a screen on the wall, it took me only seconds to understand exactly what they'd done.

"You've torn it apart," I said to the chair and his staff. Then I got up and walked out the door. There was nothing else to say. It was pointless to waste my efforts on trying to convince them.

Indeed, my only avenue, after the successful passage of the bill, was to challenge it in court. In order to make a successful claim, I had to show either that there was intentional discrimination—specifically an intent to discriminate against the minority members of my district or a discriminatory impact as a result of the redrawing. It didn't take a rocket scientist to see from the new map what had happened: they had gerrymandered my district and no one else's.

To my great dismay, and unbelievably, the Justice Department, weighing in as a party of interest in the case, opined against my position because they said we hadn't shown a historical influence of the minority community in the outcome of elections in the district. As noted previously, in all other elections that had taken place at both the state and federal levels, the precincts that made up my district had voted overwhelmingly for Republican candidates. Only in my 2008 state senate race had the minority and like-minded Anglo residents come together and elected a Democrat as their candidate of choice. On the day my attorney called to tell me that the Justice Department had weighed in by arguing that the district was not a district deserving of the protections of Section 5 of the Voting Rights Act, I was preparing to give a speech to a group of constituents. Sitting in my car in the parking lot, I was crushed. *We've lost*, I thought. There's no way we can hold the district now. There's no way we can protect its people.

On the phone, even my lawyer, Gerry Hebert, said, "I have to tell you, the chances are extremely low that we will prevail." But Gerry was a masterful litigator and such a fierce believer in the power of the Voting Rights Act to correct racial injustices that his voice literally cracked with emotion as he pleaded our case during our first hearing. And though our chances of succeeding were, in his words, probably in the 10 percent range, through his dedication and the collective hard work of Matt and J. D. Angle and Lisa Turner, along with the crucial support and assistance of LULAC (League of United Latin American Citizens), we won. Justice was on our side and I had a team of people who believed to their core that people's rights were being violated, and they fought with everything they had for justice to be served.

Our case was tried before a panel of judges in D.C. Two federal district-court judges and one federal appellate-court judge. Two of the judges were Republican appointees, not exactly adding favorably to our slim odds of winning. But in August of 2012, this panel of three judges unanimously reached a decision, finding intentional discrimination in the drawing of my district. It was remarkable. Reminiscing about what I had learned in my Warren Court class at HLS, I couldn't help but wonder about the biographical background of these three judges. Against all odds, they had ruled in our favor. Against all odds . . .

Of course, the case was immediately appealed. And my foe throughout all this? The Texas attorney general—my opponent in the 2014 race for governor. With the finding of "intentional discrimination" in the lower court, the state ultimately agreed to leave the original boundaries of the district intact, knowing it would face an uphill battle on appeal, and in the first called special session of 2013 (the same special session in which the anti-reproductive-rights bill was filed), the legislature adopted a final redistricting plan for the Texas senate reflecting that agreement. The voices of the people I so proudly represented would still be heard.

While the court was still contemplating its decision, but before my map was settled with finality when the legislature reconvened, I still had an important challenge ahead. I had to win reelection to my district in November of 2012. I knew that once again I would be in a battle for survival. The district, even though we'd managed to protect it, was still one that had originally been drawn to favor a Republican candidate. Easy Street was nowhere in sight.

Fighting to be elected to the senate, fighting to protect the seat, and fighting for reelection to the senate, together with the stresses of pushing back against a tide of controversial conservative legislation, has been a constant challenge. Thankfully, I haven't had to face it on my own—I've always had my Democratic Caucus colleagues alongside me—but I think the addition of my twelfth block vote emboldened and empowered the other Democratic members, too, creating a sea change in the way we were able to do business.

There is a part of me that believes that Greg Abbott, my gubernatorial opponent, agreed to the settlement of my redistricting case in the hopes that it would remove any incentive for me to run statewide by keeping me content in the senate. He already had his sights set on running to be the next governor, and it was widely understood that Governor Perry was unlikely to run again. The "heir apparent" wanted the clearest path possible to the governor's office. And he knew, I am sure, that I was one of a handful of people who could legitimately stand in his way.

At the beginning of the eighty-third legislative session, as is the tradition, the attorney general and other statewide elected officials joined the senators on the floor as we were sworn in to our offices again. After a long redistricting fight and a tough reelection battle, I was there among the thirty-one senators who raised our hands and swore an oath to protect the values of the Texas constitution. When I approached Greg Abbott to shake his hand, he looked me in the eye with a smile and said, "I don't think we want another redistricting battle now, do we?" He was calling a truce. *You've gotten what you fought for, now be happy with that.*

But I don't placate easily. Soon he and I would be locked in battle again—this time for the hearts and minds of the people of Texas.

EIGHTEEN

In whatever arena of life one may meet the challenge
of courage, whatever may be the sacrifices he faces if
he follows his conscience—the loss of his friends, his
fortune, his contentment, even the esteem of his
fellow men—each man must decide for himself the
course he will follow.

—JOHN F. KENNEDY,
Profiles in Courage

BOTH TIMES I RAN for my seat in the Texas state senate, there
were the naysayers, but one in particular, Ross Ramsey of the
Texas Tribune, distilled all the naysaying into one piece six months
before my 2012 reelection campaign:

The Fort Worth Democrat tops this year's list of imperiled candidates. She is running on Republican turf . . .

Davis beat Republican incumbent Kim Brimer four years
ago, leaving political observers to wonder how she did it. Did she
win the race, or did Brimer lose it? How important was the turnout in that year's presidential election?

He even created a color-coded reelection "hot list" ranking districts by the threat to each incumbent, and had me in the red zone ("Trouble walking in the door" as opposed to orange's "Trouble on the front porch" and yellow's "Trouble on the sidewalk") right up until the election. Clearly, I was being counted out of the race. Yet again.

There was no question that the 2012 election would be tough. But I'd been fighting long odds for much of my life, and certainly in politics. Each time I've fought and won, I feel a little bit like those bottom-weighted clown punching bags that, no matter how many times you hit them, just keep coming back up for more. I have never been alone in my battles. My team was once again by my side, just as they had been through every political fight before.

My reelection battle in 2012 proved to be a bitterly fought contest and an extremely expensive one—my opponent and I each spent close to $4 million in that race, one of the most, if not the most, expensive state senate races in Texas history. I had a great deal more in the way of resources in my second race. I had found in my first race that asking total strangers to donate to my campaign was difficult, but the stronger my sense of urgency about the causes we were fighting for, the easier it got to ask people to invest in that fight. Having funds meant I was able to talk to more than just forty thousand people this time, and with positive television ads I was able to share my story and my values and beliefs with voters, defining who I was and what I stood for in contrast to what my Republican opponent would say about me. He ran negative against me, raising a phony ethics charge about alleged conflicts between my role as a senator and my role as an attorney. Not only were these claims ruled "false" by a major-market television station in Dallas while the race was ongoing, these allegations were ultimately considered and dismissed by the Travis County DA when my opponent attempted, post-election, to convince them to take his allegations seriously. Even now, in my current race, those same false allegations are being circulated. I think what scares my foes more than anything is actually the opposite of what they claim: they know that the old-insiders network can't sway me. That I'm true, above all else, to the people who elected me to serve them.

The 2012 reelection was a nail-biter, and I won without a lot of room to spare—with about 51 percent of the vote—but I survived despite the strong backlash in Texas against President Obama at the top of the ticket. He lost my district by even more of a percentage in 2012 (10 percentage points) than he did in 2008 (6 percentage points). Anglo male voters particularly had come out in droves and voted against him in my district, which typically means that they check the "R" box all the way down the ballot and vote a straight Republican ticket. Once again I was glad for the intense stress and pressure of the election to be over, and after a short break while I celebrated and rested, I was anxious to get back to work—and have the honor of moving into the former office of the esteemed civil rights leader and first African American elected to the modern Texas senate, Barbara Jordan. There was so much more I wanted to accomplish. The next session was coming soon—only seven weeks away.

When I was first elected to the state senate, I wanted to connect with my constituents as though I were representing them at the local level. I tried to show them that I didn't take that seat for granted: I didn't just go meet with people and come to their meetings and hear what they wanted to talk about during election season. I aggressively represented my communities even after they'd given me the honor of their vote, and made sure that I was really helping and working directly with them, just as I had on the city council. Only, now I had about ten times the number of people that I was working for.

Being a Democrat in the Texas state senate has not been easy in the last couple of decades, and for me, ever since I've been there, I've navigated my way through an ever-present feeling of friction and tension. When I walk into the senate lounge, for example, the chilly manner of some of my Republican colleagues makes me well aware that they wish I were not a member of their elite body. I've learned to let that roll off my back. And I've found my way by forming relationships with people I respect on both sides of the aisle who are more interested in getting things done than they are in partisan politics. I am proud of the friendships I've formed with Republican members who don't come to the table predisposed to ultraconservative ideals. They're there for the same reason I am—to work hard for their constituents and to try to make our beloved state even stronger. We may have different ideas about how we get there, but we're all trying to do good work for the people we represent.

That work has always kept me focused and committed. Helping to pass bills as a Democratic senator is something I'm really proud of, whether I've authored them and gained the consent of my fellow members or whether I've supported the excellent efforts of my colleagues, both Democrats and Republicans.

One of the most important pieces of legislation that I worked on during the last two sessions, and one I was proud to gain bipartisan support for, was Senate Bill 1636, the sexual-assault evidence bill. In 2011, during the eighty-second session, I'd gotten a bill passed requiring law-enforcement agencies all around the state to go through the backlog on their evidence shelves and tell us what needed to be tested, and when we came back in 2013, in the eighty-third session, we got the audit, which showed that there were at least 20,000 untested kits. Working with one of my Republican colleagues, Senator Robert Deuell from Dallas, we secured about $11 million to test that backlog. Sadly, Senator Deuell was defeated in his reelection primary by a Tea

Party challenger. A good and true public servant now gone. But because of his help, the testing is ongoing, and law-enforcement officials say they've already gotten several hits and DNA matches as a result. Helping to bring sexual predators to justice and to bring closure to victims is incredibly gratifying.

O ne of my strongest passions is my hatred of payday loans—short-term, super-high-interest predatory lending that gives borrowers a cash advance on their paychecks. Mostly used by people with no credit or bad credit who find themselves in a sudden financial crunch caused by a health crisis or a car repair emergency, these loans can devastate families who are already struggling. Some states with tighter regulations don't even allow payday lending, but payday lenders are ubiquitous in Texas. Nearly 3,300 lending storefronts and a growing presence of online lenders made about three million payday and auto title loans in 2013 and collected about $4 billion from vulnerable Texas consumers. Regardless of the relative financial privileges I now possess, I will forevermore be that young woman who struggled to pay her bills. I will always fight for "her" because I understand how precious dollars are when you're living paycheck to paycheck. And when I see abuses of consumers because the state has failed to properly police the industry, it sets me on fire.

This is how it works: Someone who's short on cash goes to a payday lender with a pay stub to prove employment and a checkbook to prove solvency. The borrower makes a postdated check out to the lender for the entire amount that he or she (let's make our borrower in this example a man) wants to borrow. A fee—usually $15 to $20 per $100 that he's borrowing—is charged up front. If the loan is $300, there's a $60 fee, and when payday comes, the borrower is expected to pay back the entire $300.

Of course, usually he can't pay back the entire loan, since it's often the entire amount of his paycheck, or most of it, and he needs some money to live on. But when he goes to the lender and offers to make a partial payment on the loan, the lender refuses to accept it:

"Pay me nothing or all of it. And if you pay me nothing, I'll charge you another sixty dollars and roll it over until your next paycheck."

The following payday the borrower has now paid $120 in fees, so he's underwater and way outside his budget, because he never *had* $60 extra in his budget to begin with. This continues, week after week, until the insidious truth of this form of pernicious lending becomes painfully clear: high-interest unregulated loans lock consumers into monthly payments that are usually more than their family's monthly budget.

In Texas, a $400 payday loan with a 14-day term from a major payday lender means $121 in fees and interest.

That means that the total they will have paid by their first payday is $521.

That's the equivalent of an annual interest rate of 792 percent.

There are so many heartbreaking and maddening stories that we heard during committee hearings about this kind of morally reprehensible predatory lending. One involved a woman from Midland who took out a $6,300 auto title loan (a payday loan where a car is used as collateral) for her stepson's funeral and ended up paying more than $12,000 over eleven months. She was forced to declare bankruptcy and eventually called on a former employer for the last $4,000 to pay off the loan. Another involved a Houston woman who took out a payday loan of $1,400 for car repair and medical expenses. After making several monthly payments, she'd already paid more than the original $1,400 loan, but still owed $1,600.

And those are only two of thousands and thousands and thousands of examples that exist throughout the state.

If we instituted a single law requiring lenders to allow partial repayments, then people would have a chance at working their way out of their loans. But because payday lenders aren't required to accept partial payment, they just continually roll the loans over, charging new fees each time.

Some states have limited the number of times a payday lender can roll a loan before having to freeze it and allow the borrower to try to pay it off bit by bit, and some have limited the amount that can be borrowed, making borrowers less likely to get so overwhelmingly upside down so quickly. But when previous efforts attempted to shut down the ability of payday lenders in our state to abuse consumers, they found a new way to do it. Using a third-party model, the lenders started operating in what they argued was a loophole in the law. Instead of operating under the lending statute, they would operate as "consumer-service organizations" (CSOs), sanctioned in our state statute as a means of helping people repair bad credit. But this statute was never intended to cover lending practices. And for that reason there's nothing in it about limiting fees, nor are there requirements that partial repayments be allowed.

The attorney general of Texas, Greg Abbott, my 2014 opponent in the gubernatorial race, gave the green light to payday lenders to operate under that statute when he was asked to weigh in with an official opinion. Because the legislature didn't specifically rule it out, Abbott argued, payday lenders could function under the statute's cloak. And since he opened that door, there are now thousands of people who fall prey to these predatory loans—including many serving in the military.

The practice is so bad in the military that the Department of Defense conducted an in-depth study of its effects, concluding, "Predatory lending undermines military readiness, harms the morale of troops and their families, and adds to the cost of fielding an all-volunteer fighting force," which resulted in Congress capping at 36 percent the rates that can be charged to military members and many elderly folks as well. But the loophole and Texas' lax regulations had assured that this protection for the military had not been implemented. As our economy suffered a blow a few years ago, even many middle-income people, like teachers, have been trapped in one of these pernicious loans—Texans whose lives are being ruined every single month by loans they can't repay. And what they wind up doing is borrowing from another payday lender to get their first loan paid off, compounding their debt in an unimaginably precarious way.

I've been fighting the payday-lending industry ever since I got into the senate, and I can say with pride that they hate me. So much. They gave my opponent in 2012 a great deal of money to try to defeat me, and they've given Greg Abbott a lot of money, too. But I'm bound and determined to reform this industry for the people of my state. The fact that predatory lending is allowed to continue astounds and infuriates me and is in fact the deepest disappointment of my years in the senate. City councils aren't subject to the same lobbying efforts as state legislatures are, and because state legislative bodies are one step removed from their constituents, they're usually not held accountable for their votes on these issues—most of the folks they represent back home aren't even aware of their voting records and the critical ways they're affected by them. In Texas, several large cities have stepped forward and passed ordinances to curtail these abuses to pick up some of the slack. It is my desire to see that *all* the people in my state have these protections. And I won't stop fighting until they do.

In the legislature I thought I knew what it would be like to be in an environment where there's a really strong lobbyist/special-interest influence. I thought I knew what it would be like to be against the backdrop of partisanship. But I had no idea until I got into it the power that those factors can exert. On the partisan side of it, even good, well-meaning Republican members who are there trying to do constructive things for people they represent can successfully be bullied by some of these extreme conservative groups.

I call those groups the "scorecard groups."

They keep scorecards on Republican members and tell them, "If you don't line up with us on this, we will run someone against you." And in the middle of a session, if they do not feel that a member is appropriately toeing the ideological line, they'll send a mail piece out to that member's district and tell voters, "Your member's not conservative enough." Because Texas has now had two decades of Republican redistricting, most districts are drawn so purely Republican and have been gerrymandered so badly that if you're a Republican in one of these districts, the only election contest that really matters is the primary, and the people who most actively vote in the primaries tend to represent the extreme side of the party. And so Republican candidates vying against each other in these districts find themselves moving more and more to the right of each other in order to try to win election or reelection. And if their voters are told that their member isn't being "conservative enough," sadly, members working to do good things can often be beaten.

In my most idealistic moments, I believe that if legislators would all stand together, then these scorecard groups wouldn't have that power. My perspective has always been that these people have power only to the extent that they're given power. And once you demonstrate to them that they can't influence you, that you're not afraid, you take that power away from them. That said, I recently watched two of my Republican senate colleagues—John Carona from Dallas and Robert Deuell from Greenville, real leaders in the senate who were there fighting to do good things for the people they represented—get beaten. I didn't think it was possible that senators so well loved and so respected could be pushed out, but they were run against for not being "conservative enough." And the strategy was successful.

In my six years in the Texas senate, I've had to get stronger all the time. Whenever I've been battle-tested, the strength of my convictions grows. It has not diminished me. And when others try to knock me down or silence me, it just intensifies my resolve to do and say what needs to be done.

But that kind of outspokenness doesn't go unnoticed—or unscolded.

During my very first session, after I'd given a speech about the evils of payday lending during a committee hearing—how wrong and awful it is and how ashamed we ought to be that we hadn't done anything about it—the chair of the committee followed me into the senate lounge afterward and barked at me, "You know, we don't do that in the Texas senate. That's not how we conduct ourselves. We're a genteel body. We don't have debates like that."

I disagree. I think we ought to spend more time showing respect to the people who elect us than we do worrying about how we'll appear as a body. Honest political debates are a good thing; they are a way to find middle ground and to make sure all perspectives are considered. But there is strong peer pressure in the senate to follow those rules of gentility. There have most definitely been moments when I've had to push myself out of my comfort zone and take a stand on something that doesn't reflect the consensus of the body—especially in the 2013 session, when I voted against the senate's first budget draft, because it restored only $1.5 billion of the $5.4 billion that had been cut from public education, in spite of the fact that we had started the session with an $8 billion unexpected surplus because the comptroller had badly underestimated what our revenue growth would be over the prior two-year period. I was one of just two members in our thirty-one-member body who voted against it. And eventually, on May 25, we passed a budget during that session that added back $3.4 billion to our schools. I was proud, after the push and pull and all the negotiations that we went through to get there, to ultimately vote in favor of the bill's final passage.

When things like that happen, it restores my faith in the democratic process. We'd fought some along the way, but we were all proud that we had come together in the spirit of compromise to do better for the people of our state. We kidded one another that it had been the "Kumbaya" session, and we held our *sine die* party happy to be parting, until the next round, as friends.

On May 27, 2013, the same day that the eighty-third regular session ended, Governor Perry called us back to a special session to take up and consider redistricting maps. Fifteen days later, on June 11, he added another item to the special session call, an instruction to take up and consider legislation relating to the regulation of abortion procedures, providers, and facilities.

NINETEEN

It's the price of leadership to do the thing
that you believe has to be done
at the time it must be done.

—LYNDON B. JOHNSON

EARLY ON THE MORNING of Tuesday, June 25, 2013, I awoke to prepare for what I knew would be a difficult day. In a few hours, with the help of my Democratic colleagues, I would attempt to kill SB 5—a bill which, if passed, would impose on Texas women some of the most sweeping abortion restrictions in the country. If things went according to plan, I would have to be out on the senate floor by 11:11 a.m. to filibuster the bill, talking it to death for thirteen hours until midnight, when the clock would run out on the eighty-third session of the Texas senate, in order to prevent a vote. How we got that opportunity to try to stop the bill—and the strategy that went into preparing for a thirteen-hour legislative marathon—is the important beginning to the story of that incredible day.

SB 5 consisted of three provisions, each of which was clearly directed at limiting abortion access for women, creating particular hardships for low-income women. If it passed, Texas women would be forced to drive great distances in order to get their health care, since it was predicted that thirty-seven of the state's forty-two clinics would be forced to close. Texas is 773 miles wide and 790 miles long: only five clinics would be left in more than 268,000 square miles of land. That's a lot of mileage for women to cover to get health care. Having once faced the dilemma of whether I could use precious gas to go visit my mother when I was living in that trailer, I understand how the cost of gas can price women out of the ability to receive care, if they even have a means of transportation at all. For many women living on the financial edge, it makes their access to safe medical abortion care impossible. Moreover, the sonogram law that passed in the prior legislative session, requiring women to have a sonogram at least twenty-four hours before they are scheduled for an abortion, means that, for women who have had to travel a great distance for access to this medical care, an overnight stay and the expense of that stay are now also mandated.

The first provision of the bill would require that doctors who perform abortion services be provided admitting privileges at a hospital within thirty miles of the clinic where they practice. It's unusual for doctors who practice in this particular medical arena to have admitting privileges at any hospital, for two reasons. One reason is that the need for emergency services at a hospital following an abortion is extremely rare, so it isn't necessary that abortion providers ever practice in a hospital setting. In those rare instances where a woman needs follow-up care, doctors on staff at hospitals are equipped to meet those needs. The other reason is that most hospitals have some religious affiliation and many, as a rule, do not grant admitting privileges to abortion-care providers.

The second provision of the bill sought to make it much more difficult for a woman to utilize what has become a method of choice for terminating a pregnancy at its earliest stage—the drug RU-486, usually taken in two doses at home over a forty-eight-hour period. Instead, women choosing this method would now be required to make four separate visits to the clinic in order to meet new protocols.

The third provision of the bill would require that abortion clinics, already subject to very strict rules and oversight under Texas state law, would now be required to meet the same standards as "ambulatory surgical centers"—centers that serve as actual surgical facilities, requiring wide hallways for gurneys and backup generators for respiratory equipment, among other requirements. Abortion procedures are not surgical procedures. There is no administration of anesthesia or any of the other high-risk measures associated with surgery. Behind a disingenuous argument that this would somehow make women safer, this requirement would force most abortion clinics in Texas to close, because retrofitting them to meet these standards would either be impossible or cost-prohibitive. In our debate on this particular provision prior to its initial passage in the senate, the author of the bill could not offer a single reason to support the argument that these standards would in any way improve safety for women.

Had the house not amended the bill to include a ban on abortions after twenty weeks of pregnancy, it would have headed straight to the governor's desk for signature. It had been initiated in the senate. We'd already had a heated debate on its provisions. When it left the senate, the bill consisted of the three provisions I listed above, and had it passed the house exactly as it had been passed out of the senate, we would not have had the opportunity to fight it. It was that last-minute change that required the bill to return to the senate floor for layout in its newly amended form and gave us the opportunity to filibuster.

The roots of the word "filibuster" can be traced, in different forms, back to Dutch (*vrijbuiter*) and Spanish (*filibustero*), but the common meaning was the same—"*piracy*"—a fitting word for our modern intentions to tactically and relentlessly talk the bill into obstruction. Filibusters in the Texas senate are rare, not just because they can take place only on the last day of a senate session, but because they truly are a test of endurance. Unlike filibusters in the U.S. Senate, where people can take turns speaking, sit down, drink water, lean on the podium, and even leave the floor to go to the restroom while another senator fills in for them—and where germaneness isn't an issue (allowing U.S. Senator Ted Cruz to read from Dr. Seuss's *Green Eggs and Ham* during his twenty-one-hour filibuster of Obamacare in September of 2013)—the rules in Texas are very strict (and even a bit Seuss-ian): You may not touch your desk. You may not lean on your desk. You may not have a sip of water. You may not leave the floor for any reason, to eat or to go to the bathroom. You may not even have a stick of gum or a piece of candy during the day. On top of that, there's the three-strike rule: If a senator is called for three points of order for not staying on topic and talking about things that are not germane to the bill that is being heard, then the filibuster can be ended. Considering the latitude that members of the Texas senate had typically been given in the past, this seemed the least of our concerns.

How wrong we would be.

The morning of the big day came all too soon. Needing moral support, I had spent the night with Will Wynn, my then boyfriend of three years, in his apartment in downtown Austin. I bathed while listening to Bruce Robison's "What Would Willie Do," as I often do on days that I know will be tough. Its lighthearted lyrics remind me that I can overcome any challenge with the right attitude.

At 6:30 a.m., a young female doctor arrived to fit me for a catheter. Knowing why she'd been summoned, she was warm and encouraging and worked quickly to finish her awkward task. Unfortunately, though, she had not brought a urine-collecting "leg bag" with her but instead had brought a large bag that hospital patients use. The length of tubing alone was close to six feet, and I knew that getting all of it wrapped around my leg and attaching the large bag in a way that could be disguised under my clothing was going to be a real challenge, but I was game. With Will's help I did the best I could to secure it, and then, from the limited wardrobe I kept at the apartment, I picked out a dress and a long jacket to disguise it.

After I dressed, Will brought me a boiled egg, my usual quick breakfast. It's his practice to draw faces with a Sharpie pen on the boiled eggs he keeps in his refrigerator—a fun sight gag for his teenage daughters, Larkin and Kyrie, and a novel way to distinguish them from the raw eggs on the same shelf. On this morning Will brought me an egg with an angry grimace, its eyebrows furrowed, its eyes narrowed, its mouth set in a resolute line. I knew that this "badass" egg face was the perfect choice to help me start the day ahead. All it could have used was a penned-in pirate's eye patch.

Will kissed and hugged me good-bye, promising to come to the capitol later in the day, and as the door closed behind me, I looked down at the flats I was wearing and wondered if they'd have enough support for all the hours I was going to be on my feet. Worrying that they wouldn't, I ran back inside, grabbed my pink running shoes, still dusty from my frequent runs around Lady Bird Lake, and headed back out the door for a long day at the capitol. Little did I know that by the time I walked back in through that same door, my life would be forever changed, in ways I never thought possible.

When I arrived at the capitol around 8:00 a.m., my staff was still busy pulling together material for me to read, even working with other Democratic senate offices who had pitched in like true team players to help find materials and assemble them. There would be hours and hours to fill by talking or reading from relevant sources, and we had to have enough—running out was not an option. The team effort paid off. Binders bulged with previous court decisions on reproductive rights in America, expert testimony from a variety of professionals who understood the ramifications of the law that was being proposed, detailed descriptions of existing clinical standards for both abortion clinics and ambulatory surgical centers all across the state of Texas, and questions and reading materials my colleagues thought would be helpful. Most important, they contained written testimony submitted by witnesses who had hoped to have a chance to testify during committee hearings on the bill, testimony that had not been heard or read into the record. Personal testimony by women who were pleading for their right to reproductive health care that included vital tests and screenings.

In both the house and senate committee hearings held on the bill, testimony had been limited. Thousands of women and many men had signed up to speak, but the committee chairs had cut them off after several hours, with the house committee chair telling witnesses who'd been waiting for many hours for their turn to testify that their testimony had become "repetitive." Rightly, the witnesses were offended that their personal stories of pain, of having faced pregnancy-termination decisions themselves or through the experience of a loved one, would be dismissed so callously.

As the zero hour of 11:11 a.m. approached, time was running short for me to deal with a problem I knew had to be resolved before I walked out onto the senate floor. It had become patently clear that I was not going to be able to secure the tubing and the large bag on my leg in a way that would keep it from slipping below my dress and down my leg. By 8:30 my staff was reaching out to the doctor who had inserted it earlier. *Could we get a leg bag instead?* Around 9:15 a.m., a nurse arrived, we closed the door to my private office, and she changed out the bag. *Problem solved*, I thought as I continued to work with my team on reviewing the materials they'd gathered and to strategize as to how I would lay everything out when I took the floor.

But within the hour I had a realization: *Problem not solved.* Something was terribly wrong. My lower abdomen was growing increasingly uncomfortable, and when I checked the leg bag, not an ounce had drained into it. Once again my staff began making urgent calls to the doctor's office. By 10:30 we still had not succeeded in getting anyone to the capitol to determine the problem. As time was ticking toward 11:11, I began to grow desperate. In the senate ladies' lounge, I unsuccessfully attempted to remove the catheter altogether, knowing that the discomfort would be far greater with it in place than it would be going through the day without it. With minutes left before I needed to be on the floor, the nurse reappeared, breathless. Parking near the capitol had become impossible, given the thousands of people who were already arriving to lend their voices, both pro and con, to the day. She'd had to run several blocks and made it just in time to discover that there was a blockage where she had inserted the tube into the bag. Clearing it brought instant relief. I had just enough time to empty the bag, reattach it to my leg, and make my way to the floor.

The gallery was already completely full when I entered the chamber and there was a brief bit of clapping and quiet cheering when I approached my desk. Most of the people in the gallery wore burnt orange T-shirts—the only color an Austin supplier had in stock in large quantities, because it's the color of U.T.—but in the gallery above my desk, on the eastern side of the chamber, there were several people dressed in light blue, the color supporters of the bill wore. When I saw them there, I felt certain that their seating choice had been purposeful. Against the walls of the west, north, and south ends of the senate chamber, the chairs for senate staffers were fully occupied: each senator is allowed two staffers on the floor at a time, and all had come armed with the maximum assistance they knew they would need.

Because I had previously provided the lieutenant governor with the customary courtesy written notice that I would be filibustering the bill, the press was aware and had therefore gathered en masse on the senate floor to film us. Typically, on days when important issues come before us, we might have four or five press cameras on the floor. But when I walked on the floor, trying to regain my composure after the catheter debacle, I noticed that the floor was filled with cameras behind the brass railing that separates senators from others on the floor—no one other than a senator or someone from the sergeant-at-arms office is allowed inside the rail. All the cameras were set up just outside the rail on the north, south, and west sides of the chamber, with a clear view of the lieutenant governor's dais on the east side of the floor and all the action on the floor. Normally they'd stay a short while, just long enough to capture some B-roll footage to accompany television news segments, but today they settled in. Like me, they were in it for the long haul.

My heart was racing as I reached my desk, which was now missing my chair—it had just been removed to give me standing room—and I was filled with an anxiety that is hard to describe. Within minutes, the lieutenant governor called on the author of the SB 5 to lay it out as newly amended, and Senator Glenn Hegar spoke very briefly to explain the difference between the original and amended versions. Then, at 11:18 a.m., Central Standard Time, it was my turn:

I intend to speak for an extended period of time on the bill. Thank you very much.

And so it began.

Members, I'm rising on the floor today to humbly give voice to thousands of Texans who have been ignored. These are Texans who relied on the minority members of this senate in order for their voices to be heard. These voices have been silenced by a governor who made blind partisanship and personal political ambition the official business of our great state. And sadly he's being abetted by legislative leaders who either share this blind partisanship or simply do not have the strength to oppose it. Partisanship and ambition are not unusual in the state capitol, but here in Texas, right now, it has risen to a level of profound irresponsibility and the raw abuse of power. The actions intended by our state leaders on this particular bill hurt Texans. There is no doubt about that. They hurt women; they hurt their families. The actions in this bill undermine the hard work and commitment of fair-minded, mainstream Texas families, who want nothing more than to work hard, raise their children, stay healthy, and be a productive part of the greatest state in our country. These mainstream Texas families embrace the challenge to create the greatest possible Texas. Yet they are pushed back and have been held down by narrow and divisive interests that are driving our state, and this bill is an example of that narrow partisanship.

Today I'm going to talk about the path these leaders have chosen under this bill and the dark place that the bill will take us. I will try to explain the history of the failed legislation before us, the impact of that legislation, and most importantly what history tells us about these policies and the motivations behind them. They do real damage to our state and to the families whose rights are violated and whose personal relationships with their doctor and their Creator, which should belong to them and them alone, are being violated. Most importantly, today I will share with you what thousands of families have had to say about this legislation, and those bringing this legislation to the floor, when the majority of Texans want us working to press upon genuine business of the state of Texas.

L ieutenant Governor Dewhurst usually kept the senate chambers very cold—around 67 degrees—which is why I kept a blanket at my desk: I was always freezing. I worried that he would lower the temperature even more, but if he did I didn't notice. What I did notice was the sun coming through the tall windows on the north and south sides of the senate chambers, and feeling the warmth of it on me as I began. I decided to take it as a sign.

At about 1:00 p.m. I began to read the committee-hearing testimony that had been submitted but had not been read into the record. I wanted to give voice to all those who had wanted to share their stories and yet had not been heard in house the previous day. As my staff watched me moving through the binder that contained these personal stories, they began to worry that we would run out too soon and that I wouldn't be able to fill the remaining eleven hours, even with all the other materials they'd given me, if they didn't get more stories. So, unbeknownst to me, they put out a call through social media inviting people to share their stories with us. And stories started pouring in via e-mail. Heart-wrenching stories. Over sixteen thousand in all. Sixteen thousand voices wanting desperately to be heard, wanting desperately to stop this bill, knowing all too personally the devastating consequences that would follow its passage.

I'd not had time to read any of the stories beforehand. And though I thought I was prepared for the challenge I would face in wanting to do each story justice, in giving each of the people behind the stories a voice, I hadn't understood nor was I prepared for how deeply emotional each would feel to me as I read them. Simultaneously, my realization of how great the physical challenge of the day would be began to seep in. Likely as a result of both the physical stress of standing in one spot and the resulting physical stress that accompanied my anxiety, my lower back began to hurt. A nagging pain that I'd been experiencing as a consequence of being fifty years old and refusing to give up on the day-to-day pounding my body experienced as a part of my dedication to running, a pain that always flared up if was in a fixed position for any length of time. To relieve it I'd begun to walk in circles around my desk, back and forth in front of it. And back and forth behind it.

And then, right before my third hour of speaking, I came across the story of Carole M.

"No one ever thinks they're going to be faced with a decision of terminating a much-wanted pregnancy or deciding when to shut off the life support of their beloved child," her letter began. My pacing temporarily halted as I took a breath, the chambers around me disappearing as I lost focus on everything except her words, words that I felt I would know before I read any further, words that I knew would be hard to speak out loud. Still, I continued to read her tragic tale to my senate colleagues and to the hundreds of people seated so quietly, so respectfully, in a hush above us in the gallery:

On December 1, 2008, I was thrilled to discover that I was pregnant with my first child. My husband and I had recently married and decided to start having kids right away. Four months later we went in for a regularly scheduled ultrasound at twenty weeks, where we were going to find out if we were having a boy or a girl. Finding out your baby's sex is easily the most exciting time of pregnancy. And we were ecstatic to discover that we were having a girl. Unfortunately, that moment was cut short when the ob-gyn also told us that our baby was sick and referred us to the maternal fetal specialist. Two days later we were given the heart-breaking news that our daughter was not only sick but had a terminal condition, *hydrops fetalis*, in which an abnormal amount of fluid builds up in the body. Given the early onset of my daughter's illness, her condition was very grave, and we left the specialist's office with our choices. We could wait until she passed, induce my labor, or have a dilation and extraction. Knowing that your daughter is dying is heartbreaking. When you are given the news that there is nothing that can be done to save your baby's life, it feels like your soul has been ripped apart, but we had a decision to make. Even if we decided not to do anything, we were still making a decision, and we had a limited amount of time to decide. There were so many things to consider. Did I want to hold my baby? Did I want to name her? Did I want to have her baptized? Where would she be buried? Would I be able to hold her while she died, if she somehow did survive until term?

In the meantime, I couldn't eat, I couldn't sleep, and I couldn't leave the house. Every time that I left the house, someone would comment on my pregnancy. They asked perfectly normal questions about my due date, the gender, the name. I answered their questions as nicely as I could, and then I would turn around and burst into tears. So eventually I stopped leaving my house.

My voice and hands shook; I wiped tears from my eyes. It was a tale of tremendous sadness, heartache, and grief, and one that was so hauntingly familiar I could barely speak it out loud. It could have been my story. The story of Tate and what Jeff and I had gone through. And it felt as though I was reading words I could have written and as though I was exposing a pain so deep, a pain tucked in the most private of corners that was now being exposed. I did not and still do not know Carole, but I understood that she and I shared a bond that neither of us would have wished to share, and my heart was filled with an aching empathy for her. Somehow I managed to remain composed enough to continue reading aloud:

I couldn't eat because my stomach was in knots from the anxiety. I didn't know exactly what was going to happen, and I didn't know when it would happen. And I definitely couldn't sleep. I was petrified that my baby was going to die while I was asleep. I just knew that I was going to wake up one day and discover that she had died at some point during the night. The idea that I couldn't be with her and know when she had passed was more than I could bear. We decided to have my labor induced. It felt like the best path for our family.

We started making burial arrangements. We didn't have a grave plot for her because we never anticipated needing one. Instead of planning a nursery, I was picking out a headstone for my baby. Instead of choosing an outfit for her to wear home, I was picking out her burial gown. It was devastating, but there was some comfort in the fact that we were moving forward. Except we weren't really moving forward. Shortly after making our decision to have my labor induced, we were informed that it wasn't really possible. My husband worked for Seton at the time, so we had Seton insurance. As a faith-based organization, Seton would not allow us to have our labor induced while our daughter still had a heartbeat. That meant that we were either forced to wait until she passed or agree to have her heart stopped. After weeks of being crippled by grief and anxiety, I couldn't imagine waiting any longer. Our obstetrician appealed to the ethics board at Seton on our behalf, but our appeal was denied, so we made the decision to have our daughter's heart stopped.

In the meantime I prayed and begged for a miracle. A miracle that I knew wasn't coming. Every night I would talk to my baby, who we named Amber Grace, and I would tell her that I loved her—I would tell her that I loved her and that I was sorry that she was sick. And then I would tell her that it was okay to leave me.

At this point, my daughter was going to die, and it was only a matter of time when and where it happened, and if we could avoid having her heart stopped, then that is what we prayed for, but she didn't die on her own. On April 8, 2009, we went to the specialist's office. At 5:00 p.m., we took a final look at our baby on the screen, said our good-byes, and her heart was stopped less than an hour later. My labor was induced that night, and she was delivered four years ago, on April 9. I held her, kissed her—I watched her get baptized—told her that I loved her, and said good-bye.

None of our daughter's life and death went as planned or expected. I expected to have her for the rest of my life. And when that wasn't possible, I expected to be able to say good-bye to her in the way that I had chosen, but that wasn't possible either. It is very frustrating to feel like the choices you have made for your baby's life and death are not being respected. Hearing that your baby is going to die makes everything in your life feel like it is out of your control. Being told that you don't really have any control over how your baby is going to die is devastating and self-defeating.

I chose to have a baby and to bring her into this world. I should be allowed to make the very personal, very private, and very painful decision as to how she leaves it, guided by the best interest of my child and my family. If a twenty-week ban had been in place four years ago, then I wouldn't have been able to make this choice. Waiting for your child to pass is certainly a viable option for many who have been in my position. But so is the path that I chose and would choose again.

R eading Carole's story was heart-wrenching. Her family's story was so very much like my own. It shook me to my core. For an instant, I felt compelled to talk about Tate, to share my story and add it to the others I was reading out loud, to give voice to my own pain and loss and grief as so many courageous women had. But knowing such an unexpected and dramatically personal confession would overshadow the events of the day, I knew the time wasn't right. I moved on to another letter.

T he emotional toll of the day was difficult enough, but soon it became a battle of wits regarding points of order. Later I was told by one of my colleagues that the Republican members and the lieutenant governor had decided upon a strategy to find three points of order to end the filibuster by 11:45 p.m. so that they could call up the transportation-funding bill that was also on our schedule for the day, and at about six hours and nine minutes (and thirty-three seconds, but who's counting?) into the filibuster, the first point of order was called on me, leading to the first of three strikes that I would receive that day. When that happened, I knew I was going to have a real challenge on my hands. This was not the practice of the Texas senate. I was not receiving the deference typically given to a fellow senator on the rare occasions when filibusters occur. And I was pissed.

M y first strike came at 5:27 p.m., when I began to talk about how in 2011 the Texas legislature had voted to cut $77 million from funding for family-planning services and how, as a consequence of that, about sixty clinics had closed in Texas and many women had lost the only access to health care that they had ever known. It was particularly severe in some of our far-removed lower-income areas of the state, like the Rio Grande Valley. I was talking about the fact that by removing the contraceptive care, the cancer screening, the screenings for sexually transmitted diseases, Texas women were actually facing unplanned pregnancies in ways that they hadn't in the past, because the means of empowering themselves not to become pregnant had been taken away from them. Senator Robert Nichols called a point of order on the "germaneness" of the topic of abortion prevention to the bill itself, which seemed completely absurd to me, but after a brief debate about it (and I mean brief—just over two minutes), the presiding officer, Lieutenant Governor David Dewhurst, ruled in favor of the point of order. My first strike had been called. The ruling stunned me.

Never before in the history of the Texas senate had this *ever* happened during a filibuster. Even reading from a phone book had been allowed. But for me, because my Republican colleagues had predetermined that they were going to strategically find a way to end the filibuster, they applied the rules in an extreme manner. And then not only were they applying them as they had never done before, they weren't even applying them in a way that was true to the spirit of the rule. To make an argument that discussing the lack of access that women in Texas now had to preventive care somehow was not relevant to the topic of what would happen with an increase in unplanned pregnancies in Texas and therefore the need for abortion services—it was absurd. Quite a bit of debate followed that first point of order, and several of the senators who had been there for many years made note of the fact that in all their time in the senate they had never observed the application of the rules in a filibuster in the harsh way that it was being applied to me.

I took a deep breath. My resolve strengthened.

It was only the beginning.

The second point of order was called a little over an hour later at 6:35 p.m. by Senator Tommy Williams when a colleague helped me put on a back brace. I'd been rubbing my lower back, pushing on it as I was walking around my desk to try to relax the muscles that were so tight, and someone on my staff had run out to a drugstore and bought a back brace for me. Normally a messenger would bring something over to your desk for you—they're the only ones allowed to go inside the railing on the senate floor—but my colleague Senator Rodney Ellis, who sits right behind me, saw my staff member coming with the back brace, and rather than have it come to me via messenger, he just went over to the rail, got it from my staffer, and handed it to me. When I started to have trouble putting it on—keep in mind I have to keep my microphone in my hand and I have to keep talking!—he proceeded to try to help me.

Of course, what had been happening throughout the day was that my Republican colleagues would leave the floor and huddle and try to figure out how they were going to get the three strikes that would be needed under the senate rules of parliamentary procedure in order to bring an end to my filibuster. This strike was not immediately called. Instead, only after a group of my colleagues had left the floor, schemed, and then returned to challenge Senator Ellis's assistance under the rule that says you may not be assisted during a filibuster, a point of order was called over forty-five minutes later. What the rule was intended to prevent was what happens in the U.S. Senate—there can be no taking turns, no "assisting" the senator who has begun the filibuster of a bill. *You* have to be the person to do it, and someone can't relieve you and then take over. But in their desperation to find their three strikes, several of my Republican colleagues argued that Senator Ellis's act of helping me to tighten this back brace was "assisting a senator during a filibuster" and should therefore count as my second strike. At 7:24 p.m., after Senator Williams first rose to make his point of order, the chair, having called for a vote on Senator Williams's point of order, announced there were seventeen "ayes" and eleven "nays" to uphold it. I had my second strike.

After the second strike, I started getting even madder. And getting mad made me forget about everything going on around me. I wasn't thinking about my back anymore. I wasn't hearing or noticing people on the floor anymore. I was solely focused on not getting that third strike. My mind was racing, trying to stay ahead of their next move, all while making sure I continued to talk. And while I talked I had to think of what topic I would move on to next, leafing through my binders to try to figure out what would be the safest subjects that would be the least likely to draw another one of their preposterous points of order.

I was also getting nervous. I still had several hours to go, and I realized that they were playing a whole different kind of ball game than had ever been played when it came to a senate filibuster, and that they were watching me with eagle eyes to try to find some way to call the third strike on me. In fact, I could tell that they had actually assigned a Republican senator to take a certain period of time in the day when that senator would be uniquely responsible for watching my every move. I could even tell whose turn it was—I would be talking and looking around the room, and then I'd notice that one of my Republican colleagues was not taking his or her eyes off me. My Democratic colleague Senator Judith Zaffirini expressed her outrage about the ridiculous and unfair degree to which the rules were being enforced—and how the spirit of the process was being disrespected and compromised, though to no avail:

> In the twenty-seven years that I have served . . . I saw, firsthand, the traditions of this senate to support and to honor a person who was engaged in a filibuster, regardless of what side a senator was on. The question today focuses on specifically Article 4 of our rules, "Decorum and Debate of Members of the Senate, Members to Address the President."
>
> This is the rule, and the only essence of this rule: "When a Senator is about to speak in debate or to communicate any matter to the Senate, the member shall rise in his or her place and address the President of the Senate."
>
> That. Is. The. Rule. There is no other part of this rule. Allow me to repeat it: "When a Senator is about to speak in debate or to communicate any matter to the Senate, the member shall rise in his or her place and address the President of the Senate."
>
> Everything that Senator Davis has done is consistent with that rule. Now, granted, there is an editorial note. But it is *only* an editorial note. Allow me to read that to you: "A member who desires to speak on a pending question should address the chair and, having obtained recognition, may speak, in an orderly and

parliamentary way, and subject to the rules of the Senate, as long as he desires."

Everything that Senator Davis has done is consistent with that editorial note. Now, there are notes on two rulings. Those rulings were given forty-four years ago, in 1969. They are not rules, they are simply notes about another lieutenant governor's rules in 1969—again, forty-four years ago. The first note is this: "When a member has been recognized and is speaking on a motion to re-refer a bill, he must stand upright at his desk and may not lean thereon."

Senator Davis has not leaned on her desk, and you know it, because many of you are watching her every move. Her *every* move. She has not leaned on her desk. The other note is this: "When a member has the floor and is speaking on a bill or resolution, he must stand upright at his desk and may not lean or sit on his desk or chair."

Senator Davis has not leaned on her desk. She has not sat on her desk. She has not sat on her chair. And I might note, Mr. President, she's a woman. The note refers to "his desk," "his chair." So I would argue that this rule does not apply to Senator Davis.

So, members, let's be literal about this. Let's be fair. Let's honor the tradition of the Texas senate. And let's abide by the letter of the rule. Open your book. Look at your rules. Read it, and understand that everything Senator Davis has done is consistent with the rule of the senate. Please read the rule, realize how specific it is, and honor this member, and honor the tradition of the senate. Senator Davis, I applaud you for your understanding of the rules, and for your being consistent with them in every way. Thank you for your leadership.

———

M y staff now worried that I shouldn't keep reading people's stories—we had enough stories that I could have read them for
the remainder of the time, but they were afraid that my doing so
would be challenged as somehow being "off topic"—so then we all
started scrambling. Many of my Democratic senate colleagues were
coming to me saying, "What else do you need? What can we bring you
to read?" And I would give them suggestions of what I thought might
be the most pertinent material that we could defend against a point-
of-order challenge. Which worked for a while because their strategic
help was successful at keeping me tightly on topic. I even felt I was
starting to hit my stride as I spoke:

> But you can imagine, or maybe you can't, how a woman feels to
> be told that her feelings on these issues, that no matter how dif-
> ficult, no matter the circumstances that she's dealing with, if she
> can't fit into every one of these little square pegs that she's going
> to be asked to fit into by this bill, she is not going to be able to
> exercise her constitutional right. And what's so disturbing is that
> we don't seem to care. And maybe that is because so many of us
> on this floor have never ever had to face that and never will face
> it, because you don't have the equipment. And I've got it, and my
> daughters have it, and other women that I care about have it, and
> women who I don't know have it. And what I know for a fact is that
> each of them has a unique circumstance that's going to be im-
> pacted directly by virtue of the provisions of this particular bill.

Only two hours and and seven minutes would elapse until the
third point of order was called on me at 9:31 p.m. As ridiculous as the

first two were, the third point of order called was a complete travesty. I had begun referencing the sonogram bill that the legislature had passed in the prior session, which I argued was also an intrusion on access to safe, legal abortion. The point I was trying to make was that, layered on top of that law, which requires women to have a trans-vaginal sonogram twenty-four hours prior to an abortion procedure, the bill we were debating would create such an impediment to women that we were literally violating their constitutionally protected right to access safe, legal abortion care. So, like any good lawyer, I was constructing my case—starting by going back in time to 2011 when it all began and building to my crescendo to show how all these things, taken together, were creating a patent violation of that constitution-ally protected right. But before I could finish, Senator Donna Camp-bell jumped up and called that point of order, and, at 10:03 p.m., with some discussion, the chair ruled it valid.

When my third strike was officially called, the gallery erupted. A woman in the gallery shouted, "Bullshit!" For more than a minute, the audience chanted, "Let her speak! Let her speak!" Within a min-ute, Lieutenant Governor Dewhurst gestured to Department of Pub-lic Safety officers to clear offending members of the gallery.

That third strike effectively ended the speaking portion of my fili-buster. I'd spoken my last words. The rest was up to my colleagues.

We had almost two hours to fill before midnight. My brilliant, fast-on-their-feet Democratic colleagues took over in an at-tempt to eat up time on the clock. It began with a challenge to the ruling of the chair, made by Senator Kirk Watson and other Demo-crats. This challenge, used correctly, forces the removal of the presid-ing officer from the chair. With Senator Watson's quick thinking and adept use of the rules, Lieutenant Governor Dewhurst was forced to step down from his position as presiding officer while the validity of his ruling was debated. After some time, at 10:11 p.m., it was decided by the senate majority that Senator Robert Duncan would assume the role of presiding officer and would rule on Senator Watson's challenge. My colleagues did a masterful job of continuing to debate that ruling, creating a tremendous amount of chaos in the process. Meanwhile I had to continue standing, no leaning, no drink of water, no break—because if I did any of those things, the filibuster would automatically be ruled to be at an end, regardless of the outcome of the current ruling being debated. So I stood, adrenaline rushing through my body as I watched my Democratic colleagues, one by one, each in support of the other and with tremendous dedication and cunning, work to tick away the time.

As they worked, I occasionally glanced at the clock behind me, just below the gallery, on the western wall of the senate chamber. Like everyone else, I was silently pleading for its hands to move. Finally, in a desperate attempt to shut down debate, someone on the lieutenant governor's dais—perhaps Dewhurst himself—must have sent an instruction to the folks who take care of our technical issues in the chamber to turn off the microphones of Democratic senators. And so, at around 11:15 p.m., the microphones were cut off and only the ones belonging to the Republican senators would come on when they stood up to speak and demanded to be recognized and heard.

Meanwhile, as they had been throughout the day, the people sitting above us in the gallery, under the deeply coffered ceiling and the original brass chandeliers and above the treasured collection of fifteen historical Texas paintings, were watching anxiously, hanging on every word, every argument, every tick of the clock. The gallery had been full to capacity all day, with people taking turns there to allow others an opportunity to come into the chamber. Those opposed to the bill, wearing orange STAND WITH TEXAS WOMEN T-shirts, far outnumbered the few who were there in support of it, wearing light blue ones. The people gathered there had observed respectfully, with incredible decorum throughout the day, the rules of the Texas senate. There had been a few moments—particularly after the first two strikes had been called—when they would begin to clamor. But when they did so, I'd looked up and gestured for them to quiet down, which they quickly did. They were watching for my signal on things, and as soon as I would do that, the gallery would just get completely quiet again. And for most of the day, with the occasional roar that we could hear from the thousands of people outside the senate gallery who had gathered in the capitol to add their voices to the mix, you could have heard a pin drop.

But they'd been watching all day, and even a novice who doesn't really understand the intricacies of Robert's Rules of Order could see that the rules were not being applied fairly and reasonably, so the crowd was getting more and more upset—especially as the end of the evening was approaching and Democratic senators were demanding to have their debate points heard and instead having their microphones turned off. Though the nearly two hundred thousand people who watched it via Livestream couldn't hear what was happening, the people who were in the gallery saw this: the Democratic senators screaming to be recognized by the chair and the chair purposely refusing to recognize them. With his bellowing voice, only Senator Royce West had managed to succeed at getting the attention of the chair.

The crowd was already going wild. A little earlier, Leticia Van de Putte, our beloved senate colleague who'd been absent from our debate because her father had died in a car accident only a few days earlier, had driven back to Austin from his funeral in San Antonio and arrived, with a Department of Public Safety escort, at the capitol. She had planned on being with her family all day, having literally just laid her father to rest that morning. But when she heard what was going on in the capitol, she just couldn't stay away. She felt strongly that she needed to be there, to stand next to her Democratic colleagues and support us in what we were fighting for. When she got there, she headed immediately to the floor. She hadn't expected to say anything—she just wanted to add her presence as a symbol of support—but she became so frustrated watching what was happening that she, too, began screaming to be heard. At 11:44 p.m., sixteen minutes before midnight, *still* not being recognized—"Did the president hear me or did the president hear me and refuse to recognize me?"—she finally asked this question:

At what point must a female senator raise her hand or her voice to be recognized over the male colleagues in the room?

She'd had to shout that, of course, but as soon as she did, the gallery erupted. She'd brought the house down. It was the perfect statement. It beautifully summed up the frustrations we'd all been feeling. And the gallery could be silent no more. The spectators jumped to their feet and started screaming, and by then—because *I* had reached *my* breaking point and my patience point, too—rather than try to quiet them, I encouraged them. They had been obeying the rules all day while I'd watched my Republican colleagues breaking the rules, having no respect for the decorum of the Texas senate—or any of our other rules, for that matter—and I'd had enough. So I started gesturing in the opposite direction as I'd done previously when trying to quiet them—"Keep it up! Keep it up!" I was shouting up to them—and the rest of my Democratic colleagues joined around me. We knew if we could keep them going and keep a vote from being taken, we could get to that midnight deadline. Which is exactly what happened.

At about fifteen minutes before midnight, in the midst of this chaos, the presiding officer finally ruled that the third point of order had been appropriately sustained—a debate over parliamentary inquiry that had started at 10:06 p.m. The third strike had been ruled successful. My filibuster had, with certainty, finally come to an end. But the "people's filibuster" had just begun. As Senator Duncan shouted to the secretary of the senate to begin taking the roll-call vote, the roar of the crowd in the gallery rose even more. And they were joined by the chorus of thousands of voices in the building, outside the chamber. I could feel the floor shaking under my feet with the thunderous noise they were making. And beautifully—poetically, almost— something truly democratic occurred. People, thousands of people, were demanding that their voices be heard. And heard they were. As Patsy Spaw, the secretary of the senate, began taking the roll-call vote, Republican senators were screaming to be heard, running up to her at the dais to register their "yes" votes in favor of the bill. Needless to say, the Democratic senators were not doing the same. Amid the confusion, the presiding officer gaveled and said, "SB 5 has now passed," and tried to adjourn the body, but my Democratic colleagues and I, especially Senator West, who was consulting his own cell phone, which read the time as 12:00, and balking at the obvious discrepancy between it and the clock on the senate wall, refused to go quietly.

"Mr. President! What time is it? What's the time? We can't take a vote after midnight! Constitutional point of order!" And a whole debate ensued over which clock was actually correct.

Typically, when a vote is taken and recorded, the secretary of the senate enters it into the computer and it is time-stamped. The original time stamp on the recorded vote matched reality. It was 12:03 a.m. SB 5 was dead. But within just a few minutes—and it is still unknown how or why—a new time stamp was entered. This one showed that the vote had been taken at 11:59 p.m. Our night was therefore far from over. And a debate raged on, with Senator West taking the lead on the floor, each of the senators huddled around him as they argued back and forth with the presiding officer about whether the bill had actually passed before the midnight deadline. At some point, while that went on, I left the floor, sat down for the first time all day, and ate a bite and drank some water, both offered by my kind and nurturing colleague Senator Zaffirini.

Ultimately, the senate, as a "caucus of the whole," reconvened in the Betty King Room just behind the senate chamber, and argued our positions. Fairly quickly, after a comparison of the original time stamp (thanks to someone on social media who had captured the proof of that original stamp) and the second time stamp, the lieutenant governor and my Republican colleagues conceded that the bill had not passed by the deadline and that there was no way they could reasonably defend an interpretation otherwise. But then a great debate ensued about what the lieutenant governor would say about why he was changing his ruling in order to save face. It was ludicrous. The words the lieutenant governor agreed upon, after a tremendous amount of back-and-forth and a great deal of wordsmithing, were delivered by him as he retook the dais at sometime past 3:00 a.m.

Shortly before he did, and before we all gathered on the floor to hear him officially declare the bill dead, I had texted Cecile Richards, the executive director of Planned Parenthood and the daughter of our now-deceased but much-beloved governor, Ann Richards. Cecile was in the rotunda, surrounded by the crowd still gathered there awaiting word. My text read as follows:

"The Lieutenant Governor has agreed that SB 5 is dead."

Cecile quieted the crowd and read it aloud to them. And they erupted with tears and laughter and excitement.

Very quickly after receiving the official ruling from the lieutenant governor on the floor, my Democratic colleagues and I exited the senate chamber, where we were met by hundreds and hundreds of people, joyously shouting. We were embraced by them and cheered by them as we spoke and thanked them. There was so much emotion that it's hard to even describe what that moment felt like. It was surreal. Who among us could have possibly predicted the events of the day? We were awed by it all—by the outcome, yes, but more by the fact that each of us had played an important role in protecting the health of Texas women. I was grabbed and hugged and wept on by people, once strangers, who were now allies in combat. And we had won. Later we all gathered on the southern steps of the capitol to speak to the press. We were surrounded by so many people from the media that we couldn't see over them through the night's pitch-black sky to the throngs of people who were there, cheering, crying, applauding. So we borrowed the bullhorn that Cecile had been using to communicate to the crowd in the rotunda and took turns, aiming it high in the air so our voices would be carried, giving our brief thanks for the support and the work of all who had participated in the journey of that day and the weeks that had led up to that day. Speaking to the crowd is a moment I will never forget:

> Today was democracy in action . . . Today was an example of government for the people, by the people, and of the people. And you all are the reason that happened. You were the voices we were speaking for today from the floor, and we are so proud as a group of Democrat senators to have represented your interests on this issue today.

We Texans have lived under a couple of decades of steamroller-type leadership, where the interests of a special few insiders tend to supersede those of millions of Texans and their families. It's gone on so long that, quite honestly, sometimes fighting the battles to push back against that tide has felt futile. Many people around the state have become accustomed to governing being done without their input or influence and they've resigned themselves to the fact that that's just the way things are. Even for myself and my senate Democratic colleagues—there have been days we've gotten up and fought for things that we knew in our hearts were a losing battle, finding it hard to muster a high level of enthusiasm for what we know will be a fight that leads to a foregone conclusion.

But the events of that day of June 25, 2013, led to an awakening.

And it was the awakening of an energy that can't be immediately tamped down. It wasn't just about reproductive rights. It was about a group of citizens, all over the state of Texas, who were fed up with those folks on the inside who aren't listening to them. June 25 was different. People across this state were inspired to believe that when they do stand up and when they *do* cry out, they *can* be heard and they *can* make a difference.

A beautiful blog post written by Rachel Farris, an Austin resident, powerfully described her feelings about the moment that the people in the gallery rose to their feet that day:

> I have been asked if it was planned. If we were encouraged by someone. If we knew it was coming. The truth is this: when you have no words left, when every word spoken has fallen on deaf ears, when the representative you have chosen to speak is no longer allowed to do so, sometimes all there is left to do is scream. The final twenty minutes of the people's filibuster was a manifestation of the impact of every word that had been said but not truly heard in the Senate that day. Because while the Republicans in power chose not to listen, we had been listening. We had been sitting. We had been waiting. We had no words, but we stood and we had a voice.

And even though that awful bill restricting women's reproductive rights passed just a few days later when a second special session was called, people were empowered by what they'd been able to accomplish that day—not what *I* accomplished but what *they* accomplished. And I see that now everywhere I go in Texas—an awakening to what it means to participate and how empowering that can be, and a new understanding and acceptance of the fact that we cannot cede our values simply because we may not win every time we speak out. And an understanding that there's a much larger collection of those values out there than maybe we've known. Because when you're sitting quietly reading the newspaper, thinking, "There they go again!" you don't know that there are hundreds of thousands of people across the state feeling the same disappointment and disgust in their leadership. But last June these people found one another, and this is what they said:

Look at all of us! Look at what we can do.

The Monday following the filibuster, we were called back to a second special session. A rally convened on the capitol lawn, with people raising cleverly worded handmade signs above a sea of orange T-shirts. I spoke, some of my colleagues spoke, and we were joined by our fellow Texan and outspoken advocate for women's issues Stephanie March (best known for her role on *Law & Order: SVU*), who also spoke. There were six or seven thousand people on the capitol lawn that day, and longtime Department of Public Safety officers said they hadn't seen a turnout of the public like that since the LBJ era, when he would speak at civil rights demonstrations. It was just amazing. And so powerful. And the most overwhelming part of it for me, then and now, isn't the media frenzy or all the Twitter memes and the videos and the songs. It's what I still witness almost every single day as I travel around my much-loved state.

A young woman—and it's almost always a young woman—will come up to me, trembling, and look me in the eyes and start crying. As Rachel Farris so beautifully described it, they have "no words" to put to what that moment meant to them, what finding their voice means to them, what having someone who's speaking for them means to them. It's so humbling and so inspiring to know that as lonely as these battles have sometimes felt over the years in the Texas senate, they're not really lonely battles at all.

TWENTY

"Oh, Pooh. If ever there is a tomorrow
when we're not together, there's something
you must remember."

"And what might that be, Christopher Robin?"

"You're braver than you believe, and stronger than
you seem, and smarter than you think. But the most
important thing is: even if we're ever apart, I'll
always be with you. I'll always be with you. Always
be with you . . ."

—A. A. MILNE

O N AUGUST 5 of 2013, I gave a speech to the National Press
Club in Washington, D.C. Afterward, I received a text from my
dad, who had watched it online, that read: *"Simply amazing at the
NPC! So in awe of you and so proud, I wept!"* Exactly one month later,
in the early-morning hours of September 5, I said my final good-byes
to him as I watched him take his last breath. And I wept. And wept
and wept.

Not even two weeks after he sent me that text, my dad was taken
by ambulance to a local hospital in Fort Worth. Suffering from acute

abdominal pain, he had driven himself to one of those twenty-four-hour doc-in-the-box places, and was quickly transported to the hospital. He had a severe bowel obstruction that had caused a part of his colon to twist around on itself and die. Emergency surgery went well and we were told he'd be going home in just four or five days.

I was traveling as part of exploring whether a run for governor would make sense. "I'll be fine," he'd said to me. He wanted to know the details of where I'd been, how it had been going. He was excited for me. And he was anxious to know what I would decide. As I checked in on him from the road, everything seemed to be going well. But on day five, things started looking a little worrisome. A lifelong smoker, he was having difficulty breathing—his lungs were suffering post-surgical effects. My stepmother, Suzi, was reassuring when we spoke, but by the time I landed in Fort Worth the following day, I discovered that things were much more serious than she'd understood. At almost the exact time the wheels of my plane hit the tarmac, my dad was being intubated and put on a respirator, beginning a downward spiral from which he would never recover.

In the days that followed, I was with him every moment that I could physically manage, as were my siblings, Chris, Joey, and Jennifer. As was my half sister, Kathy, my dad's firstborn, who had flown in from Rhode Island to be with us. As were many of his grandchildren. As was my stepmother. As was my mother. We kept vigil, each of us taking turns in his room, watching his labored breaths. We slept in the hospital and took turns going home to shower and catch a few hours of solid sleep in a real bed. Meanwhile, my dad fought a valiant fight to stay with us. There were only a couple of days during those two weeks that I got to see his warm brown eyes. His doctors had tried him off the respirator, bringing him out of the sleep state that they'd kept him in. And though I could see his beautiful eyes, and though he spoke to me, he was off in another place still, fighting the demons who were trying to take him away. They were getting the better of him, leaving him reintubated with a machine taking over the fight on his behalf.

Miraculously, it seemed, my family and I watched my father defy all the odds. At one point, his entire body had started shutting down. He had emergency surgery on his heart, which the doctor predicted he would have little chance of surviving. He pulled through nonetheless. A separate doctor was assigned to every possible part of his system—his kidneys, his blood, his heart, his lungs . . . his brain. We thought our prayers had been answered when, one by one, each started to improve. We became experts in reading the outputs of the machines that were monitoring him, understanding what the numbers meant and seeing for ourselves that he was turning around. We took turns talking to him, whispering in his ear as he slept. We watched as the nurses turned and bathed him with such loving care. We kissed his face and his hands. We ran our fingers through his thick wavy hair. We rubbed his feet. We moved his arms and legs, trying to prepare him for the physical challenges we knew he would face when he awakened. We played CDs for him, favorites of his that Joey and I had retrieved from his collection. We sang to him, along with his favorite performers.

And we spent more time together as a family than we had since our parents had separated and divorced. We reminisced. And we laughed. And cried. My mother and Suzi, who had long since become friends, supported each other in the most beautiful way. We kids said to my mom, "Tell us about the time when . . ." and she would tell us, either leaving us all laughing hysterically at some funny tale or crying at a sentimental one. Joey and I worked the crossword together like old times.

Our moods lightened each day as the doctors would come to us, shaking their heads in disbelief at my dad's recovery. Every organ was improving. Finally, a decision was made to remove the respirator for the second time. Now we would only need to wait for the drugs that had kept him in his deep slumber to wear off. And so, we waited. And we waited. The doctors were reassuring: "He's been on a great deal of medication. It will take time." But after a couple of days with no sign that he was awakening, an MRI was ordered.

And then, just when we all thought we'd be preparing for the long-term care and rehabilitation that we thought he would need, we found ourselves instead preparing to say good-bye to this giant of a man we all loved so much. Tragically, during my dad's silent sleep-filled battle, he had suffered a series of strokes. As the neurologist showed us images of the damage to his brain, we held on to one another and wept. Though he'd managed a miraculous recovery in all other respects, his brain had suffered irreversible damage. He was gone. Our father would never be our father again. Over the next day, the neurologist patiently waited for us to absorb and process the information she had shared. He was gone. And we knew what we had to do. Because we all knew our father. We knew what he would want.

Nonetheless, Jennifer and I went to our father's home. He and Suzi, though still married and still very close, had been living apart for several years. We wanted to see if he had written a living will, and we looked through the entire house, every drawer and closet, without success. What we found was a simple two-page Last Will and Testament that he had typed up himself on his computer, describing how he wanted his modest belongings divided. That he wanted to be cremated. That he wanted his ashes to be joined with those of his most cherished dog, Ziggy, who had died before him, and spread over the Grand Canyon by his family.

Back at the hospital, we gratefully received prayers from the hospital's clergy. And we prepared to have my dad moved to palliative care. And then, miraculously, as we watched the nurses carefully move him into a transport bed, my dad gave us a parting gift. With all his might, he had fought to climb out of the deep, dark place where he'd been and he looked at us all with those deep brown eyes of his one last time. We were standing outside the room, watching the nurses do their work, when I saw his eyes flutter open. And in an instant, we were all beside him—my siblings, my mom, and Suzi. Each of us cried out to him, sobbing, telling him how much we loved him, desperate to fill these precious moments with nothing but our intense love for him. He stayed with us for as long as he could manage—a few minutes at most. But it was enough. He had shown us, one final time, how much he loved us all.

Later, the doctors would tell us that they had seen it before, the miracle of what happened with my dad. They could not explain it. But we didn't need an explanation. We were not surprised that my dad had managed it. He was magic, remember?

In the palliative care unit, as we prepared to say our final good-byes, the doctors told us he might hold on for a few hours, maybe a day. But true to the fighter that he had always been, my dad hung on for almost three days. We each, my siblings and I, took turns swabbing his mouth with a small sponge dipped in water. We watched as Amber massaged his hands and feet with lotion. And, as he began to slip away from us, we took turns privately whispering to him, kissing him as tears fell from our faces to his.

When it was my turn, I found myself contemplating the symbolism of his "bread and butter" superstition. And, knowing what we were facing—that soon we would come to confront a physical separation unlike one we had ever known—those were some of the final words that I whispered into his ear.

"Bread and butter, Dad. Bread and butter."

Until we are together again . . .

EPILOGUE

A Ritual to Read to Each Other

If you don't know the kind of person I am
and I don't know the kind of person you are
a pattern that others made may prevail in the world
and following the wrong god home we may miss our star.

For there is many a small betrayal in the mind,
a shrug that lets the fragile sequence break
sending with shouts the horrible errors of childhood
storming out to play through the broken dyke.

And as elephants parade holding each elephant's tail,
but if one wanders the circus won't find the park,
I call it cruel and maybe the root of all cruelty
to know what occurs but not recognize the fact.

And so I appeal to a voice, to something shadowy,
a remote important region in all who talk:
though we could fool each other, we should consider—
lest the parade of our mutual life get lost in the dark.

For it is important that awake people be awake,
or a breaking line may discourage them back to sleep,
the signals we give—yes or no, or maybe—
should be clear; the darkness around us is deep.

—WILLIAM STAFFORD

I N LATE AUGUST of the year that Jeff and I said our good-byes to Tate, he and I joined our dear friends Mike and Annette for a round of golf. They had always been important to us, but had become even more so as they helped us to work through our grief. It was a clear, crisp day. With winter approaching, the trees were losing their leaves and there were enormous piles of them along the sides of the fairways where the grounds crew or the wind had blown them. I walked along with Mike, searching through them for my wayward tee shot. After a time, moving the leaves to and fro with the head of my 7-iron, I located my ball, bent down to clear a path of leaves from which to hit it, and stood over it, eyeing my shot to the green. As I gripped my club, lining up my shot, something magical happened. There, where I stood, the wind picked up and swirled the leaves around me. I was standing in the middle of their tornado-like vortex as they encircled me, in perfect cylindrical form. As they did, I looked up and around and through them at the sky above, transfixed. And I felt her. I was sure of it. Tate. Moving through me, saying her good-byes to me. Letting me go.

In the weeks and months since my father died, I have wondered whether I would experience something similar. Would he, too, make his way through me, release me on his journey to the great beyond? I have waited, especially in the quiet of the middle of the night when I awaken, thinking of him, listening for him. Will he move through me, release me as Tate did? Perhaps he knows I still need him here with me as I travel this next chapter in my personal journey. Perhaps he's watching over me, waiting until he knows I am ready for him to let me go.

Not yet, Dad. Not quite yet.

Like the leaves swirling around me on the golf course that brisk fall day, there have been many people whose lives have intertwined with mine and who have left a lasting imprimatur on the person I became. All of those that I have written about, whether they are still here or are now gone, played an integral role in assuring that I would not get lost in the dark as I traveled on my journey. My story is a story of each of them and the role they played in shaping the kind of person that I am. Because of their light, I avoided a darkness that kept me from missing my star. Instead, through them, because of them, and the values each instilled in me, I found my voice. I found my fight.

And somewhere, along the way, I forgot to be afraid.

ACKNOWLEDGMENTS

I am eternally grateful to the thousands of women and men who have shared their deeply personal stories with me before, during, and after the filibuster because they believed that the telling of their experiences could make a difference. Through them, I found the courage to tell my own.

My deepest appreciation goes to Laura Zigman, who taught me to believe in the strength of my own writing, and who thoughtfully coaxed, guided, and shaped the telling of my story. I am thankful for the many hours she spent with me in an effort to understand the heart of how I became who I am, and for her efforts to put my story into words. Most important, I am grateful for the care with which she listened to my story, helping me to move through yet another stage of my grief in losing Tate and my dad. This book would not have been possible without her talents and her compassion.

I am tremendously thankful to Paul Fedorko, my agent at N. S. Bienstock, who gave me the encouragement I needed to believe I was capable of putting my story into book form. Though I received many calls about writing a book after the filibuster last year, Paul was the one agent willing to show up at my door and ask how he could be of help. Through the writing process, Paul has been my biggest cheerleader and supporter, and through his encouragement, stepped into a small part of the void my father would have filled had he still been alive. My thanks also to Paul's assistant, Sammy Bina, for making sure we were always in touch.

I am also grateful to David Rosenthal and Aileen Boyle, as well as the rest of the team at Blue Rider Press, including assistant editor Phoebe Pickering; our chief copy editor, Linda Rosenberg; senior copy editor Marie Finamore; copy editor Maureen Sugden; managing editor Meredith Dros; and art director Jason Booher. When David and I agreed to do this project together, he assured me that he would handle my story with great care and deference. He has proven true to his word in that regard and I am pleased to have trusted my instincts when deciding that David's team was the right one to partner with in order to turn the idea of telling my story into the reality of a book.

Tremendous thanks also go to Lisa Turner, Sonya Grogg, J. D. Angle, and Taylor McCarty, Graham Stadler, and Russell Langley, who helped to provide research assistance and moral support in the telling of my story. Each has long been an important part of my team, and, once again, they've proven that in all ways, they always have my back.

ABOUT THE AUTHOR

Wendy Davis is the Democratic candidate for governor in Texas. She represents Fort Worth and surrounding cities in the Texas senate and previously served on the Fort Worth City Council. In June 2013 she held a historic filibuster to block legislation that would create harsh abortion restrictions on Texas women.

An index for this book can be found at
Penguin.com/ForgettingtoBeAfraidIndex.